Craft Sewing

For Fun & Profit™

Mary Roehr

PRIMA HOME

An Imprint of Prima Publishing

3000 Lava Ridge Court • Roseville, California 95661

(800) 632-8676 • www.primalifestyles.com

Library of Congress Cataloging-in-Publication Data

Roehr, Mary.
  Craft Sewing for fun & profit / Mary Roehr.
      p.   cm.
  Includes index.
  ISBN 0-7615-2043-0
  1. Sewing.   I. Title. II. Title: Sewing for fun and profit.
TT705.R64 2000
746—dc21

                                                                                    99-057534
                                                                                    CIP

00 01 02 03 04 ii 10 9 8 7 6 5 4 3 2 1
Printed in the United States of America

How to Order

Single copies may be ordered from Prima Publishing, 3000 Lava Ridge Court, Roseville, CA 95661; telephone (800) 632-8676. Quantity discounts are also available. On your letterhead, include information concerning the intended use of the books and the number of books you wish to purchase.

Visit us online at www.primalifestyles.com

Contents

Introduction v

Part One: For Fun 1

   1: The Joy of Craft Sewing 3
   2: Getting Started 19
   3: Setting Up Your Personal Workspace 41
   4: Creative How-To's 57
   5: Creating Your Craft Sewing Projects 81
   6: Your Crafts Vision 117

Part Two: For Profit 127

   7: Profiting from Your Talent 129
   8: Pricing Your Craft Sewing 141
   9: Selling Your Craft Sewing 153
  10: Marketing Your Craft Sewing 191
  11: A Mini-Course in Crafts-Business Basics
         by Barbara Brabec 211

Glossary 291
Resources 293
Index 315
About the Author and Series Editor 323

The FOR FUN & PROFIT™ SERIES

Craft Sewing For Fun & Profit

Decorative Painting For Fun & Profit

Holiday Decorations For Fun & Profit

Knitting For Fun & Profit

Quilting For Fun & Profit

Soapmaking For Fun & Profit

Woodworking For Fun & Profit

Introduction

WHEN I WAS STUDYING for a degree in clothing and textiles in the 1970s, authorities in the field predicted that by the year 2000 we would all be wearing molded plastic spacesuits and there wouldn't be a need for sewing. They were wrong!

Technology has provided us with all types of fabric glue, bonding agents, and fusing systems, but nothing seems to work as well as a good old needle and thread. The popularity of sewing as a craft and the need for sewn items are bigger than ever.

According to the Home Sewing Association, an organization that encourages all facets of sewing, the United States now has 33 million sewing enthusiasts. These are not just people who own sewing machines but people who are actively sewing. That represents nearly one-eighth of our total population.

Now I understand why so many women I meet say they sew or used to sew at some point in their lives, quite often when their children were growing up. Some say how they received a sewing machine as a gift for high school graduation or as a wonderful anniversary surprise from their husbands. The machine may be tucked away in a closet, now unused, but they have never once considered giving it up because they already understand the benefits of sewing.

Perhaps you've just admired the handiwork of others and wondered what is involved, how you could get started, and what kinds of things you could create. If you have not yet explored the world of sewing to find the possibilities it can hold for your life, you are in for a great adventure. I'll warn you, though: it can be addictive—but in the best sense of the word.

This book is for people who may not have the time or desire to sew everything they wear but who would enjoy creating sewn crafts or accessories. You'll certainly be able to progress to garment sewing later, but for now my focus will be on craft sewing.

Even though you may tend automatically to associate sewing with making garments, countless other useful and aesthetic items are sewn. Take the time to look around and notice how sewing has enriched your life.

Walking through my home, I discover sewn items everywhere, starting in the kitchen with curtains, a tablecloth, and matching napkins. Some of the small appliances are concealed under fabric covers, and even the refrigerator magnets are crafted from tiny bits of fabric and stuffing. Cooking and cleaning up would be difficult without pot holders, dish towels, and dishrags.

Tapestry valances above the windows, decorative pillows on the sofa and chairs, and a fringed cloth lampshade on the lamp enhance the living room. The dining room table is set with a runner and coordinating placemats.

My bedroom is embellished with sewn items, from the bed with its dust ruffle, bedspread, and accent pillows to the closet with garment, shoe, and tote bags. Curtains on the windows and a patchwork wall hanging set the theme for the entire room. In the bathroom my monogrammed towels hang next to a shower curtain made from a Battenberg lace tablecloth, and I've organized my cosmetics in a zippered bag.

Even my office is decorated with pictures in colorful fabric frames, and the chair I sit on is more comfortable because of a padded cushion. In the garage, my tennis racquet cover as well as the head covers for my golf clubs—each one resembling a colorful tropical bird—were all custom designed. I use my fanny pack, visor, or baseball cap constantly whether I am a spectator or actively involved in the recreation of the day.

I personally have sewn all the items I've mentioned, but if you are beginning to think I am a Martha Stewart clone, I'm not. I simply love to sew and enjoy expressing myself through my craft. I started out not knowing how to sew a single stitch, and if you're a novice, you can certainly learn, probably faster than I did.

No matter what your skill level, even if you are a beginner, I am going to show you how to have a lot of fun sewing and how you can make money, too, if that is your intent, in the second half of this book. I have made money selling many of the items I sew.

Hobby and Income— The Perfect Combination!

It has been said that if you do what you love, the money will follow. This has certainly been true in my life. But, even though I make my living from the items I sew, in the beginning I didn't particularly like sewing or take to it quickly. Later I'll tell you about experiences while learning to sew, but for now I want you to know that I hung in there through the frustrations and I'm glad I did. One small success led to another, and my enthusiasm grew quickly for my new hobby.

I started designing and sewing garments, stuffed animals (does anyone remember poodle skirts and autograph dogs?), pot holders, doll clothes, pillows, and just about anything else that would fit in my sewing machine. Friends began to notice my one-of-a-kind projects and asked me to sew for them. I was delighted they liked my handicrafts and astounded that they wanted to pay me! Creating something worthy of admiration and then getting paid for doing it was thrilling. I was hooked.

When I started out, I had no master plan or any aspirations for a business. It just happened naturally. More than 40 years and countless projects later, I am still making money from my hobby. If you sew items you love to look at and/or enjoy using, there's a good chance others will feel the same way. This creates an automatic outlet for you to sell what you sew—the perfect combination of hobby and income.

A Little Craft Sewing History

Whether you have sewn before or are just starting out, you'll be proud to know that sewing was probably the first handicraft practiced by women. Elizabeth Barber, an archaeologist and an avid sewer, describes in her book *Women's Work* how 40,000 years ago after the great Ice Age, creative hunter-gatherers began producing novel tools like awls (sharp hole-punching implements that we still use today) and pins. A mere 20,000 years later bone needles had become common for fastening beads of shell, tooth, and bone to hide garments. And we thought fabric embellishment was something new!

At the same time, the first bits of twisted fiber, the precursor to modern thread, started to appear. This new medium replaced sinew and thin strips of leather that were previously used to attach and fasten things together. The art of sewing had begun.

Everything was sewn by hand for thousands of years—mostly by women—until the invention of the sewing machine in 1846. In less than 200 years, sewing machines have taken a quantum leap from treadles that operated without electricity, to computerized models that actually embroider and perform some functions without manual guidance.

At the Tucson Historical Society in Arizona, a whole room is devoted to needlework samplers, an obligatory part of every pioneer girl's education. The squares of cloth were filled with rows of tiny hand stitches, starting with simple straight stitches that could be used to join cloth together and progressing to more complicated techniques like making gathers or buttonholes. This was a standard way for young girls all over the world to perfect their sewing skills before tackling larger projects.

Strangely enough, the advent of wars in our nation's history was one of the greatest contributors to the progress and development of sewing as a handicraft and hobby. Prior to the Civil War, women devoted most of their time to making clothes for their families, but the need for uniforms led to the development of clothing factories. Further demands during World War I and World War II, along with the Industrial Revolution, created what is now our modern ready-to-wear system. This development gave women more time to sew simply for fun and relaxation.

The trend toward craft sewing has really caught on. The Hobby Industry Association in America examines all aspects of crafting and hobbies in the annual Nationwide Craft/Hobby Consumer Study that revealed that in 1998, 80% of households reported that at least one of its members engages in a craft/hobby. The various needlecraft-related activities continue to be the crafts with the most widespread participation. And, 24% of those polled do craft sewing!

Craft sewing is more popular than ever, and if you choose to join this movement, you'll become part of one of the largest and friendliest groups of kindred souls today. People everywhere are rediscovering ways to enhance their modern lives with this ageless craft. Come along with me—the best is yet to be!

Using This Book

My foremost goal in writing this book is to provide you with a guide that will lead you on the path to craft sewing for fun and profit in an easy step-by-step progression. I'll tell you why sewing is one of the most satisfying and popular hobbies, and I'll show you how to get started whether you are new to sewing, want to refresh your skills, or would like to cross over from some other craft.

You'll learn all about the necessary tools, how to set up your own personal workspace, and the basic how-to's of sewing. Then you can practice your new skills with fun and simple projects I've designed especially for you. These are all easy and attractive items that anyone could use and enjoy. Later I'll introduce you to the possibilities of profiting from your talents, including your craft vision, business savvy, pricing, and selling what you have made.

Second, I hope this book will be an inspiration, because I'm going to encourage you to uncover and release those secret dreams and hidden talents. I know you'll enjoy hearing about others who have done the very same thing in all manner of planned and unplanned ways.

Last, I hope you'll see *Sewing for Fun & Profit* as a companion along your path to creativity. If you're like most hobbyists, you may often be by yourself without much interaction or feedback from others. Some solitude is necessary for concentration and actually helps to free your imagination, but too much can lead to isolation. Since I have spent a lifetime sewing and selling my crafts, I've tried to anticipate your questions before you ask them, and I've also provided you with resources for further input and exploration. SEW, let the fun begin!

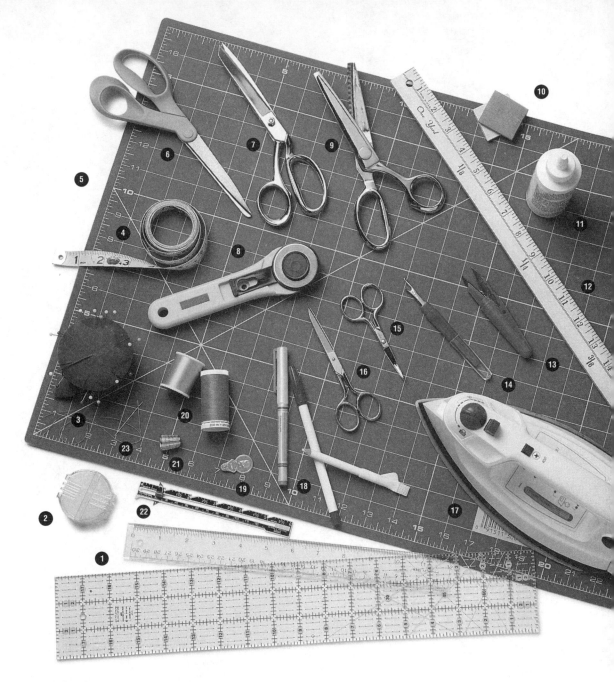

Basic Tools for Craft Sewing

1 Rulers
2 Beeswax
3 Pins & pincushion
4 Tape measure
5 Rotary-cutter mat
6 Standard cutting scissors
7 Dressmaker's shears
8 Rotary cutter

9 Pinking shears
10 Tailor's chalk
11 Fabric glue
12 Yardstick
13 Thread snips
14 Seam ripper
15 Embroidery scissors
16 Sewing scissors

17 Iron
18 Marking pens
& pencils
19 Needle threader
20 Thread
21 Thimble
22 Seam gauge
23 Needles

Part One

For Fun

The Joy of Craft Sewing

▼▼▼

YEARS AGO WHILE TRAVELING through North Carolina, I took a side trip to Old Salem, a restored eighteenth-century town originally settled in 1766 by Moravians fleeing religious persecution in their native Czechoslovakia. I was attracted to the area because Moravian women were known for their beautiful lace and other needlecrafts made without the conveniences of electric lights or sewing machines.

One of the shops offered a short class on how to re-create some of the age-old techniques like making simple lace and fancy finishes for the edges of cloth. My interest in the class was obvious because I had sewn all my life, but as I talked to the other five women, I was surprised to find that none of them had sewn before. "Then why are you doing this?" I questioned, since most of the techniques are rarely used in modern sewing. "Because it's fun!" they unanimously answered.

The American Sewing Guild is a national organization dedicated to sewing. Every state offers chapters, and I highly recommend that you join a group in your area if you are interested in any aspect of sewing (see Resources). Each year the Phoenix, Arizona,

GLENDA'S STORY

Glenda Sparling, author of the popular book on fabric embellishment, *Wrapped in Fabriqué,* is one of those people who overflows with enthusiasm and self-confidence. When I asked her to contribute some inspirational advice for this book, I was surprised to learn that she struggled with insecurity for years.

"As a child I experienced many of the negative messages that parents many times do not know they are expressing to their children," Glenda told me. "As a result, I was convinced that I was totally uncreative and filled with self-doubt. A seventh-grade home economics teacher encouraged me to follow my love of sewing, and that encouragement was the stimulus I needed to pursue an outlet for self-expression long stilled within me. I followed this path and eventually achieved a degree in home economics and a teaching career.

"As the years progressed, my husband saw in me many abilities and creative capabilities that I never saw. His continual support, assistance, and encouragement helped me develop many aspects of my life that were hidden and possibly would never have been seen. I developed a large,

chapter holds an annual retreat in which members converge at a nearby resort to sew for the weekend. Everyone sets up their machines in one huge ballroom, and they literally sew around the clock, finishing projects and starting new ones. A bystander once asked why they did that, and, of course, the answer was "Because it's fun!"

Sewing combines so many good things that it can't help being fun. Come with me while I explain just a few.

successful sewing pattern company that grew from humble origins in Eugene, Oregon, to an international market including the entire United States, Canada, and Australia. My main focus during this exciting time was on instructing home seamstresses to fit and design their own patterns, and although in the past I had always been challenged to find new and creative possi-

bilities, now the difference was that I knew I was creative. I was able to turn off those negative messages and strive to be as good as I could possibly be. This freedom allowed me to release my creativity and develop a totally abstract direction to my sewing—fabric embellishment—which led to the publication of my book.

"I encourage you to listen to your inner voice and awaken hidden skills that will fill your life with reward and achievement. Surround yourself with people who see your talents and appreciate your contributions. Learn to turn your sewing into that pat on the back that says, 'Well done!'"

The Friendly Hobby

If you sew, you automatically have more than 30 million new friends, whether you know them all or not. They are around you everywhere, just waiting to meet and discuss your common interest.

Every time I'm at a party or social gathering, running errands, or strolling through the neighborhood on my evening walks, I know that as soon as I tell someone I sew, the conversation will be off and running. Sewing impacts the lives of everyone daily. We all wear clothes, and we all make use of sewn items constantly. If people I meet don't sew themselves, they all have mothers, grandmothers, aunts, or friends who sew, and their stories about these people are always warm and animated.

There are countless guilds, clubs, organizations, classes, conventions, trade shows, and special events (see Resources) where people converge to celebrate their love of sewing. They are just waiting for you to join!

You can even participate without leaving your home via magazines, newsletters, videos, and books. I'm sure you've run across one of the numerous sewing shows if you've ever channel-surfed. The Web is filled with people eager to exchange ideas, offer helpful tips, discuss sources for materials, or just relate to others with the same interest. You'll find numerous sewing Web sites with chat rooms in the Resources.

If I had to name the number of friends I have met through sewing, I couldn't do it. The list would be impossibly long and the omissions many, but even though I may not have talked with some of them for years, I know we could resume our friendships instantly because of our shared hobby. If you already sew, you know what I mean. If you don't, there's always room for one more!

Silk Purses from Sows' Ears

Last summer I taught a group of children ages 8 through 12 at the Boys & Girls Club in our town how to sew covers for computers. The thrill these youngsters experienced after rummaging through the bag of old fabric I had brought and ending up with something they had made from what they thought was nothing was evident. Some begged to make another cover, while others started to fashion little doll dresses, headbands, and pouches from the leftover fabric scraps. When their rides showed up, no one wanted to go home. They bombarded their parents with exciting stories about their first sewing experiences.

Adults are no different no matter what their age. I'll never forget a young woman in her 20s who took one of my adult sewing classes for beginners. After completing her first project, an embellished tote bag, she shared her amazement and delight with me when she said, "I never knew I could actually do this, create something from nothing!" She had learned what all people who sew know: how to take a pile of cut-up fabric pieces and turn it into a masterpiece.

Enhancing Other Activities

Watching TV has become such a popular pastime that we've coined a new term for someone who does it all the time: *couch potato*. If you sew while you watch TV, you can do so much more than sit and vegetate. If you're sharing the set with someone else, you'll probably have to limit your activity to hand sewing, but I guarantee TV viewing will be a lot more fun when you're working on a good project—especially when it is someone else's turn to select the program!

Because hand sewing doesn't make any noise, you can do it unobtrusively while talking on the phone or sitting at a sick friend's bedside. Better yet, use it to salvage what normally would have been wasted time like sitting in the doctor's office or waiting for the car to be repaired.

I constructed the top for my first quilt during airline flights by designing separate blocks that could be hand appliqued and hand quilted individually. When they were completed, I simply sewed

> **Handy Hint**
>
> Take along a hand-sewing project to make the time pass much faster in case you get stranded at the airport or on a long car, train, or bus trip, or need to fill the time while waiting to pick up a child from some activity.

them all together on my machine at home and hid the seams and edges under purchased quilt binding. I actually looked forward to flying, an activity I previously dreaded, and I produced a valued heirloom.

One of people's greatest talents is the ability to do more than one thing at a time. Sewing lets us shine in this area, and when we're done we always have something beautiful to show for our efforts.

Using Other Talents

Sewing is fun because we can incorporate other needlecrafts that we already know how to do. *Sew News Magazine* is one of the most popular sewing publications in North America (see Resources). A recent issue showed how to use individual quilt squares as pockets to decorate an otherwise plain apron. If you've ever taken a class or already practice another needlecraft, you may have samples or small items left over that alone serve no purpose. Sew them together or sew them onto something else, and you've turned them into an object that is useful and can be shown off at the same time.

I went through a period when counted cross-stitch was my passion. I was so proud of my creations that I framed them all, but soon my house started resembling a cross-stitch museum. I took some of the pieces and sewed them onto other items such as eyeglass covers, tote bags, and even my tennis racquet cover. Now I use and enjoy them much more and so do all the people who never had the chance to visit my "museum"!

My friend inherited a bag of beautiful crocheted squares when her mother passed away. She couldn't possibly part with them, but an afghan, which her mother originally intended them for, just didn't fit into her decorating scheme. By brainstorming together, we found several fun ways to use the squares including sewing some together for a winter scarf and as patchwork covers for pillows. Two

How Many of These Needlecrafts Have You Tried?

- Quilting
- Embroidery
- Needlepoint
- Counted cross-stitch
- Lace making
- Tatting

- Appliqué
- Embellishment
- Smocking
- Weaving
- Knitting
- Crocheting

Sewing puts them all together!

squares sewn together with stuffing inside made a pretty pincushion, my friend's gift to me for my part in the projects.

Colorado is home to many talented weavers, and *Hand Woven*, a magazine dedicated to their craft, is published in Loveland (see Resources). While at a sewing convention in the area, I saw an exhibition of many beautiful items that had been made from hand-woven cloth, including scarves, bags, wall hangings, holiday decorations, and more. I remember thinking what an important part sewing played in the process. If you enjoy other needlecrafts and would like to find a new way to use or display them, craft sewing could be a fun and easy solution.

The Benefits of Sewing

Sewing is probably the most user-friendly of all hobbies. It requires simply no qualifications except the desire and willingness to participate. You can stay at home, and there's no dress code or specific hours of operation. It never gets boring because there are so many options and you can do as much or as little as you please. The investment is low, and, unlike insurance policies in which something bad has to happen before you get the benefits, sewing delivers every time and any time you do it.

Self-Expression

The Home Sewing Association has found that the number-one reason people sew is for creativity. We no longer sew from necessity or to save money but as an outlet, a way to express ourselves. In most cases, because of our high-tech lifestyles, anything that affords us an opportunity to create something by hand is all the more valuable.

Sewing is self-expression personified. In fact, you cannot sew anything *without* expressing yourself. Since we are all individuals, whatever item we craft will carry our own personal touch. I have noticed in my sewing classes that no two people will ever make identical items even when everyone starts with the same materials and pattern. There is no one in the world quite like you, so even if you tried to copy someone's idea exactly, it would still have your own distinct imprint.

Customizing the items we sew is another way of giving them our own personal touch. In addition to embroidering or monogramming initials or names on our handicrafts, sewing provides us with a way to make them more convenient or comfortable. I added just the right size and number of pockets to the fanny pack I made, and when the raincoat I fell in love with didn't have a hood, I fashioned my own from coordinating fabric and attached it with snaps hidden under the collar. My neighbor sewed appliques to her plain sweatshirt, and in one walk around the neighborhood she received five orders!

Do you know people who you love to hate? They always seem to do things you wish you could do, or they have created something so simple yet wonderful that you wonder why you didn't think of it first. They are simply expressing themselves, and that is what sewing is all about.

Sense of Accomplishment

When we accomplish something, we are raised to a higher level, we see things from a new vantage point, and, in the process, we learn new skills that will be with us forever. Nothing is quite so satisfying as the sense of accomplishment that comes from creating something ourselves.

My neighbor Pat grew up in Iola, Kansas, where she learned to sew in 4-H. During one of our many conversations about sewing, I asked her what her biggest accomplishment had been. She immediately lit up while describing her first project, an apron. She won't let me mention her age, but that was over 35 years ago and she remembered every detail including the color of the fabric, the gathers around the waist, the special ruffle she designed herself and added to the top, and even how many times she had to rip it out before it was done. "Talk about accomplishment," she exclaimed. "Nothing could top sewing that apron and winning a ribbon for it at the state fair!"

One of the most poignant sewing stories I know took place at a battered women's shelter where mothers and their children could go when conditions at home became unbearable. The insightful administrators launched a pilot program to teach both the women and their children how to sew various handicrafts with the idea of selling them for a fund-raiser. The program was an overwhelming success not only from the money it raised for the shelter but mostly for the women themselves. Battered women characteristically suffer from low self-esteem, but many blossomed with the sense of accomplishment and the pride they took in creating something of value that they could actually sell. Some gained the courage to improve or leave their painful relationships, and a few even started sewing businesses of their own.

There is no doubt that finishing a successful project builds self-worth and contributes to a feeling of empowerment. I personally believe that if every child in our country learned how to sew (or do some other handicraft), there would be much less vandalism, violence, and crime in our schools today.

Sewing Is Therapeutic

I have dedicated my career to sewing and have taught thousands of students how to sew and start businesses of their own, so I have been around a lot of people who sew. By far the most common comment I hear is that sewing has been their therapy.

Whether it has served to take their minds off family tragedies, given them something to do during a lonely period in their lives, or relieved tension after a stressful day, it has gotten them through the difficult times. Today's life is hectic, but sewing allows us an escape to refresh and restore ourselves. Linda, a sewing buddy in Seattle, discussed how sewing gives her a boost at just the right time. "I always leave my sewing machine set up in a corner of the guest room," she told me. "Just sitting down and sewing for a few minutes relaxes me and gives me a quick pick-me-up whenever I need it."

John Gray, in his popular book *Men Are from Mars, Women Are from Venus*, describes how men need to "go to their caves" (i.e., garages, dens, basements) to escape and regroup from the pressures of daily living. In my opinion, women are just the same. My sewing, wherever it might be located in the house, is a retreat, a time-out from whatever the current crisis may be, and I know thousands of women would agree.

The Busy Woman's Sewing Book, 10-20-30 Minutes to Sew, and *Sewing Express* (a book and video) were all written by Nancy Zieman (see Resources) for women who don't always have as much time to sew as they would like. She breaks down sewing time for popular projects into smaller intervals and shows us how we can steal away to enjoy brief sewing encounters.

I often meet people, just in the course of doing my daily errands, who seem bored or half asleep at their jobs. If sewing happens to enter the conversation as it usually does when I'm around, they perk up and jabber as if a light has come on. Just talking about their hobby uplifts and refreshes them.

Sewing always brings outward tangible results. We actually see, touch, and use what we have created. The process is so rewarding and pleasurable that we want to do it again and again. Remember when I said sewing was addictive? If sewing weren't fun, it certainly wouldn't be therapeutic.

Sewing Is the "Feel-Good" Craft

Do you suffer from any of these symptoms?

- Boredom with the old routine, even if there isn't one

- Inability to laugh at really funny jokes or missing the punch line altogether

- Incurable munchie attacks

- Tiredness all the time, even after a double latte

- Crankiness

- Excessive whining

- Bad hair days

- Broken fingernails

- Forgetting your best friend's name, your husband's name, your name

- The urge to laugh hysterically during meetings, church, or other events where you're supposed to be quiet

If so, you probably need to sew something!

Learning Problem-Solving Techniques

In 1995, I published my book *Sew Hilarious*, which is filled with cartoons about sewing. Most of them were inspired by actual humorous events that had happened in my classes or that I had heard about over a 20-year period from people who sew. The dedication reads, "Dedicated to the sewers of the world: The only people who can do something inside out, upside down, and backward, and have it turn out right!"

Prior to finishing the book, I had been chatting with some women after a Sewing Guild meeting about all the different skills we have garnered and used from our sewing. We, as women, tend to underestimate our capabilities and sometimes don't give ourselves credit for all that we have accomplished.

Because sewing is so enjoyable, we never really stop to think how many problem-solving skills we have developed or used because of it. Decision making is used when selecting a project, envisioning an end use, and implementing a plan for procedure. While sewing, we are constantly figuring where the pieces should go, how to attach them, and in what order to do it. Of course, we make mistakes—that's what ripping is for—but we always survive and go on to bigger and better projects.

For you beginners—not to worry! I was in my late 40s when this conversation occurred, and I realized all my learning experiences had been painless or relatively so. In fact, with each little roadblock has come a small achievement, the results of which just add up to help me the next time around. That's one of the great benefits of sewing: We grow as we sew!

Benefiting Others While Benefiting Ourselves

In addition to giving personal satisfaction, sewing can also benefit humankind. Nancy Zieman, an author I mentioned earlier, is also the originator of a popular mail-order sewing supply catalog called *Nancy's Notions* (see Resources) and the hostess of the public television program *Sewing with Nancy*. In February 1988 she introduced the *Sew a Smile* series, which focuses on volunteer groups who sew for those less fortunate. Over 15,000 people from every state and Canada responded to the program and sent letters describing their charitable activities that were benefiting all ages from newborns to the elderly at homeless shelters, emergency agencies, hospices, and schools.

The movement to help others through sewing has grown and expanded to huge proportions including thousands of clubs and organizations. A neighborhood group of the American Sewing Guild in Philadelphia sewed stuffed animals as well as hats for premature babies in the critical care unit at St. Mary Medical Center, while in another part of the city, Brownie Troop 1234 presented 40 hand-made teddy bears to the Emergency Department at Brandywine Hospital.

The Suncoast Tampa Bay Chapter of the American Sewing Guild makes curtains, bedspreads, pillows, and many other home-decor items and donates them to a home operated by Religious Services in their area. "People who are down on their luck, both individuals and families, may arrive with nothing but the clothes on their backs," Phyllis Reynolds, the current president of the guild told me. "We even sew little ditty bags filled with soap, shampoo, a toothbrush, and other personal items," she continued, "and when they leave they get to take everything with them to furnish their new homes." The same group sewed hundreds of brightly colored oversized bibs for a nursing home; made sleep sacks for the children at homeless shelters; sewed a new outfit for all the children at Stepping Stones to wear on the first day of school; and donated scores of hand-sewn items such as vests, quilts, and wall hangings to be raffled at a charity event. That's not even the complete list of their activities, and there are hundreds of other groups nationwide!

Two women in Minnesota, Bonnie Ellis and Mary Hess, started a grassroots effort sewing thousands of soft, stylish Comfort Caps for cancer patients who often lose their hair during chemotherapy. Their combined efforts with sewing groups and corporate sponsors (such as the Husqvarna Viking Sewing Machine Company, Jo-Ann Fabric Stores, and the Minnesota Division of the American Cancer Society) to create free hats for every cancer patient in the state has now expanded to include the whole country.

The touching and heartwarming stories go on and on. If you would like to get involved by helping others through sewing, you'll find plenty of ideas in the Resources section of this book.

Did you know???

In the late 1990s, the Home Sewing Association unveiled a new program called Sew for the Cure to raise funds for breast cancer research and education, while also helping to publicize the benefits and fun of sewing. All members of the home-sewing industry searched for ways to raise funds through sewing-related products or activities.

What You Can Expect to Create After Learning How to Sew

What can you expect to create with your newfound skill? Just take a look at your life and pick an area that appeals to you.

Do you have children? How about bibs, sun hats, baby blankets, crib liners, sleep sacks, backpacks, cloth play books or book bags, stuffed animals, cloth dolls or doll clothes, and puppets? Here's your chance to make that Halloween costume they've always begged for. There are hundreds of cute patterns for accessories that can be worn with regular clothing to create scary monsters or sweet fairies and more.

What's your favorite sport or hobby? I've already mentioned my tennis racquet and golf club covers, fanny pack, visor, and baseball cap. Add to that a wrist or ankle keyband for jogging; water bottle holders; bicycle packs; beach bags; rowing mitts; fishing vests; tool belts; money belts; butterfly nets; tote bags; garment bags; and sunglass, camera, and binocular cases.

Would you rather just stay at home and relax? We've already talked about many easy and fun home-decor items, but there are also lawn chair and stool cushions, shower satchels, computer covers, bookmarks, silverware bags, and dish caddies. If you do happen to get too chilled—literally, this time—doing all that, sew up a sturdy log tote and put another log on the fire!

You don't have to sew entire garments to spice up or enhance your wardrobe. Try adding a scarf, belt, shawl, hat, hair scrunchie, turban, or purse. Believe it or not, you can even sew jewelry—cloth pins, necklaces, earrings, and bracelets.

Are you beginning to realize that thinking of things to sew will not be a problem? I'm sure you have plenty of ideas already. Let's get started!

Getting Started

▼▼▼

SEWING IS A RELATIVELY INEXPENSIVE hobby to start. I'm going to list and describe essential tools, supplies, and equipment, but remember, since sewing supplies don't go out of date, they don't have to be new, just in good condition. Shop yard sales and thrift stores for bargains that may be used but are in good condition. Perhaps you've inherited a relative's or friend's sewing basket or machine, so here's your chance to use them. Most people already own some of the necessary equipment (e.g., an iron and ironing board), so that will be a savings, too. For additional tools or equipment that you can't find in the usual stores, or for those who don't live near convenient shopping areas, I have listed mail-order sources in the Resources at the end of this book. Aside from fabric and thread, almost everything you purchase for sewing will last a lifetime, so there won't be many repeat expenditures once you're set up.

Tool Tips

Sewing tools should save you time and make each task easier and neater. I'm going to stay with the essentials, but if you're a gadget lover, you'll find an endless variety in craft, fabric, and sewing machine stores. Most of these tools are featured on page xi in the front of the book. Many of these items will be onetime purchases, so shop with the attitude that you are making an investment rather than trying to find the lowest price. Most stores that sell sewing supplies have regular sales, so if you're not in a hurry, shop for the best item, compare prices, and purchase when it's to your advantage. I recommend getting on stores' mailing lists so you will receive flyers with notices of upcoming sales and coupons.

Measuring Up

Measuring tools play a key role in sewing because they are used in every step of a sewing project, from layout and cutting to sewing and finishing. I'm limiting this list to those used for craft sewing, so if you want to progress to making garments later, you may need additional items.

A *tape measure* is the most familiar and indispensable measuring device. The best choice is made from coated fabric or plastic that is flexible and will not tear or stretch, is 60 inches long, has numbers on each side, and has metal tips on the ends. Check your tape measure periodically against a yardstick to be sure it hasn't stretched.

A *seam gauge* is a small, 6-inch metal ruler with a sliding marker. This tool usually costs less than a dollar and is used to retain measurements that must be made over and over, such as to keep hem widths even or to place trim an equal distance from the edge of the fabric such as in fringe on a pillow. My seam gauge is more than 30 years old, and although it is somewhat bent and worn, it's still very serviceable.

You'll need a *ruler* for measuring and marking when a yardstick is too long. I prefer a good old 12-inch plastic ruler from my school days, but newer models are available in transparent plastic up to 18

Tools Needed for Craft Sewing

- Tape measure
- Seam gauge
- Rulers
- Yardstick
- Standard cutting scissors
- Bent trimmers or dressmaker's shears
- Pinking shears
- Sewing scissors
- Embroidery scissors
- Thread snips or clips
- Rotary cutter and cutting mat

- Seam ripper(s)
- Marking pens & pencils
- Tailor's chalk
- Pins
- Needles
- Needle threader
- Pincushion
- Thimbles
- Beeswax
- Fabric glue
- Iron

inches in length. (Later we'll be talking about straight edges used with rotary cutters that can double as rulers.)

Yardsticks are used for taking long, straight measurements and for checking the grain line (see chapter 4 under Fabric Preparation). Select metal or wood that is smooth-shellacked or painted. Wooden yardsticks are breakable, and the markings on both wood and metal can wear off eventually. Wooden yardsticks are a popular giveaway item during store promotions, so I stock up then. I can't remember having ever actually bought a yardstick!

Creative Cutting

Rotary cutters—tools resembling pizza cutters but used for cutting fabric—have greatly impacted sewing, and even though they have great features and make some tasks much easier and faster, there's still a need for traditional scissors in your sewing toolbox. I'll explain the benefits of each and also introduce you to implements for ripping (removing stitches you've already sewn)—an inevitable part of sewing.

Bent trimmers or *dressmaker's shears* have angled, bent handles that allow fabric to lie flat while being cut. The most popular blade lengths are 7 or 8 inches. Even though rotary cutters are now widely used in place of shears, you will still need a good pair of shears to cut certain angles that cannot be reached with cutters or if you simply prefer them to cutters. Select the blade length most appropriate to your hand—7 inches for smaller hands and 8 inches for larger hands. All sewing scissors and shears are available in left-handed models.

Pinking shears cut zigzag, ravel-resistant edges on fabric and are also used for decorative finishes. Seven inches is an average blade length. Pinking shears can be expensive as well as heavy and difficult to use, so a lightweight alternative is a rotary cutter with a pinking blade. Since pinking shears are mainly used for preventing raveling on seam edges, you may want to select another seam finish such as machine zigzagging and make this an optional item.

Sewing scissors contain one pointed and one rounded tip and are used for clipping and trimming seams. Five- or 6-inch lengths are most common.

Embroidery scissors measure 4–5 inches in length, and the two sharply pointed blades are useful for hand sewing and detailed or intricate work.

Thread snips or clips cut thread quickly and easily. Their spring action feature instantly reopens the blades after each clip. Although thread snips are very popular and are made for that specific purpose, I don't own them. I grew up using sewing scissors to cut threads at the machine and embroidery scissors to cut threads while hand sewing.

Rotary cutters are extremely popular with quilters because they cut straight lines easily and accurately, but they also work well for cutting crafts and garments. The blades are available in different sizes (45 millimeters is the most popular) as well as with pinking and wave edges. They must be used with special plastic mats, and fabric weights are often used instead of pins (see chapter 4 for instructions). Recent ergonomic designs make the newest rotary cutters very easy to grasp. If you are going to be cutting a lot of straight lines (as required in most of the projects in this book), you will need a straight edge or durable plastic guide that won't be harmed by

Scissors and Shears Quality and Care

Invest in the best-quality scissors and shears you can afford, and they will last a lifetime with proper care.

- Scissors are shorter than shears and have round handles of equal size. Shears have longer blades and contoured handles for more comfort and leverage in cutting.

- The best quality are made of heat-forged, high-grade steel. Blades should be joined with a screw, not a rivet.

- Never cut anything but fabric as paper or other materials will dull the blades and ruin their alignment.

- Test before you buy. Find a pair that cuts smoothly and evenly from the tip of the blades to the backs and that is comfortable in your hand.

- Occasionally lubricate the screws with a drop of sewing machine oil and wipe them clean with a soft, dry cloth.

- Store them in a case or pouch, or use blade covers that come with some brands.

- Have them professionally sharpened at the first sign of dullness. Most fabric stores can recommend a service, and some have certain days of the month when service is available in the store. If not, contact the manufacturer for referrals.

Rotary-Cutter Mat Must-Do's

- Purchase the largest mat you can afford, or purchase two smaller ones that clip together.

- Store mats flat—never roll them.

- Self-healing mats are the best.

- Heat is the biggest enemy of mats, so never use or store them in direct sunlight.

cutter blades. Rotary cutters, mats in various sizes, weights, and straight edges are available anywhere fabric or sewing supplies are sold. Rotary cutters are extremely sharp. Always take special care when using them, and never leave them within reach of children.

Ripping is probably the least favorite task in sewing, because many people don't realize that traditional *seam rippers*, which aren't extremely sharp in the first place, get dull and must be replaced periodically. Many sewing professionals use pocket knives or single-edged razor blades instead because they are much sharper and last longer. Olfa, a rotary cutter manufacturer, produces a tool called the Rotary Point Cutter. It was originally designed for cutwork and appliqué, but many people use it very successfully for ripping. I give detailed instructions for ripping in chapter 4, so you may want to read them before making a purchase.

Marking Magic

Marking tools enable you to determine which pieces of your projects fit together and where to sew. You'll be sewing on several types of fabrics, so you'll need a variety of marking tools. Thanks to technology, there's a great variety of tools that make marking fast and easy. These are all inexpensive items, so I suggest you purchase one of each so you can "test-drive" them to determine your favorites.

Marking pens are available in two versions: one with water-soluble ink (usually blue) for washable fabrics and the other with evaporating ink (usually purple) that disappears within 48 hours.

Tailor's chalk, a more traditional form of marking, comes in pencil form or small, flat cakes. Marking pens are definitely more convenient, but chalk lasts longer and is less expensive over time.

Marking How-To's

Before starting a project, always test-mark a small swatch of fabric to determine the best marking tool to use. Marks should dissolve, fade, or brush off without leaving stains or residue.

- Pressing may set marks permanently, so test first to see whether this will be a problem.

- If you're using an evaporating marking pen and your work gets interrupted, seal the project in a plastic bag that zips shut, taking care to squish out the air first.

- Always replace the covers tightly on marking pens, or you'll return to find the contents have dried out or evaporated.

- Tailor's chalk in cake form is available in two types: chalky, like chalkboard chalk, and waxy, like soap. The chalky type brushes off, and the waxy type vanishes when touched with an iron, although it can leave residue or grease marks on some fabrics, so test first. Sharpen both with a razor blade.

Pins, Needles, and Hand Tools

Most of these items are small and inexpensive but very essential to sewing. Invest in quality, and you'll save time and effort in the long run.

Pins are available in several lengths and styles. I highly recommend purchasing the type with round heads instead of flat heads and in lengths of 1¼ to 1½ inches. They are much easier to see and grasp and won't get lost in carpets. Glass heads are slightly more expensive than plastic heads, but they won't melt if touched by the iron.

Most of our projects include very little hand sewing, but you'll need a pack of *needles* when the time arises. Sharps are all-purpose, medium-length needles used for general hand sewing with sizes ranging from 1 to 12; I prefer a size 7. Both needles and pins should be rustproof and made from brass, nickel-plated steel, or stainless steel. For easier needle threading, purchase a *needle threader*.

Pincushions provide safe places to store pins, and some contain emery packs that clean and sharpen needles and pins. You've probably noticed or own the popular tomato pincushions that come with emery-filled strawberries. Wrist models keep pins handy, and magnetic versions are wonderful for preventing or picking up spills. Over the years I have made many cherished pincushions from squares of brightly patterned fabric and fiberfill stuffing. Decorative as well as useful, I keep them at different areas in my sewing room.

Until about 170 years ago, when a machine was invented to cut and shape pins from a single piece of wire, pins were uncommon and valuable. Pincushions, originally filled with sand, were also valued possessions.

Thimbles protect your middle finger while sewing and provide a firm surface for pushing the needle through the fabric. They are available in many materials, including plastic, metal, various durable fabrics, and leather. The fabric and leather varieties provide more ventilation. Decorative ceramic thimbles are some of the most popular sewing collectibles, but they aren't used for sewing.

Beeswax coats thread with a smooth finish to make it stronger and prevent tangling during hand sewing. It is an actual byproduct made from honeycombs, and I'll be showing you how to use it in chapter 4. Beeswax makes a tasty snack for some dogs, so if your pet keeps you company while you sew, you may want to purchase the kind with a plastic holder.

Miscellaneous items, which I call *"sewers' helpers,"* speed sewing and make it easier. Fabric glues fasten pieces together until you sew them (instead of basting them by hand) and are either temporary or permanent. They are packaged in bottles or sticks that can be daubed onto fabric. In general, I prefer temporary glues that are guaranteed not to gum up machine needles. Fray Check is a colorless plastic liquid that prevents the edges of fabric from raveling. It's a time-saver but can darken light colors, may become stiff, and is permanent, so always test it on a swatch of your fabric first.

> ### Did you know???
>
> *Thimble* is the contraction of the term *thumb bell,* which was invented in Holland and originally worn on the thumb.

Fabrics and Thread

You've probably heard the popular expression "He who dies with the most ____ (fill in the blank) wins!" For sewing, *fabric* would be the operative word. People who sew love to look at, feel, and buy fabric whether they need it or not, and we call our treasured collections "stashes." Many cartoons and jokes have been written about stashes, and you probably won't sew long before you start one of your own.

Shopping for fabric can be confusing, so I'm going to sift through all the names and categories to simplify the process for you. You may want to skip ahead to chapter 4 and read about fabric preparation prior to sewing before you make your fabric purchases. Basically, all fabrics are made from fibers, and all those fibers are either natural (occurring in nature) or synthetic (artificially made).

Natural Fibers

The four most popular natural fabrics—cotton, silk, wool, and linen—were our mainstays from prehistory until almost 1900. They are known for their absorbency, comfort, versatility, and relatively low static electricity. Modern science has tried to create synthetic fibers with all the same characteristics but has been unsuccessful in duplicating them exactly.

Cotton

Cotton is, by far, the most popular natural fiber because of its ability to breathe and its durability. Cotton's tendency to wrinkle and shrink has been greatly improved thanks to new fabric finishes, but these characteristics are still the biggest drawbacks. Luckily it has the ability to blend easily with other fibers and can add strength, absorbency, and washability, while other fibers can override cotton's negative qualities. Cotton is a good choice for craft projects because of its strength and versatility.

Silk

Silk, which is made from the cocoons of silkworms, is the most luxurious natural fiber. The Chinese, who first cultivated silk, kept the guarded techniques secret for 3,000 years and created a mystique and demand for it that still exists today. Because silk is expensive to produce—each cocoon must be unwound and processed repeatedly—scientists have tried to duplicate it chemically more than any other natural fiber. This has greatly confused consumers because synthetic fibers and fabrics are often described as being "silky" or are even called "silk" when they are not. Silk can add a unique luster to craft items, but lighter weights aren't very durable.

Wool

Wool, which comes from sheep (which produce a new coat each year), has been called one of nature's masterpieces because the surface is highly absorbent but also tends to shed water. Its scaly outer surface can cause liquids such as rain and snow to bead and roll off, while those same liquids together with perspiration and humidity from the air will be absorbed under the scales if allowed to contact the surface long enough. In general, wool is not washable because agitation causes the scales to felt, or bind together and shrink, but new treatments as well as blending it with other fibers have produced washable wools. Wool's natural crimp makes it the most resilient natural fiber and the easiest fabric to press. Some people are allergic to wool and cannot wear it next to their skin without irritation, but when it is used for accessories or craft items, this reaction is not a problem. Felt is a very popular fabric for crafting because it does not ravel, but wool felt is expensive, and many synthetic felts are now available.

Linen

Linen, which was once worn only by the wealthy, is one of the oldest fabrics and was produced 3,000 years before cotton. Made from the flax plant, which has been called the "golden yarn" because of the flax plant's beautiful golden color, linen's absorbency makes it cool and comfortable to wear, but its biggest drawback is wrinkling. Wrinkle-resistant finishes applied to linen have been somewhat successful, but people who wear linen clothes usually must have a high tolerance for the wrinkled look. Using linen for craft sewing can add strength and texture.

Synthetic Fibers

The world became aware of synthetic fibers when nylon was first used for parachutes and rayon replaced wool and cotton because of rationing during wartime. Polyester reached popularity in the 1960s with the infamous leisure suit and the explosion of knits. Synthetic fibers are advantageous because they can be produced year-round,

Fabric Facts

- Fabric comes in 36-, 45-, 54-, or 60-inch widths that are listed on the ends of the bolts. In general, the wider the fabric, the less you'll need for a project. Fabric stores have width conversion charts to figure the equivalent yardage for each width. Fabric is cut in 1/8-yard increments.

- Also listed on bolt ends are the price per yard, the fiber content, and care instructions. You'll need this information for preparing and caring for your fabric later.

- Fabric is grouped together in stores in various categories such as knits, home-decor fabrics, bridal fabrics, bottom weights (usually for making pants), suit weights, and so forth. Most stores sell many types of fabrics, but some specialize in one kind, such as in upholstery fabric or quilting fabric.

- Get to know the different weights and textures by walking around and feeling the fabrics. Some are heavy, some light. Some stretch; some don't. Try to visualize how a particular fabric would look made up in the project you're doing. Crush the fabric in your hand. Does it bounce back or stay wrinkled?

- Select the best quality you can afford. Poor-quality fabric never justifies the time and effort you spend on it.

- If you can't make up your mind or have questions, ask a clerk or another customer in the store. They are all there because they love to sew and will usually gladly help.

indoors, and in relatively little space. Quality is easier to control, and they can be produced in any length and thickness. Synthetics can be superior to natural fibers in color-fastness and wrinkle resistance, but blends of both combine the best qualities of each.

In general, artificially made fibers are synthesized from either natural materials such as cellulose or protein or from completely chemical sources. Rayon, the first synthetic, was developed by fiber scientists who were trying to make "artificial silk." Other well-known synthetics are acetate, triacetate, acrylic, nylon, polyester, spandex, and the new microfibers. The confusing part for consumers is that each fiber may have several brand names that offer no clue to the fiber origin, such as polyester marketed under Dacron, Fortrel, Trevira, and other names.

Fabric stores are required to list the contents of fabric on the ends of bolts, so this makes identification easier. Luckily, the natural fibers are always listed in their generic names as cotton, silk, wool, or linen. I have described the general characteristics of these so you know how they will perform. If they are blended with another fiber, the percentages of each will be listed. It's impossible to learn and keep current on all the trade names for synthetics, but just be aware that *anything other than a natural fiber listed on the label will be a synthetic,* and they have probably been combined to enhance the best qualities of each.

Fabric Construction

The way fabrics are constructed will make a difference in how they perform, so I'm going to give you some essential facts. Most fabrics are either woven or knitted. A woven fabric is composed of two sets of yarns that are woven together at right angles. As a child, did you ever make potholders on a simple metal loom? That was simple weaving and will give you an idea of how woven fabric is made. In general, woven fabrics do not stretch at all or very little and are appropriate for all the projects in this book.

Knitted fabrics are made from a series of interlocking loops that allow the fabric to stretch. Have you ever seen someone knitting a sweater? Knit fabric is produced by a similar method, only mechanically and on a much larger scale. T-shirts, jogging suits, swimsuits, and socks are all made of knitted fabric. Knits are used mostly when stretch is needed, such as in sportswear, so wovens are better choices for the projects in this book.

Grain

All knitted or woven fabrics have direction, or *grain,* that is established by the position of the yarns from which the fabric is made. The lengthwise grain goes up and down on the fabric, parallel to the selvages, or tightly woven edges of the fabric, and the crosswise grain goes back and forth, or perpendicular to the selvages. Grain affects the way garments or any items made from cloth hang and perform. If you've ever had a pair of jeans that twisted around your legs, you've experienced fabric that was "off grain" when it was cut.

Modern methods of fabric manufacturing have greatly reduced this problem, but the easiest way to detect it is by simply looking at the fabric in the store to see whether it looks straight. For wovens, the threads should be at right angles to each other without curves, bends, or distorted lines; for knits, the little loops should do the same. If a fabric looks crooked in the store, though it may be possible to straighten it (see chapter 4), I wouldn't advise buying it.

Very few synthetic fabrics, such as vinyl or fake leathers and suedes, are bonded, a process in which textile fibers are fused together with an adhesive or bonding agent. Sometimes they can be cut without regard for grain, and since there are no yarns to unravel, they can be sewn without finishing the edges. Samples of several of the eyeglass cases in chapter 5 are made from bonded fabrics—they were fast and easy.

Special Surfaces

Fabrics with nap, such as corduroy, velvet, synthetic suedes, velour, fleece, and fake fur, have raised, textured surfaces. They usually appear light, shiny, and smooth when brushed in one direction and darker and rougher when brushed in the opposite. The smooth side usually goes down the body when making garments, but for craft sewing, you can sometimes select whichever direction you prefer. Working with napped fabric is more challenging because the fabric tends to shift when you are sewing two pieces together. You need patience and a lot of pins, or sometimes hand basting is required.

Thread

All of the projects in this book will require all-purpose or general-purpose thread available in cotton-covered polyester or 100% polyester, both being very adequate. When shopping for thread, read the spool ends carefully to make sure they fit these specifications, because thread racks will also contain lightweight thread, topstitching thread, button and carpet thread, and thread for decorative stitching. If you can't find a thread to match your fabric exactly, buy a shade darker. You will need only one small spool for each project in this book, but if you anticipate sewing a lot in the future, you may want to purchase larger spools of basic colors like white and black. Don't be tempted by bargain bins of thread while walking down the store aisles unless you have carefully read the labels on the spools. They often contain inferior-quality thread or smaller than normal amounts per spool and aren't a savings at all.

For Your Information

Interfacing is special fabric used to reinforce and support outer fabric to maintain shape and firmness. In general, try to select fabric that is the proper weight for your project, but if you fall in love with a piece that seems too lightweight, you may be able to interface it to achieve the results you desire. Ask a clerk to help you choose the appropriate interfacing.

Pressing Equipment

Pressing is essential for a professional look in all sewn items, and I'll be giving you instructions on how to press in chapter 4, but first I want to discuss pressing equipment. I usually turn my iron on first thing in the morning and use it all day while sewing my projects, so it is an indispensable tool.

Irons

If you already have an operative iron, you're ahead of the game; otherwise, you may be shopping for a new one or want to upgrade. Technology has provided us with wonderful new irons that make this traditionally dreaded task much easier and quicker. Weight, which provides leverage for pressing, used to be a key factor when purchasing irons, but because modern irons produce so much steam, weight is now merely determined by personal preference. The most important feature in any iron is steam production, and manufacturers have responded to this need by offering variable steam settings, bursts of steam, vertical steam, and more steam vents in soleplates. If you'll be using your iron to press clothing, you may want the feature that enables you to spray a stream of water on garments that are very wrinkled.

The new trend in irons is toward steam generators with separate high-capacity water tanks that provide stable bases for the irons. Steam is delivered to the iron through a thick cord. The iron can be lighter and smaller than a normal iron because the high volume of steam makes pressing faster and easier.

Pressing Surfaces

No matter what pressing surface you use, try to allow yourself the largest pressing area possible. You may want to start out with an

Checklist for Purchasing an Iron

☐ Heat—wide range of variable temperatures

☐ Steam production—burst of steam, variable steam settings, ample steam holes in soleplate

☐ Water—tap or distilled; directions should clearly indicate what is required

☐ Soleplate—nonstick and/or scratch-resistant finish; grooved border for pressing around buttons

☐ Handle—comfortable to grasp

☐ Settings—easy to reach and adjust

☐ Weight—not important if there's adequate steam

☐ Warranty—one year or more

☐ Cord—swivel or pivoting, adjustable for left-hand pressing, or cordless

☐ Extra features—stream of water, self-cleaning, automatic shut-off

☐ Manual—clear and easy to comprehend; name, address, and phone number of manufacturer or service center

ironing board and, if your hobby develops, then progress to a pressing table. An ironing board should be sturdy and level with collapsible legs that are easy to operate. Believe it or not, wood is the ultimate pressing surface because it absorbs moisture, so if you have an old wooden ironing board stored in the attic, here's your chance to use it. Most modern ironing boards are metal, but they contain holes or mesh surfaces to allow for escaping moisture. Foldout ironing boards that fit into walls or retract into their own cases are available if space is very limited.

I prefer using a pressing table instead of an ironing board for craft sewing because tables are more stable and provide larger surfaces to lay out the pieces of my projects. My sewing room is large, so I padded and covered a door (without the doorknobs) that I purchased at a building supply store and placed it on two filing cabinets for support. In the past, when my sewing areas were smaller, I simply cut a piece of plywood to fit in whatever space I had, padded and covered it, and set it on one or two filing cabinets or tables, whatever worked best.

Many options also exist for small and folding press boards. June Tailor Inc. sells both the Quilter's Square (18 × 24 inches) and the Quilter's Square 'N Press (12 × 18 inches), covered and padded, dense fiberboards, that can be placed next to your machine or carried with you to another part of the house. Handler Textile Corporation markets Space Boards (available in 21 × 27 inches and 33 × 51 inches) for pressing that are portable and can be folded in half for storage (see Resources for both).

Most experts agree that cotton covers are best whether you're covering a pressing table or an ironing board, because cotton dissipates the heat evenly. Synthetic or metallic covers can be slippery and may produce hot spots. Traditionally the best pads were cotton or wool because both absorb moisture, but the new hydrophobic pads made from nylon are engineered to wick moisture away, just like some outerwear fabrics that wick moisture away from the body. They are uniform in width, won't get matted down, and can be washed by hand (see Resources).

Press cloths are used between the iron and the fabric to prevent shine marks. They are available for sale in fabric stores, but you could use a handkerchief, diaper, or piece of cotton cloth as well. Always press a small corner of your fabric before ironing the entire piece to determine whether a press cloth is needed.

Sewing Machines

Your sewing machine will be an important tool and a trusted companion for years to come, so I'm providing a mini-guide to help you find the perfect one. Following is a basic overview of machine types, a list of specific features, and some tips for machine maintenance.

Buying a Machine

Before shopping for a machine, take the time to determine your individual needs. Consider your skill level, how much time you want to devote to your hobby, and your budget. If you are a beginner and not sure you'll be sewing much more than an occasional project, many basic, very adequate, and inexpensive machines are on the market, some costing less than $100. If you want to make a major commitment to your new hobby and possibly turn it into a money-making venture, or if you have sewn for a while and want to upgrade your machine, the sky is the limit for computerized models with all the bells and whistles. Modern sewing machines are divided into two categories: mechanical, which means you turn dials, and computerized, which means you push buttons—quite a change from grandmother's treadle!

Just about any basic machine will allow you to sew two pieces of fabric together, but additional features will enable you to do it faster and easier, and perhaps with more style. Simpler and less expensive mechanical machines do basic straight stitches, zigzag stitches, and probably several decorative stitches. More expensive and complex computerized machines do all of the above plus buttonholes, embroidery, and a multitude of decorative stitches. In general, the more features they have, the more expensive they will be both to purchase and to repair.

The Serger

An alternate type of sewing machine, the serger, was introduced to the home sewing market in 1984. Its outstanding feature is the ability to trim, finish (overcast the edges), and sew all in one motion. Although sergers can be used to stitch entire garments or sewn items, they have not replaced regular sewing machines. Many people, particularly those who sew clothing, own sergers in addition to their regular machines, and all sewing machine dealers now carry them.

The best way to shop for a machine is to visit a variety of sewing machine stores (Sears, JC Penney, and other department stores also sell machines), see machine demonstrations, and actually sew on the machines yourself. If you have sewn before, take some samples of your own fabric because the samples used in stores for demonstrations are always the most foolproof. Make a list of popular features and compare them from brand to brand. This will help you decide which is the best buy for the price. I've prepared a basic list to help you, and if you're a beginner, some of the terms may be a bit strange now, but you'll quickly become familiar with them during your first demonstration. Refer also to the sewing machine illustrations to spot the principal parts of machines. Be sure to have a firm idea of your needs and goals *before* you go into the store because the salesperson will want to sell you the fanciest model.

Try not to be dazzled by features that you'll never really use. It's amazing to see a machine stitch rows of yellow ducks, but how many times would you actually use that feature? I once bought a $3,000 machine mostly because of the great buttonhole it made. At home I could never seem to duplicate the one in the store demonstration and learned an expensive lesson I have never forgotten: never buy on impulse!

Talk to other people about their machines, what type of projects they sew, the features they like and don't like, and who their dealer is. One of the most important factors in purchasing a machine is the availability of service and repair in your area. Most dealers offer classes, which is the best way to get to know and use your machine. If you don't live near a dealer, investigate fabric stores or community colleges for basic sewing and machine operation and repair classes.

Machine Maintenance

Caring for your new machine will ensure years of dependable use. Manufacturers claim that 80% of all repairs could be avoided with regular maintenance. Follow these handy tips:

> **Did you know???**
>
> In 1855, the first year sewing machines were actively marketed, 883 were sold. By the end of 1856 that number had increased to 2,564. According to the Independent Sewing Machine Dealers Association, an estimated 1.5 million machines were sold every year during the 1990s in the United States alone, and many people who frequently sew own two or more machines!

- Learn to clean and oil your machine if necessary according to the manual instructions.

- Wipe the surfaces with a clean cloth and cover the machine when not in use.

- Change the needle regularly. Some machines make a slight clunking sound when the needle is dull. Use the appropriate needle and thread for each individual project.

- Read and follow manual directions for even the simplest tasks. Turning dials the wrong way or even threading the machine improperly can cause damage, jamming, or timing problems.

- Always make sure the machine is turned off and out of the reach of children when not in use.

- Have your machine serviced regularly—about once a year for optimum performance.

Sewing Machine Features

☑ Easy to thread

☑ Accessible and easy-to-fill bobbin

☑ Straight, reverse, and zigzag stitches

☑ Number of decorative stitches—built-in or on cams or disks

☑ Dials and buttons that are easy to identify and adjust

☑ Movable needle positions

☑ Feed dogs that can be dropped or covered

☑ Attachments that come with the machine, extras available

☑ Portable or built-in cabinet

☑ Length and terms of warranty

Buying Used Machines

Buying a used sewing machine is just like buying a used car. There are great bargains to be had, but always check them out with a reputable repair shop before making the purchase. Ask the previous owner whether the machine was ever registered for a warranty, and check to see that all extra and necessary attachments are included along with the instruction manual. Sewing machine dealers are a great source for used machines and almost always offer extended warranties with every sale.

Setting Up Your Personal Workspace

▼▼

EVERY WOMAN WHO LOVES SEWING dreams of a place all her own where she can be free to visualize and create. Whether you have the luxury of an entire room or must carve out a special area somewhere within your home, find a place that will be yours alone—a haven, a retreat, a sewing sanctuary. I am going to show you how to claim that special space and use it to the utmost advantage, no matter what the size.

Location

While locating and arranging your space, remember that you are creating a special area that will bring hours of enjoyment, satisfaction, and relaxation for years to come. Each item you select will help build and contribute to your accomplishments. This is not a self-centered or selfish idea—women in general spend their lives caring for others—it is a chance to take time out and devote some attention to yourself.

Analyzing Your Needs

Probably the most important aspect of analyzing your needs is determining how much time you will spend sewing. Do you want to limit your sewing to strictly a hobby? Do you want to enjoy sewing mainly as a hobby but make some items to sell occasionally, or would you like to develop your sewing into a full-time career? In general, the more time you want to devote to sewing, the more space you will need.

What is your personal style for engaging in a hobby? Do you need solitude, preferring to work alone, or do you like to be in the center of activity, perhaps preferring or needing to keep an eye on what's going on around you? I have talked to some people who sew who "just can't think straight" unless they are alone in a quiet place, and others purposely locate their sewing spaces in the kitchen or family room because they like to have company around them all the time.

Think about your tolerance for clutter or your desire for neatness. Do you prefer finishing one project before completing the next, or are you happiest when several projects are going at once? Do you like to own every available tool and gadget, or do you operate with the bare essentials? Do you throw away scraps or save everything hoping to find that special use for it someday? Each style has different space requirements, and if you are a collector, you may need room to expand in the future.

If you don't live alone, consider the feelings of those around you. It would greatly detract from your sewing experience to have your husband constantly asking you to clean up the clutter or to stop sewing so he can hear the television.

Working with the Space You Have

After analyzing your basic needs and personal style, walk around your living space (both inside the house and out) to find an area that's just right for you. Entire rooms are the obvious first choice, but if these are not available, search creatively and don't rule out the smallest nook or cranny. Consider parts of rooms—closets, walls, counters, or corners—and don't leave out hallways, laundry rooms, sunrooms, basements, and garages. Some of the most loved and used sewing areas I have seen were made from alternate spaces like an old tool shed or gardening room. One woman set up shop in the family motor home, and I remember her proudly opening the storage compartments underneath to reveal stacks of fabric and sewing supplies.

While searching for a location, it's natural to think bigger is better, but that's not necessarily true. I have had nine different sewing spaces during my career ranging from entire rooms to very small areas, and by far the most efficient was a linen closet that measured 4 × 9 feet. The shallow built-in drawers previously used for storing linens worked perfectly for hiding fabric, projects in progress, and sewing supplies. Everything was within an arm's reach, and I could sit and sew for hours without getting up. The advantage of a larger room is more space for storage, shelving, and cutting and pressing areas, but remember a basic physics law as it relates to sewing: The more room you have, the more stuff you'll fill it up with!

Essential Areas

Before you claim your special space, make sure it has room for certain specific operations. Every sewing space, no matter what the size, ideally needs four essential areas: cutting, sewing, pressing, and storage. We'll be discussing each in detail later, but for now I'll give you the minimum requirements. (Note: Throughout the rest of this chapter, I will refer to items or places that are listed in the Resources at the end of the book, so refer to it whenever you need more information.)

Essential Areas Checklist

☐ Sewing—Your "Control Central"

☐ Pressing—Accessible and convenient

☐ Cutting—Can be in a different location

☐ Storage—Never enough!

Sewing Space

For sewing, you'll need space for the machine and an area large enough to accommodate a chair, which might be on wheels. If you're in a hallway, under a stairwell, or in some other area with traffic flow, you can move the chair to another location when you're not sewing. Just make sure there is enough space to move the chair up to and away from the sewing machine easily without tripping on it or having it block your path.

> ### Handy Hint
> The cutting area requires the most space—probably at least a square yard for the smallest project.

Pressing Space

Depending on the nature of your sewing projects and the equipment you already own or want to purchase, you will require at least a small area for pressing. I discussed ironing boards and alternative pressing areas in chapter 2, so refer back to it as needed.

Cutting Space

Cutting, though it needs the most space, is the task that can most easily be done in another area such as on the kitchen or dining room table, so if you find a great location that is smaller than you'd like, a cutting area is not a necessity. I have an entire room set up for sewing now, but I still do my cutting on the dining room table so I can allocate what would have become a cutting space to other activities within my sewing room itself. In a previous home—the one with the linen closet sewing room—I did all my cutting on a Ping-Pong table in the basement. That was several flights of stairs away, so I simply cut as many projects as possible at one time to save on trips.

Sewing machine cabinet manufacturers offer a variety of space-saving, fold-down cutting tables. One of the most popular is made by the Sew Fit Company from heavy-duty cardboard that is lightweight and collapsible. Folding aluminum tables are another alternative when space is limited.

Storage Space

Every sewing area needs storage, and there are endless possibilities and options for you to consider. While doing so, take into account

How to Get Organized

Before you start your projects, take a few moments to plan for a pleasurable experience.

- Organize the tools you'll need beforehand—always keep tools in the same place so you won't lose them and spend time searching.

- Buy duplicate items so you won't have to carry them back and forth.

- If you're working on more than one project at a time, store each in a separate plastic container.

- Keep a swatch of fabric from each project and staple it to an index card listing the date, cost, problems, techniques, improvements, and other information.

- If you're a beginner, don't get overwhelmed—break your project down into steps: cut one day, machine sew the second, hand sew and finish the third.

- When done, leave your work area tidy and ready for your next sewing adventure.

your comfort level for clutter and neatness, and to what extent you want to develop your hobby. Aside from a comfortable place to sit and sew, storage is probably the most important consideration in selecting an area, and I'll be giving you plenty of attractive and fun ideas for that.

Setting Up an Efficient Workspace

Most kitchen designs feature a sink somewhere in the middle flanked by a refrigerator on one side and a stove on the other. This U-shaped layout is considered efficient because a minimum number of steps are needed between tasks. A sewing space is no different in that ultimately everything should be within easy reach or a few steps away. Start by situating your sewing machine and chair between the areas for laying out project pieces and pressing, and include other details as needed. You may want to create a diagram of your ideal sewing room so you can mark off the dimensions on graph paper and move them around to explore the layout options. Smaller spaces take less time to design and can be very efficient.

Furniture

A comfortable chair is probably your most important piece of furniture. I probably sat in 50 or more chairs before I finally decided to purchase one, and even after all that research, I still bought and returned several before I found just the right one for me. I'm going to give you some basic facts that will help you narrow down the field before you visit the store. Most important, a chair should be ergonomic, or adjustable to the individual needs of your body. The optimum width for the seat of the chair is about 16 inches from front to back, and the ideal seat height ranges from 14 to 21 inches above the floor depending on your height. For sewing, the front of the seat should be tilted upward about 15 degrees to reduce back strain and pressure on the thighs, and the chair should swivel. The back of the chair should be adjustable in every direction and contoured for lumbar (lower-back) support. A five-leg base with quality castors is the most stable. Fully adjustable chairs may cost a little more than ones with fewer features, but they are worth the expense in the long run.

Handy Hint

You may need to purchase a plastic chair mat if your sewing space is carpeted.

Whether your sewing machine is portable or is contained in its own cabinet will determine how much extra furniture you need for actual sewing. If your machine is portable, you will need a stable surface to prevent machine vibration. This could be as simple as a desk or table or as elaborate as an entire sewing cabinetry system, depending on the size of your space and your budget. If you are just starting out, I recommend keeping it simple in the beginning until you decide how involved your hobby will become. It will also be easier to determine your needs more accurately after you have actually sewn several projects, but you will need some extra space around the sewing machine to lay project pieces, tools, and supplies that you are using at the time.

If you're not purchasing cabinetry made especially for sewing, visit the cheapest and best furniture showroom around—your own home! The attic, garage, and basement are particularly good sources, especially for furniture that has been retired, but I have found other pieces that weren't being used or wouldn't be missed in the lived-in areas, too. Even if they weren't made especially for sewing, they probably have personality and can be modified to fit your needs by adding extra shelves, drawer dividers, or blocks of wood to make them the right height.

Home centers, kitchen and bath shops, antique malls, and office supply and computer stores all offer many items that can be used as they are or combined with furniture you already own. Two filing cabinets have been with me through all my moves—sometimes they stand on their own in different parts of the room or are hidden in a closet, or they make a great sewing, cutting, or pressing table by putting a board or piece of countertop over them. Hardware, closet, storage, and container stores carry endless options. Yard sales are also inexpensive treasure troves for furnishing your space.

Storage

You will never have enough storage. I have always found a way to completely cover every square inch of my sewing areas with usable storage, and I could always use more. Again, the storage system you use will depend on your personal style, the amount of sewing you do, your budget, and the size of your sewing space. This is an area where creativity helps as much as a full pocketbook, so explore the options and then let those creative juices flow. The key words are accessibility and convenience, so try to make everything easy to identify and easy to reach.

Pegboards and/or corkboards have been part of every sewing room I've had as well as adjustable shelving in all lengths and widths. I also use clear plastic tubs in many sizes to hold nearly everything I'm not using and stack them on shelves, counters, or inside closets. They allow me to see what's inside without opening them, and I can carry a tub to a location, use what's inside, and return it without misplacing anything. My first sewing area did not have enough wall space to hang a spool caddy, so I put all my thread in two oversized brandy snifters—one for light colors and one for dark—and placed them on the table behind my sewing machine. This made the spools so easy to see and accessible that I've never changed the system.

Storage with Style

- Use metal cookie tins, canisters, or ice cube trays to store buttons, snaps, needles, and other small sewing notions.

- Add extra shelves or cabinets to closets to utilize the maximum space.

- Create a great sewing basket from a fishing tackle box or picnic basket.

- Hang wire baskets and pot racks from the ceiling and fill with supplies or drape ribbon, trim, tape measures, and so forth.

- Install shelving 12 to 15 inches below the ceiling for decorative storage; use colorful baskets, boxes, or other containers to hold supplies.

- Place screw-in wall pegs where needed.

- Buy or have a lumberyard cut additional shelves for existing bookcases; get extra brackets to customize your shelf heights.

- Fill a plastic garbage can with new fabric or leftovers; top it with a round piece of wood and a circular tablecloth.

- Search your local hobby and craft stores for many sizes and shapes of partitioned display racks that can be mounted on a wall.

- Install shelving above windows and doors.

- Cover empty popcorn or potato chip cans with fabric and use for storage or waste cans.

- Don't forget other areas of the house such as under beds, inside window seats, or in the refrigerator (just kidding, but it's probably been done!).

Safety in Sewing

People who have sewn for a long time know there are safety issues associated with sewing—and many have learned the hard way.

Keep in mind, though, that in the overall picture these are merely areas that demand a little extra attention and won't overshadow the pleasure that sewing provides. Following are some reminders for the experienced and some precautions for beginners.

- Never sew over pins—they can break and the point may fly into your eye.

- Don't sew over your finger. This may seem somewhat comical, but almost everyone who has sewn for awhile has done it. Prevent this from happening by not sewing when you are rushed or fatigued, and by not shoving or forcing the fabric through the machine.

- Always push a seam ripper away from your body while ripping, just as you always cut away from yourself with a knife.

- Always store sewing shears under cover or in protective cases that many of them come with when they're new.

- Develop the habit of covering rotary cutter blades immediately after use. Rotary cutters are the sharpest and most dangerous cutting implements used in sewing. Some new rotary cutters have blade guards that snap into place as soon as the cutter leaves your hand.

Because of these safety issues, it is important, if children are a part of your life, to find a way to protect them from potential harm (see sidebar, Sewing, Safety, and Children, on page 51).

Creature Comforts

Patrick Grant of Tiara Furniture Industries, manufacturers of sewing furniture, says that a sewing space should really be called a "fun" space, and what a great description that is! In addition to arranging the furniture and storing all those wonderful materials and tools, you'll want to create an environment that provides a comfortable and pleasant place to sew. Let's start with flooring and work our way up.

Sewing, Safety, and Children

If you think children may ever be part of your sewing experience at one time or another, here are some tips to consider:

■ Try to sew during nap time or after bedtime, or trade baby-sitting with other sewers who have children.

■ A sewing space contains many items that can be harmful to children—irons, electrical cords, scissors, pins, needles, rotary cutters, seam rippers, and so forth. Take extra precaution to store or shield these items by child-proofing the area.

■ The sewing machine is a very tempting "toy"—remove the cord and needle between projects if necessary.

■ Make your sewing space or parts of it "off limits."

Floor Coverings

Vinyl, probably the most popular floor covering for sewing spaces, is affordable, easy-care, and provides a firm but not hard surface. Hardwood flooring is more luxurious and expensive, but dropping pins can easily scratch it. Ceramic tile, although attractive and distinctive, is hard, and its uneven texture makes moving in a chair and standing difficult and uncomfortable.

Carpet is warmer and softer to stand on, but pins can become buried easily. The best carpet for a sewing space is commercial grade with low, dense pile and little or no padding. If your sewing space already has flooring that you are unhappy with and changing it is not an option, use area rugs to soften harder surfaces and chair mats to protect carpet. Dropped pins, threads, and fabric scraps are all part of sewing, so if clean floors are your priority, you may want to stash a small hand vacuum nearby.

Wall Treatments

Whether you select paint or wallpaper for the walls of your sewing space, I recommend you keep them light in color and subdued in design. You will want them to reflect as much light as possible because you will probably cover a substantial portion of them with storage systems or decorations, and distinct patterns would only detract as a backdrop.

Covering a wall or a portion of one with fabric is a fun, colorful, and very appropriate accent for a sewing space. Quick Trak, a plastic channel that holds fabric in place without glue or stiffeners, allows you to display fabric and change to another piece easily without damaging it. What a great way to dream about and visualize your next project or preserve an unusually beautiful piece!

Lighting

Proper lighting is probably the most important creature comfort for your sewing space. You will need to supplement natural light even if your area is filled with windows. Everyone is familiar with incandescent lighting, the most popular and least expensive method. Halogen bulbs were high profile several years ago because they use half the power of incandescent bulbs and last up to seven times longer. Unfortunately, they can become very hot and even fade surfaces, so their popularity has waned.

Fluorescent lights are cooler and use 60% less energy than incandescent lights, making them environmentally more sound, but some people are sensitive to the particular glare they can give off. I replaced the standard fluorescent tube above my pressing table with a Vita-Lite fluorescent tube. It is full-spectrum (very similar to natural sunlight), gentler on my eyes, and is wonderful for color and shade matching.

Painting Parameters

■ Paint is the least expensive and most dramatic way to change the look of an area. Unless your space is very large, paint your moldings and baseboards the same or a similar color as the walls to avoid chopping up areas.

■ Select brighter colors for areas with northern exposures and duller colors for ones with southern exposures.

■ To make a low ceiling appear higher, paint it lighter than the walls; to appear lower, paint it darker.

■ Camouflage cracked or chipped walls by adding a textured surface available at paint and hardware stores, or use textured wallpaper, fabric, or sponge paint.

■ Steer clear of intense colors for flooring, walls, and ceilings—unless you don't mind running outside to match fabric and thread! Any color other than a very light neutral changes the color of thread and fabric substantially.

■ Consider the effect you want before choosing high-gloss or semigloss paint. High-gloss paint is more dramatic than semigloss or flat; however, semigloss and gloss are easier to wash.

You can't be around sewing circles very long without hearing about the new technology in lighting—the Ott-Lite. Ott-Lites produce low-heat, nonglare, full-spectrum light that rivals natural daylight, enabling you to see colors without distortion or fading. They are very energy-efficient—a 13-watt Ott-Lite produces about the same amount of light as a 60-watt incandescent bulb—and are available in bulbs to fit normal household lamps or in special Ott-Lite lamps where the bulbs resemble small fluorescent tubes. Ott-Lites seem expensive when compared to other lighting, but they will last up to 10 times longer and deliver far superior light.

Whatever your light sources, you'll need both ambient or overhead lighting and task lighting to highlight smaller areas. You may want to use a combination such as florescent tubes in the ceiling and Ott-Lites or incandescent bulbs for task lighting. Even though most sewing machines include built-in lights, you will probably need extra lighting near your machine and in any other area that requires close-up work. Lynette Ranney Black's book, *Dream Sewing Spaces*, gives excellent ideas for balancing your sewing space lighting including wattage requirements, light positioning, and accent lighting.

Temperature Control

Heating, cooling, and ventilation are important comfort considerations for your sewing space. Irons and pressing equipment as well as lighting can all contribute heat, so depending on your climate you'll need a way to dissipate it by using a fan, air conditioner, or an extra vent if you have central air. Steam irons also produce moisture that can make sewing uncomfortable in humid climates. Small, freestanding air conditioners are available in some appliance stores or by mail order from catalog companies such as Harmony. Some fabrics, glues, and backing materials used in sewing can give off odors, so if you are sensitive, you may need to have extra ventilation. For cooler climates, you may need to add another heating vent or use a space heater, especially if your flooring is vinyl, hardwood, or tile.

Electricity

Sewing machines require very little electricity, but irons, space heaters, and air conditioners all use a lot of power. If your space has a shortage of outlets, power strips work well for sewing machines and lights, but ideally irons and air conditioners should have their own circuits. If you live in an older home or apartment, always consult a qualified electrician before plugging in your equipment—it's not worth taking a risk!

Clutter Control

You'll enjoy sewing and look forward to your hobby more if your sewing area is neat and clean. Place wastebaskets near areas where you'll cut, trim, and sew to make cleanup convenient. I received a colorful can covered with photos of vintage Singer sewing machines for a gift, and it has become a valued and useful part of my decorating scheme. A variety of thematic waste cans as well as little bags for collecting thread and fabric scraps that connect to sewing machines are available in fabric and sewing machine stores.

> ## Handy Hint
>
> When wiring a new room, install at least two circuits—one for the iron, and one for a general outlet.

Even the most proficient "neat freak" can have trouble keeping a sewing space tidy all the time, so if you can't close the door and walk away, you may be able to camouflage the area with a colorful screen, a large potted plant, fabric curtains, or some other type of room divider. I have seen hundreds of sewing rooms and have never met an owner who didn't apologize for the mess. In fact, if a sewing space looked too neat, I would automatically assume the owner of the room hadn't been sewing lately!

Creative
How-To's

▼▼

IF YOU ALREADY KNOW HOW to sew, perhaps you learned from your mother, grandmother, another family member, or a friend. My mother decided school was the best place for me to learn, so I started sewing in an eighth grade home economics class. It's a miracle I ever got past the first project, a tea towel (now we call them dish towels), which simply involved cutting out a square of fabric and turning the edges under to make a hem. I didn't think that was fun at all, and I ripped out the stitches so many times that sections were threadbare! Luckily I persevered and eventually made projects I loved and found useful.

If you are just beginning, I want to make your first sewing experiences fun and easy from the start. We'll build on the basics and go on to simple projects that are attractive, useful, and salable—itcms almost anyone would love to own. Those of you who have sewn before may want to skim this chapter and then proceed directly to the projects in chapter 5.

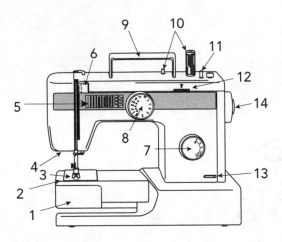

1. Door to bobbin
2. Throat plate and seam guide
3. Presser foot
4. Light
5. Built-in stitches
6. Tension dial
7. Stitch-length regulator
8. Stitch selection
9. Fold-down handle
10. Spool holders
11. Bobbin winder
12. Stitch-width regulator
13. Reverse sewing
14. Hand wheel

Figure 1. Standard sewing machine and parts.

Machine Sewing

Congratulations! You've decided you want to sew, and you've made the commitment by setting up your sewing space—now the real fun begins. If you're slightly nervous, I understand why. Many women aren't mechanically inclined or don't consider themselves to be. I am definitely in that category, but when it comes to my sewing machine, I am a master mechanic, and you can be, too. I don't mean that you'll be disassembling the parts and repairing your machine—that's what service centers are for—but you'll be operating it smoothly and easily in not much time at all if you start with the basics and master each step as you go. I have provided a diagram of a sewing machine with parts labeled (figure 1) for easy reference.

Read the Manual

If you took some basic lessons when you purchased your machine, you'll be one step ahead of the game, but if you didn't, nothing is more important than reading and following the manual for your specific machine. Some features are common to most machines, but each also have their own idiosyncrasies, so consult your manual as we go.

In addition to explaining sewing basics, manuals also furnish a wealth of additional information such as how to use specialty feet and stitches, project ideas, simple maintenance, and troubleshooting. You'll also learn what size and type of needles to purchase, recommended thread, and adjustments for different fabrics. Whenever I move, I find a special place near my machine for my manual, because even after many decades of sewing, I still refer to it often.

Threading the Machine

A machine takes two threads to sew a stitch: the upper thread that comes from the spool and the lower thread that comes from the bobbin. It sounds simple, but improperly threading the machine causes people learning to sew more problems than anything else. The thread must go through all the right parts in the right order, or the machine won't sew, so make this the first thing you learn by heart. If necessary, open the manual and go step-by-step until you're familiar with the process. Before threading the machine, check to make sure the needle is medium weight (sometimes called universal) for general sewing, which is what we'll be using for all the projects in this book. They are standard in all new machines, and extra needles are available at dealerships or any fabric store.

Put the presser foot in the up position and the needle in its highest position, and start by filling the bobbin, which holds the lower thread. It is important to regulate your control pedal so the bobbin winds slowly and evenly. Thread can actually stretch if you wind it too quickly on the bobbin, leading to puckery stitches when you sew. After it's filled, hold the bobbin case in your left hand and load the bobbin with your right (some machines wind the bobbin while it is in the machine, thus eliminating this step). Put the bobbin case in the machine, leaving about 4 inches of thread hanging out of the case. Close the bobbin case.

For the upper thread, place the spool on the holder with the slash down—the slash is for securing the thread after sewing. Grasp the spool lightly with your right hand while pulling the thread through the machine with your left hand. This puts slight tension on the thread, and you'll be able to feel whether it has entered the various grooves correctly. After you've gone through the needle, leave about 4 inches of thread before you cut the tail.

Next you'll need to raise the bobbin thread by holding the upper thread firmly in your left hand while turning the handwheel with your right. As the needle goes down, gently pull the upper thread back and the bobbin thread will become looped and be drawn up through the hole. Pull both the upper and lower threads to the back of the machine, and you're ready to sew.

Handy Hint

For easier threading, cut the thread at an angle. Some machines have built-in needle threaders, or you can purchase a separate needle threader to make this step easier.

Stitch Length and Tension

Stitch length is calibrated by the number of stitches per inch—the more stitches, the stronger the seam. Some machines actually let you set the stitch length by numbers, and some have other ways to mark it, such as in millimeters. We will be using a medium stitch length, which is about 12 stitches per inch for most of the sewing in our projects, but we may change the stitch length to make it longer for topstitching (discussed later in this chapter) or shorter when extra reinforcement is needed. Locate your stitch regulator, and turn it to a medium setting (most new machines will be preset to this length).

While sewing, the upper and lower threads must interlock evenly in the center of the fabric layers or have the right tension. When one of the threads is tighter or looser than the other, the tension is off (this should be discussed further in your sewing machine manual). Start sewing with the tension regulator set in the middle position for general sewing. Some new machines regulate the tension automatically, but you should still know how a seam sewn with uneven stitching looks when the tension is off. Tension can also be adjusted on the bobbin case by turning the screw to the right to make it tighter and to the left to make it looser. It is almost never necessary to adjust the bobbin tension, and I would only attempt it as a last resort.

Sewing Seams

When I teach children to sew, I give them paper drawn with various lines, and they practice sewing on the lines of the paper before sewing on fabric. If you're an adult beginner and don't have extra fabric scraps yet, I recommend this technique for you, too. Use graph paper or notebook paper for straight lines (figure 2), and progress to curved lines (don't make the curves too small at first) when you've mastered that (see figure 3). Using a basic straight stitch, start sewing with your right hand on the fabric while gently pulling the threads behind the needle with your left hand (see step SS-1). After you've sewn several stitches, guide the paper lightly

Pinning Tips

- To prevent slippage, pin at right angles to the stitching line at 3-inch intervals (see step PT-1) unless you feel you need more pins to secure the fabric.

- Never sew over pins—remove them as you go; sew up to a pin, remove it, and proceed.

- Don't put pins in your mouth—aside from the safety issue, they can become covered with lipstick or Chapstick that can stain the fabric.

with the fingertips of both hands. Sew to the end of the line and stop with the needle down in the paper. Raise the presser foot and pivot the paper at right angles so you can sew over to the next line (see step SS-2). When you're done stitching, always raise the needle to the highest position before lifting the presser foot, and pull evenly on the two threads for a few inches before you cut them. This is a good way to get the feel of the machine without worrying about ruining fabric.

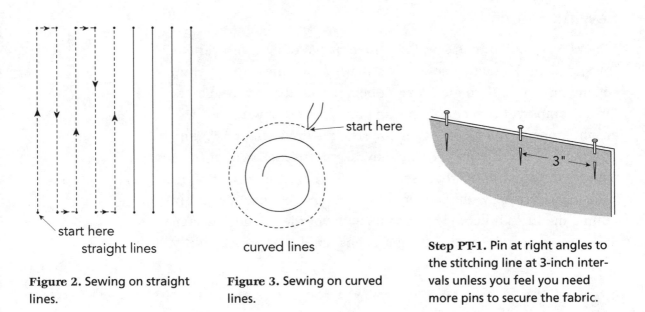

start here
straight lines

curved lines

Figure 2. Sewing on straight lines.

Figure 3. Sewing on curved lines.

Step PT-1. Pin at right angles to the stitching line at 3-inch intervals unless you feel you need more pins to secure the fabric.

When you feel comfortable with the machine, sew some small square or rectangular pieces of fabric together. Use wovens rather than knits because wovens are more stable and won't stretch. Now you can begin using the seam guides that are marked on the throat plate of the machine. Normal seams are ⅝ inch wide, and the seam guides are marked at ⅛-inch intervals from the center of the needle. When I was just beginning to sew, my mother put a piece of masking tape along the ⅝-inch groove on our old Singer to help me, and although I stopped needing it after a few months, I never removed the tape because of the pleasant memories it recalls.

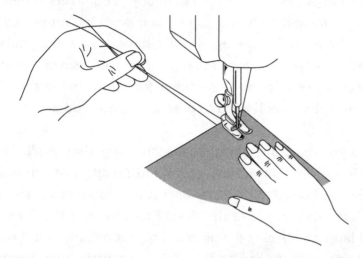

Step SS-1. Using a basic straight stitch, start sewing with your right hand on the fabric while gently pulling the threads behind the needle with your left hand.

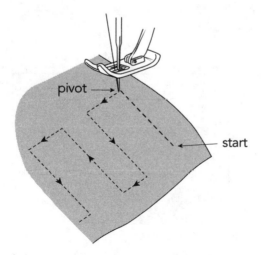

Step SS-2. Raise the presser foot and pivot the paper at right angles so you can sew over to the next line.

Sewing in Reverse and Backstitching

All sewing machines contain levers for sewing in reverse, and you'll need to locate yours if you haven't already. The levers sometimes operate by spring action and can be activated by simply pulling down on them while sewing. Others have levers that must be pushed up or down and stay in that position while sewing. You will rarely need to sew in reverse except for backstitching, which I describe next, but you'll need to practice before you begin sewing projects.

When you're joining two pieces of fabric together, you'll need to backstitch to prevent the seam from pulling apart or unraveling. Many sewing books tell you to backstitch as soon as you start sewing, but this can cause the thread to jam, and if the seam is trimmed later, the backstitching could be cut off. Instead, I recommend sewing in about five or six stitches, backstitching for several stitches, and then proceeding (see step BS-1).

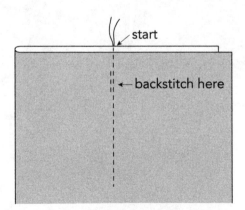

Step BS-1. Sew in about five or six stitches, backstitch for several stitches, and then proceed.

▼▼

Common Problems

Most stitching problems are not serious, and many can be remedied if you stop sewing at the first sign that something is wrong.

■ Improper threading results in uneven stitches, needle or thread breaking, or bad tension. Always rethread your machine—top thread and bobbin—at the first sign of trouble.

■ A damaged needle, either bent or blunt, usually makes a clunking sound and can throw off the machine's timing. Replace needles after several projects, and be sure to insert them correctly.

■ A dirty machine, one that is filled with lint or dust, will lead to jamming and caught threads. Never try to force a machine if it won't sew—remove the bobbin case and dust the area, gently pulling any caught threads. If they can't be removed easily, see a repair person.

▲▲

Seam Finishes

Seams must be finished on the edges to prevent raveling, for durability, and to contribute to the overall neatness of the project. To determine whether your fabric needs the seams finished, gently pull the threads along a cut edge to see how easily they fray. In general, woven fabrics will need to be finished, while knits, fleece, vinyl, and synthetic suedes won't. The most basic seam finish is to pink the edges with pinking shears or a pinking cutter. For an even more secure finish, you can stitch ¼ inch from the pinked edges (see figure 4). Another way to reinforce and finish raw edges is to use a zigzag stitch (see figure 5) or serging if you own a serger. You can also overcast the edges by hand (see the Hand Sewing section later in this chapter), but this technique is time-consuming and not very durable.

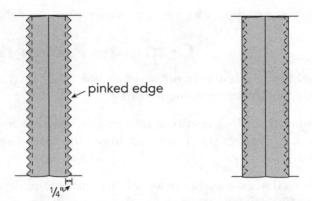

pinked edge

¼"

Figure 4. Pinked edges with machine stitching (seam finish).

Figure 5. Zigzag seam finish.

A "down and dirty" way to finish seams is to use Fray Check, which I mentioned in chapter 2, but it can leave the seams stiff and abrasive, so I prefer using it for spot reinforcement only. Experiment with the fabric for your various projects to determine which seam finish is most appropriate.

Topstitching

Topstitching is stitching that is done on the surface of an item and always shows, unlike other stitching that is not visible from the outside. We will be topstitching different areas in our projects to accent seam lines, to make them more durable, and to keep them flat. Although thicker topstitching thread is available and used mostly for garment sewing, regular thread will be suitable for our projects. Topstitching can be done close to the edge of seams or garments, or it can be done at wider widths, usually ¼ or ½ inch. It's your choice—there are no set rules. Some machines come with separate topstitching feet, but this necessitates changing the feet, so I usually use the edge of the presser foot as a guide. On most machines it is usually about ¼ inch from the needle, which is an average width for topstitching. Practice on fabric scraps from your project before you do the final topstitching to determine what width you prefer. When topstitching, stitch slowly while guiding the fabric with both hands.

Fabric Preparation

Now that you're comfortable with the machine, you're anxious to create your first project, but you'll need to take some preparatory steps first, and with sewing, that means preshrinking the fabric. I learned this lesson early—it is an essential step in the sewing process and a key to success.

Preshrinking the Fabric

All washable fabrics must be preshrunk prior to sewing according to the care instructions on the end of the bolt. If a fabric is machine washable, preshrink it by washing and drying it in the machine. Iron it if it has become wrinkled.

Straightening the Grain

If, after preshrinking, your fabric appears crooked or off grain (see figure 6), you will need to straighten it before cutting (refer to the Grain section in chapter 2). Your goal is to have all four corners form perfect 90-degree angles (see figure 7). Pull a crosswise thread near the top and bottom of the piece of fabric (see step SG-1), and cut following the thread (see step SG-2). Then pull the fabric in the opposite direction from the way the ends slant until the corners form right angles (see step SG-3). You may need to fold the fabric on the lengthwise grain, right sides together, and pin the

Handy Hint

Some home-decor fabrics made from cotton, polyester, or other washable fibers may be labeled "dry clean only" because they have been treated with sizing or fabric protector to preserve a crisp finish. Do not use these fabrics for projects that must be washed frequently, such as an apron, because the fabric will soon lose the look and feel it had when new.

three edges that aren't a fold. Then press the piece to complete the process (see step SG-4).

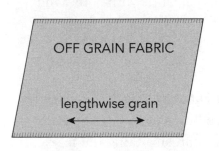

Figure 6. Off grain fabric.

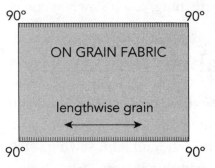

Figure 7. On grain fabric.

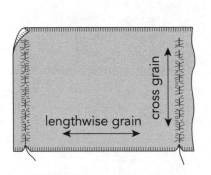

Step SG-1. Pull a crosswise thread near the top and bottom of the piece of fabric.

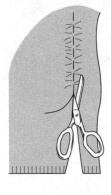

Step SG-2. Cut following the thread.

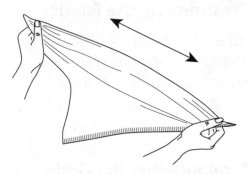

Step SG-3. Pull the fabric in the opposite direction from the way the ends slant until the corners form right angles.

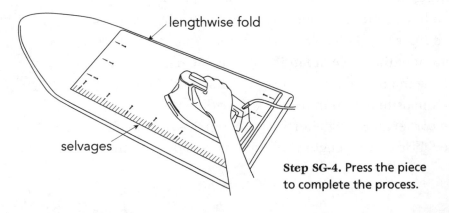

Step SG-4. Press the piece to complete the process.

Layout

In general, fabric is folded or rolled on bolts with the right side to the inside, and this procedure is followed as fabric is laid out for cutting. Sometimes, particularly after preshrinking, it is difficult to distinguish the right from the wrong side. Prevent this by putting a safety pin in the right side before you wash it, or take it into natural light for a closer look. If you can't decide which side is the right side, the solution is simple—just pick the side you want. In fact, sometimes the wrong side of the fabric will be more appealing, and you may want to use it instead of the right side.

To prepare the fabric for cutting, fold it on the lengthwise grain with the right sides together and smooth out any bumps or creases. Commercial pattern pieces are marked with arrows that denote the grain line, and they should correspond to the lengthwise grain of the fabric. I have indicated these grain lines on our project pieces when necessary. Use a ruler to make the grain line of the pattern parallel with the grain of the fabric (figure 8).

Pin the pattern to the fabric by putting the pins at right angles to the seam allowances of the pattern pieces. If you are using a rotary cutter, be sure to lay your fabric on top of your cutting mat, and

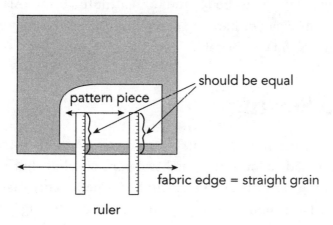

should be equal

pattern piece

fabric edge = straight grain

ruler

Figure 8. Layout on the grain.

distribute the weights evenly on the pattern pieces. It is perfectly acceptable to use pins instead of weights with rotary cutters; just make sure they aren't near the edges.

Cutting

When cutting with shears, keep them at an upright angle, and don't lift the fabric from the table. Try to move slowly and evenly while holding the fabric down with the opposite hand. When I first started sewing, I didn't think that $\frac{1}{8}$ or $\frac{1}{4}$ inch made much difference, but I have learned that accuracy in cutting is extremely important to the success of a project. You'll only be cutting once, so take your time—your patience will be rewarded!

If you haven't cut with rotary cutters before, it will take some getting used to but is definitely worth the effort. Scissors or shears are still needed for small corners or detail areas, but you can cut everything else much easier and faster with rotary cutters. The most important thing to remember is that rotary cutters are very sharp. Newer models are equipped with a spring action that covers the blades automatically as soon as you're done cutting. If yours doesn't have this feature, train yourself to retract the blade instantly when you finish cutting a project. As with shears, cut smoothly and evenly away from your body, and do not tilt the blade. Also be sure that your fabric is not hanging over the mat, or you may misjudge the overhang and cut the table—a costly mistake!

Hand Sewing

Machine sewing and the availability of special stitches and attachments has made a lot of tedious handwork obsolete, but you'll still need to know a few basic hand stitches. I personally dislike hand sewing, so I am going to give you all the tips I've learned to make it faster, easier, and more enjoyable.

Threading a Needle

A single thread is used for quick or delicate work such as basting or hemming, and a double thread, which is more durable, is used for fastening things together such as the edges of a pillow after stuffing it. Cut a strand 18 to 24 inches long for sewing with a single thread, and double that amount for sewing with a double thread. Cut the thread at an angle just like we did when threading the machine.

If you're like me, the holes in needles get smaller every year. I used to laugh at my students who had trouble threading their needles, but I don't think it's funny anymore! Hold the needle in one hand and push the thread toward it with the other. If you just can't seem to get it, needle threaders are available in fabric stores as well as self-threading needles that have a groove cut through the top of the eye so you can just pass the thread through (see figures 9 and 10). I have not had much luck with the self-threading needles though because the thread can pop back out when pulled with pressure.

open notch
in top

Figure 9. Needle threader.   **Figure 10.** Self-threading needle.

Using Beeswax

One of the most frustrating parts of hand sewing is when the thread knots up or tangles. Beeswax prevents these problems and strengthens the thread at the same time. To use beeswax, first thread your needle (don't knot it), and then draw the thread over the beeswax holding it down with your thumb to coat it. Plastic beeswax holders contain grooves that act as guides. You will see the thread becoming stiffer and smoother after making several passes. Knot the thread and sew as usual. When sewing with a single strand of thread, knot the end you cut to prevent tangling. (see figure 11).

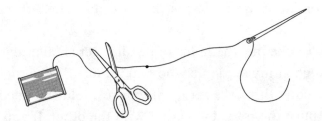

Figure 11. When sewing with a single strand of thread, knot the end you cut to prevent tangling.

Tying a Knot

Hold the thread between the thumbs and index fingers of both hands (see step TK-1). With your right hand, bring the thread over and around your left index finger, crossing it over the thread end (see step TK-2). Gently push your left thumb over the crossed threads toward your fingertip while pulling with your right hand (see step TK-3). This causes the thread end to roll around the loop. Finally, slide the loop off your fingertip, pinching the rolled end be-

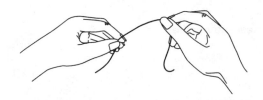

Step TK-1. Hold the thread between the thumbs and index fingers of both hands.

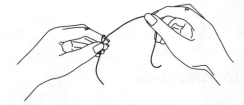

Step TK-2. With your right hand, bring the thread over and around your left index finger, crossing it over the thread end.

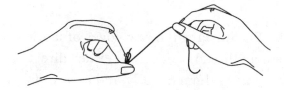

Step TK-3. Gently push your left thumb over the crossed threads toward your fingertip while pulling with your right hand.

Step TK-4. Slide the loop off your fingertip, pinching the rolled end between the thumb and the index finger, while pulling the long thread to set the knot.

tween the thumb and the index finger, while pulling the long thread to set the knot (see step TK-4).

Basting

Basting is temporarily attaching two pieces of fabric until you sew them permanently; it is often used when pinning won't hold the pieces adequately or if you want a realistic idea of how the seam will look when it is sewn on the machine. For basting we use a single thread and a running stitch, weaving in and out of the fabric evenly. Basting stitches can be about ¼ inch or up to ½ inch if you are basting a very long seam (see figure 12).

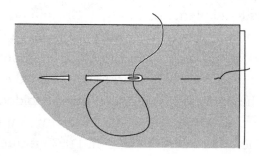

Figure 12. Basting.

Overcast Stitch

This stitch is used primarily for finishing the raw edges of fabric so they won't ravel. Using a single thread, work from either direction and take diagonal stitches, spacing them equally and at a uniform depth, usually about ¼ inch apart (see step OS-1).

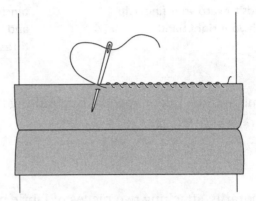

Step OS-1. Using a single thread, work from either direction and take diagonal stitches, spacing them equally and at a uniform depth, usually about ¼ inch apart.

Slipstitch

This is a nearly invisible stitch that is used to join two folded edges or one folded edge to a flat surface. It is widely used for hemming in garment sewing, so most books will tell you to use a single thread, but craft sewing requires more strength and durability, so I advise using a double thread and plenty of beeswax. Our pillow project requires us to join a folded edge to a flat edge to close up the pillow after stuffing it. Working from the right to the left (or opposite if you are left-handed), bring the needle out through the folded edge, catch several threads on the flat side, and go back into the folded edge immediately. Run the needle inside the fold for about ¼ inch before surfacing to catch the other side (see step SL-1). Continue until the two pieces are joined and tie a good knot at the end.

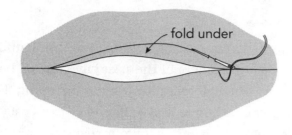

fold under

Step SL-1. Run the needle inside the fold for about ¼ inch before surfacing to catch the other side.

Tying Off

To end your hand sewing, take a tiny stitch directly over your last stitch, and then tie a knot by pulling the thread to form a loop (see step TO-1). Run the needle through the loop and pull the thread to form a second loop (see step TO-2). Put the needle through the second loop and draw it tightly, forming a knot at the base of your stitches (step TO-3). Practice tying off on scraps to perfect the technique before starting your projects.

Handy Hint

After tying a knot, run the needle back through the fabric and gently pull until the knot is drawn inside the fabric. Burying the knot this way protects it from wear and tear and prevents it from unraveling.

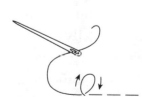

Step TO-1. Take a tiny stitch directly over your last stitch, and then tie a knot by pulling the thread to form a loop.

Step TO-2. Run the needle through the loop and pull the thread to form a second loop.

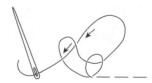

Step TO-3. Put the needle through the second loop and draw it tightly, forming a knot at the base of your stitches.

Ripping

Ripping is an inevitable part of sewing, and unfortunately, some perfectionist sewing teachers of the past have turned beginners off because of their overzealous attitudes about ripping. I'm going to give you the updated scoop to make ripping fast and easy so you can correct errors quickly and get on to your sewing.

Traditional Seam Rippers

When ripping, many sewers fear cutting the fabric, and understandably so. To lessen the possibility for errors, pull seams gently apart while ripping away from the sewn item, not toward it. As I have previously mentioned, traditional seam rippers work well when new, but you should replace them every 6 months to a year, depending how much you rip.

Alternate Seam Rippers

In an attempt to find better implements for ripping, many people who sew use single-edged razor blades or even small pocket knives, because the blades are much sharper. I have used single-edged razor blades (available in beauty supply or hardware stores) for years and have talked with others who also use them successfully. They last longer and are less expensive to replace than traditional rippers.

In the late 1990s, Olfa, a leading rotary cutter manufacturer, introduced the Rotary Point Cutter, which was originally developed for cutwork and appliqué but has become widely accepted as a perfect tool for ripping. It is much easier to grasp than a traditional ripper, is much sharper, and comes with replaceable blades. In addition, the blades are retractable, making them much safer than razor blades. Rotary Point Cutters are available in most major fabric stores and sewing catalogs (see Resources) and are used like traditional seam rippers. They are also handy for maneuvering under sewn edges, such as pockets, that have been sewn incorrectly.

Using any type of seam ripper takes some practice, and I recommend using old or discarded clothing for that purpose. You won't be as fearful because you won't be concerned if you ruin the item, so it is a great way to perfect your technique. Soon you'll be ripping with confidence and hopefully won't dread that part of sewing.

Warning: Remember that all ripping tools are sharp, so handle them with care, and be sure to store them in a safe place if children are near.

Removing Threads

Broken threads resulting from ripping can be difficult to remove from the fabric as well as a messy irritation. If you are using a razor blade or Rotary Point Cutter, turn the blade at an angle and brush over the embedded threads to loosen and remove them. You can then use a piece of masking tape wound around your fingers to gather them up. Or, make a handy thread grabber from an 8-inch strip of Velcro. Use the hook side of the tape and sew the ends together to make a circle. Fit it around your hand for grabbing threads as you brush it over the fabric (it can snag some fabrics, so test first).

Pressing

Pressing is essential to sewing. It doesn't matter how perfectly you sew your seams—if they aren't pressed properly, your meticulous work won't show. Locate your pressing area close to your sewing machine to make pressing convenient. I am going to show you how to use your iron as a tool and how to get professional results in all your projects.

Temperature and Steam

Irons all come equipped with variable heat settings for different types of fabrics. The problem is, the same fabric can come in different weights, such as lightweight cotton blouse fabric and heavy cotton denim, and this variability sometimes makes temperature settings irrelevant. I have developed the practice of leaving the heat setting of my iron at the steam setting (usually a colored symbol) all the time. This provides enough heat to make steam but greatly reduces scorching and shine marks. This will also save electricity and greatly extend the life of your iron.

In general, I always iron and press with the steam setting turned on. The addition of steam will make your tasks easier and faster, as will irons that have a shot or burst of steam. Always read the manufacturer's instructions for the proper water type and amount required. It is important to let the iron heat up properly before using steam (some irons have light indicators for this purpose), or it can drip or spit, leaving water marks on the fabric.

Did you know???

The number-one cause of iron problems is dropping the iron. This can damage the temperature regulator as well as the water tank, which leads to dripping and spitting.

Pressing Procedures

Irons perform two functions that are each very distinct: ironing and pressing. Ironing, sliding the iron back and forth without a lot of pressure (see figure 13), is done to remove wrinkles. Pressing is used to permanently shape and mold areas into place by applying pressure in an up-and-down motion (see figure 14). Most people think they are pressing, but they are really ironing, and now that you know the distinction, you'll be able to use your iron in its full capacity.

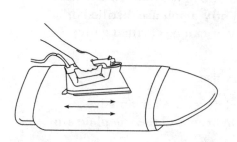

Figure 13. Ironing.

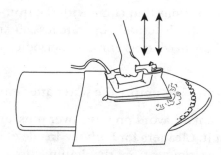

Figure 14. Pressing.

For best results, iron directionally, or with the grain of the fabric. It is the natural tendency to iron back and forth in the crosswise direction, but this can pull the fabric off grain and cause diagonal pull lines or puckers. When pressing, press straight down in one area, pick the iron up, move it to another area, and press down again.

As soon as you have sewn a seam, turn to your pressing area and press it. This is important because when two previously sewn seams are joined, they will not lay flat if they both haven't been pressed first. This results in the "happy hands at home" or homemade look.

Here is a tip that many experienced seamstresses don't know: After you have ironed or pressed anything, you need to "set the press." This means you must let the item become cool and dry in that position before you move it. This sets the press or makes it permanent. Simply feel the item to see whether it is cool, and then you are free to proceed with the next step.

▼▼▼▼▼▼▼▼▼▼▼▼▼▼▼▼▼

Handy Hint

Always press as you sew—this is the creed of experienced seamstresses.

▲▲▲▲▲▲▲▲▲▲▲▲▲▲▲▲▲

Care of the Iron

■ Always read the directions that come with the iron. Some new irons are designed to take tap water and will actually operate less efficiently if you use distilled or bottled water. Others need to be emptied periodically or can be cleaned with a special button.

■ To extend your iron's life, empty the water after every use.

■ To protect the soleplate, avoid pressing over pins, and never use an abrasive cleanser to clean it. Cleaners for both the inside of the iron and the soleplate are available in fabric stores or from the manufacturer.

For Future Reference

Two of my favorite how-to books on sewing are *The Vogue Sewing Book* (Vogue Patterns) and *Reader's Digest Complete Guide to Sewing* (The Reader's Digest Association). Both offer timeless techniques and can serve as handy references if you need more instruction on some aspect of sewing.

Creating Your Craft Sewing Projects

▼▼▼

I'M EXCITED ABOUT THE FOUR wonderful projects I've designed for you: an eyeglass case; table linens including placemats, napkins, and a table runner; accent pillows; and an apron in adult and child sizes (see the color insert in the center of this book for a look at these finished projects). I had so much fun making the samples and hope you'll be inspired to sew each one, adding your own personal touch. Since none of them are age- or gender-specific, they will appeal to the vast majority of people, making them wonderful gifts and potentially salable items. All can be customized in endless ways, and I'll give you several examples of how, but I doubt you'll need much advice from me; just let your imagination run free and you'll be surprised at the ideas that start to flow. I've arranged them by degree of difficulty; if you're a beginner, I recommend starting with the eyeglass case and proceeding from there.

 ## Eyeglass Case

This is a fast, fun project that will give you instant success and confidence. An eyeglass case is something that almost everyone can use. Regardless of whether they wear prescription lenses or not, most people wear sunglasses—I've even seen babies in strollers wearing sunglasses! Most glasses and sunglasses don't come with cases, and if they do, they are usually plain and utilitarian. I have chosen this for our first project because it is easy, inexpensive, useful, and it can be sewn in a wide variety of fabrics. Personalize it in endless ways—you can really let your creativity flow on this one!

Recommended Fabrics

Virtually any medium-weight fabric will do—the sky's the limit! Let me describe my samples to give you some ideas (again, see the color insert in the center of the book for a look at these eyeglass cases). The daisy-embellished blue case is sewn from hopsacking, a heavy cotton fabric—it would be perfect for my aunt who loves to garden. I cut the orange-patterned case from a textured piece of upholstery fabric that is sturdy and decorative. The yellow fish case is vinyl—it's waterproof for the beach. The purple and teal cases came from the same reversible piece of Polarfleece, one cut on each side—a great choice for an athlete, sports fan, or anyone who just wants to keep their glasses warm. I had my niece in mind for the heart and lace-trimmed cotton broadcloth, and the blue-and-white striped denim matches the apron I made for my brother—the perfect accessory for the man who has everything!

Your choices are unlimited; just walk through a fabric store and see what catches your eye. Don't forget the remnant bins filled with leftover pieces from the ends of bolts—they're usually a fraction of the original price. This is going to be a very inexpensive project anyway, but it's fun to see how little you can spend. Keep in mind that ¼ yard of fabric will make at least four eyeglass cases, so you can sew extras to give away or sell. If you're a veteran sewer, rummage through your scrap bag.

Profit Potential of an Eyeglass Case

One year I made every person at our family Christmas gathering a personalized eyeglass case for a stocking stuffer (total of 27). What an easy and inexpensive gift— I had made them all throughout the year from scraps left over from other projects. They were the hit of the party, and even though I hadn't planned on it, six relatives placed orders for more to use for both themselves and as gifts. Before the day was over, I taught an aunt and niece how to make their own. I was surprised and happy to see how much enthusiasm my homemade project raised.

Eyeglass cases are probably the most potentially profitable of all our projects because they are so fast and inexpensive to produce and can be used by people of any age or sex. Let's run some numbers and see the possibilities. I'm going to just pick $10 as an average price per yard for fabric and divide that by 4. That's $2.50 for ¼ yard. You can make four cases from ¼ yard of 36-inch-wide fabric, so divide $2.50 by 4 and you get a cost of $0.63 per case. And they get even cheaper if you use wider fabric—you can cut five from 45-inch fabric and seven from 60-inch fabric. Throw in a few more cents for thread, and we'll round it off to $0.70. We'll talk more about pricing in later chapters, but even after adding in the cost of your labor, this is an inexpensive item to produce— one of the most important requirements for something that sells well.

Materials

¼ yard fabric, any width
1 small spool of thread

Time

Approximate cutting time: 15 minutes
Approximate sewing time: 15–30 minutes

New Skills

Backstitching

Sewing curves

Trimming seams

Finishing seams

Embellishing

Fabric Preparation

If you anticipate washing your eyeglass case, preshrink your fabric first. Some fabrics, like the orange case I made from upholstery fabric, aren't washable. I spray items made from dry-clean-only fabrics with fabric protector such as Scotchguard to keep them clean longer.

Note: In the illustrations throughout this chapter, the right side of the fabric will be shaded, and the wrong side will be plain (see figure 15).

Layout and Cutting

I have provided an actual-size pattern for you to simply copy or trace onto paper (see figure 16), so you will want to do that now. Fold the fabric on the lengthwise grain, right sides together, and pin the pattern to the fabric as shown in figure 17. Cut with shears or a rotary cutter.

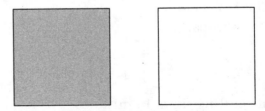

Figure 15. Samples of right side and wrong side of fabric in illustrations.

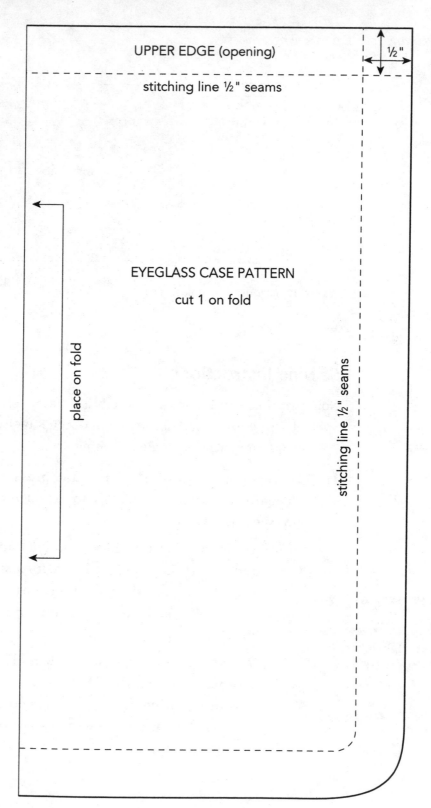

UPPER EDGE (opening)

stitching line ½" seams

½"

EYEGLASS CASE PATTERN

cut 1 on fold

place on fold

stitching line ½" seams

Figure 16. Pattern for eyeglass case.

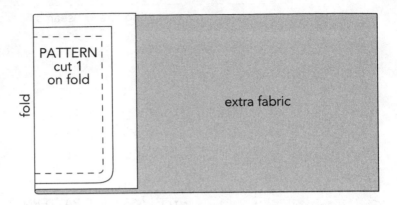

Figure 17. Layout for eyeglass case.

Sewing Instructions

Note that these directions are for fabrics that ravel. See the section Special Directions for Fabrics That Don't Ravel (such as vinyl, Polarfleece, or synthetic suedes) coming up.

1. Turn the upper edge under ¼ inch and press. Turn under ¼ inch again and press. Stitch close to the edge and press when done (see step SW-1).

2. Fold the case right sides together, and stitch at ½ inch. Start the stitching line with a small row of zigzags, or backstitch several times to reinforce (see step SW-2). Backstitch at the end of the stitching line also.

3. Trim the seam allowances to ¼ inch and zigzag around the edge to finish the seams (see step SW-3). If your machine doesn't zigzag, you can overcast the edge by hand (see chapter 4) or serge the edge if you own a serger.

Handy Hint

For production sewing, fold the fabric twice and cut two cases at once.

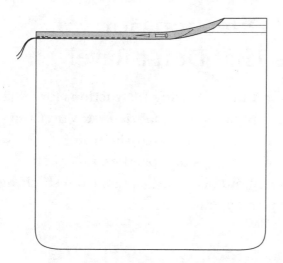

Step SW-1. Turn the upper edge under ¼ inch and press. Turn under ¼ inch again and press. Stitch close to the edge and press when done.

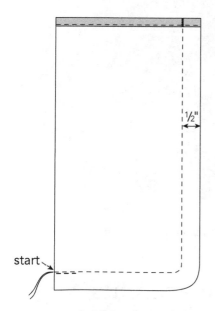

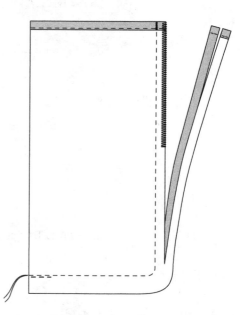

Step SW-2. Fold the case right sides together, and stitch at ½ inch. Start the stitching line with a small row of zigzags, or backstitch several times to reinforce. Backstitch at the end of the stitching line also.

Step SW-3. Trim the seam allowances to ¼ inch and zigzag around the edge to finish the seams.

Special Directions for Fabrics That Don't Ravel

1. Follow step 1 under Sewing Instructions for fabrics that ravel—be sure to test your fabric first. Vinyl and other synthetics will melt if touched by the iron.
2. Fold the case wrong sides together and stitch.
3. Trim seam allowance away ⅛ inch from stitching line (see step FS-1), and you're done!

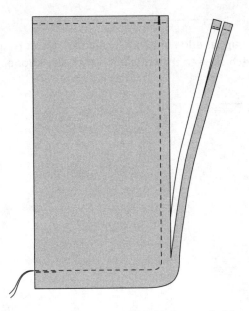

Step FS-1. Trim seam allowance away ⅛ inch from stitching line.

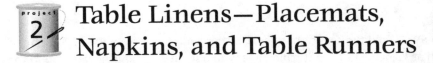 # Table Linens—Placemats, Napkins, and Table Runners

Table linens are traditionally made from linen, the most wrinkly fabric, but who has time to wash and meticulously iron them any-

Customizing Your Eyeglass Case

Adding trim or other decorations to your eyeglass case is easy—here are some tips:

- Sew on ribbon, lace, or other trim before you sew the case together.

- Use permanent fabric glue to attach large trim such as the daisies in my piece after the case is completed.

- Search fabric and craft stores that sell hundreds of appliqués and initials, both sew-on and iron-on (as on the Polarfleece case). If you select the fusible type, make sure your fabric is ironable.

- Use scraps for accessories. I cut the fish appliqué for the yellow vinyl case from a scrap of fabric, sealed the edges with Fray Check, and sewed it on before sewing the case together.

- Take the opportunity to use those fancy decorative stitches on the machine or hand embroider for a special touch.

- Embellish with fabric paint, glue glitter, or fusible gems, all available in craft and fabric stores.

more? Luckily we can now choose from a huge selection of alternate fabrics that are attractive and easy to care for. There are even linen look-alikes that don't wrinkle for people who want a classic look.

For this project we will make two sets of linens: one for the kitchen and one for the dining room. I realize some people may not own a dining room table or never use it (the same could be true if you don't have an eating area in the kitchen), but I am distinguishing between the two by making the kitchen set more casual (the napkins are also slightly smaller) and the dining set more formal. These are just generalizations, however, so read through the projects to see which version best fits your needs.

Sewing your own table linens is an easy and fun way to make any table special. The fabric you select will set the tone whether it is bright, subdued, whimsical, or romantic. You may want a delicate floral, a warm and welcoming country motif, or even the rugged and casual look of denim. Theme fabrics with a holiday, travel, or hobby motif can be cheerful and a great conversation starter. So many options are possible that you will have difficulty narrowing them down to choose one.

First consider the color and pattern of your china or dinnerware. If it is boldly patterned or geometrical, you might need solid-colored linens. If it is all one color, your choices are limitless. I always take a plate with me when shopping for table linen fabric, and then I know exactly how the two will look together.

My dining room table is in an open area next to my living room, so I made placemats and a table runner from the same fabric that I used for pillows in the living room. Since I live in Arizona, I chose fabric with a regional Southwest theme. My sister, who lives in Florida, selected a tropical print, while my girlfriend in Seattle made a cute breakfast set from fabric covered with umbrellas and falling rain.

Also consider the color of the room, whether it is painted or wallpapered, and other accessories in the room such as curtains, draperies, upholstery, centerpieces, or flower arrangements. Your table linens will need to blend or coordinate with all of these.

Kitchen Placemats and Napkins

This is the fastest and easiest way to make table linens—we'll simply stitch around the edges and fray the fabric by hand. Although this is considered a more casual look, I have made dining room table linens in this manner; they can look very formal, depending on the fabric you select.

Table Linens—The Perfect Gift

Who wouldn't be thrilled with a personally handmade gift at any of these events?

- Housewarmings
- Weddings
- Showers

- Christmas or holidays
- Anniversaries
- Parties (hostess gifts)

The instructions make four placemats, four napkins, and an optional table runner if you purchase 45-, 54-, or 60-inch fabric. My kitchen table is so small that there isn't room for a table runner, but if yours is larger, you can cut a runner from the leftover fabric. I have made matching dish towels from the extra side piece—those from 100% cotton become soft and absorptive. If you need more than four placemats and napkins, an additional ½ yard will make one placemat and one napkin.

Recommended Fabrics

Almost any woven 100% cotton or cotton blend fabric works well such as broadcloth, gingham, poplin, denim, or chambray, to name a few. Knits are out—they do not fray. Many suitable fabrics can be found in the general sections of fabric stores, but the home-decor section is also a good source. Just make sure your fabric is washable and soft enough for napkins. Some fabrics like denim feel stiff in the store but soften after washing. If you can't decide, ask a clerk for recommendations.

Materials

1¾ yards of 36- or 45-inch fabric; 1¼ yards of 54- to
60-inch fabric (I have allowed ⅛ yard extra for shrinkage)
1 large spool of thread

Time

Approximate cutting time: 30 minutes to 1 hour for
    all items
Approximate sewing and fraying time: 30 minutes
    per piece

New Skills

Zigzag stitching
Fraying fabric
Machine hemming

Fabric Preparation

Preshrink your fabric by washing and drying it in the
dryer. Iron if wrinkled. Straighten the grain if necessary (see
chapter 4).

Layout and Cutting

Lay out your fabric right side up and cut according to figure 18 or
figure 19 (depending on the amount of material you have). Do not
include the selvage in your project—it must be cut off and discarded. If you would like to make a table runner from the extra fabric on the side, arrange the placemats on your table after you have
cut them out, and then measure the space you have left to determine the size of your runner.

Handy Hint

For patterned fabric,
select thread
that matches the
predominant color or
the color you like best.
Or choose thread in a
contrasting color for a
decorative effect.
Having options is one
of the advantages of
sewing!

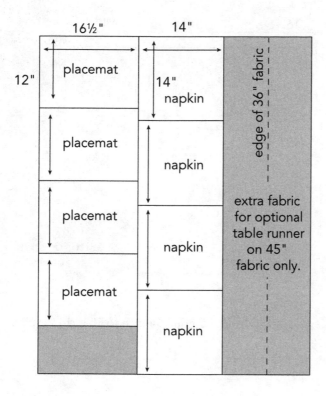

Figure 18. Layout for utilizing material (36-inch to 45-inch) for placemats and napkins.

Sewing Instructions

The frayed edges around the placemats and napkins (and table runner if you're making one) can be any width you choose—from a minimum of ¼ inch up to 1 inch from the edge of the fabric. You can use the edge of your presser foot, one of the grooves on the seam guide, or a piece of masking tape as your guide. My fabric has lines spaced about ½ inch from the edges, so I am using them as my sewing lines.

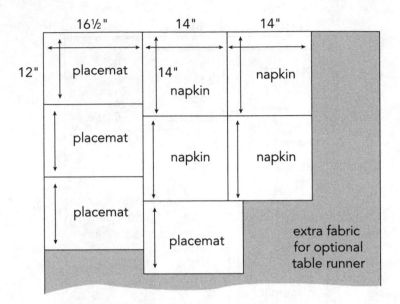

Figure 19. Layout for utilizing material (54-inch to 60-inch) for placemats and napkins.

If your machine does zigzag stitches, use a small narrow stitch. Stitch around the placemats and napkins, stopping and pivoting at each corner. Backstitch at the end. For machines without a zigzag stitch, select a very small stitch length (about 20–22 stitches per inch), and stitch around the item twice (however far from the item you wish to fringe), pivoting at the corners. Backstitch at the beginning and end.

Fraying Instructions

Pull a few strands from one side of the item and then go on to the next, working your way around all four sides continuously a few threads at a time until you're done (see figure 20). Fraying is a good project to do while watching TV, riding in a car, or anytime an activity doesn't need your full attention.

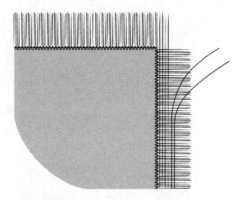

Figure 20. Pull a few strands from one side of the item and then go on to the next, working your way around all four sides continuously a few threads at a time until you're done.

Dining Room Placemats, Napkins, and Table Runner

For this option I've added a table runner and made the napkins a little larger, which can look more elegant. We'll be hemming the edges of all the pieces on the machine for a clean finish.

Recommended Fabrics

All of the fabrics I mentioned for the kitchen set are appropriate for the dining room set; however, if you are looking for something more formal, you may see many lovely home-decor fabrics that must be dry-cleaned. If you fall in love with a dry-clean-only fabric, you could use it for placemats and a runner—these don't need to be cleaned frequently—and purchase or sew coordinating napkins in a washable fabric. Just be sure to look at the measurements for the items and recalculate your yardage requirements if you mix and match.

Handy Hint

Fraying is a great time to let children or other family members help. People cannot sit and watch you without wanting to help— I once had the whole Super Bowl party fraying edges!

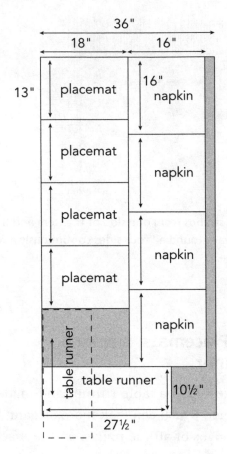

Figure 21. Layout for utilizing material (36-inch) for dining set.

Materials

2⅛ yards of 36-inch fabric if you cut the table runner on the crosswise grain, 3⅜ yards if you cut it on the lengthwise grain (see figure 21); 1⅞ yards of 45-, 54-, or 60-inch fabric
1 large spool of thread

Profit Potential of Table Linens

Whether you are rushed with take-out food or have time to linger, table linens make eating an event. They add a festive touch and dress up the simplest meal and can enhance any function where food is served. All the finer restaurants realize this and make much of their beautiful and appealing table settings.

A sewing buddy of mine who lives in a ritzy suburb of Houston hosted an afternoon tea for her ladies' group. She dressed the table with a lovely flowered runner and napkins that coordinated with her tea set. We laughed when she recalled overhearing a conversation between two guests. They were both going to order custom-made table linens from their interior designers the next day. No one realized my friend had made them herself, and they would have been even more amazed to know the price—just under $10 for the whole set! She purchased the fabric on sale, but even at full price, making your own linens can be very cost-effective, especially if you want to sell them.

Visit the table linen section of any department store, and you'll notice the limited number of colors and designs that are available. Many commercially made linens look cheap because they are made from inferior fabric or are finished with seams that aren't appropriate and will soon unravel. Furthermore, the prices can be exorbitant. Unique designs, quality fabric, color coordination, and a reasonable price—these are all selling points that you can offer customers who want to improve their dining experience. Wait until your friends see the custom set you just made, and be prepared to take some orders!

Time

Approximate cutting time: 1 hour
Approximate sewing time: 45 minutes to 1 hour per item

Fabric Preparation

Preshrink fabric, press, and straighten the grain if necessary (you're getting good if you already know all these terms by heart—give yourself a gold star!).

Layout and Cutting

For 36-inch fabric, lay out and cut according to figure 21. For 45-, 54-, and 60-inch fabric, use the layouts in figures 18 and 19, but make the placemats 13 × 18 inches and the napkins 16 × 16 inches. Cut the table runner on the lengthwise grain from the extra fabric on the side. The table runner I made measures $9\frac{1}{2} \times 26\frac{1}{2}$ inches finished or $10\frac{1}{2} \times 27\frac{1}{2}$ inches before hemming. My table is 60 × 42 inches, so measure yours and adjust accordingly.

Sewing Instructions

Fold the edges of the items under ¼ inch and under again ¼ inch. Depending on your experience, you may be able to do this as you sew, or you may have to press the edges under and pin them all around first.

Sew with an average stitch length, backstitching at the beginning and end. The fabric may be difficult to maneuver under the pressure foot when sewing around the corners, so try this handy tip: thread a hand-sewing needle with about 8 inches of thread (do not knot it); push the needle through the corner (see step S-1), and pull on the thread ends as you sew to guide the fabric under the presser foot (see step S-2). This prevents the machine from "eating" the

Other Uses for Table Linens

- Dress up a breakfast in bed tray with a cheerful placemat and matching napkin.

- Make custom-fit placemats for TV trays.

- Placemats and napkins add a festive touch to patio and picnic tables—use overall patterns that disguise stains from ketchup and barbecue sauce!

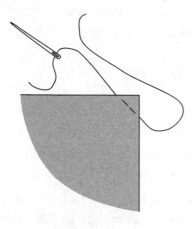

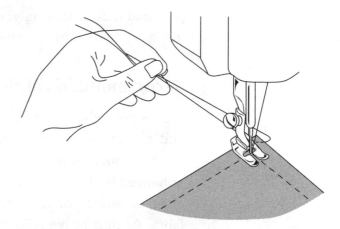

Step S-1. Thread a hand-sewing needle with about 8 inches of thread (do not knot it); push the needle through the corner.

Step S-2. Pull on the thread ends as you sew to guide the fabric under the presser foot.

fabric at the corners or pulling it down inside the machine and jamming. Press the items when done, and you're ready to set a beautiful table!

3 Accent Pillows

Accent pillows can add a lively and inexpensive touch to any decorating scheme and allow you to change the mood in a room instantly without spending a fortune. They can also perk up areas that have become dated by adding fresh color, texture, and pattern. In this project, I'm going to show you how to make two variations: one with fringe and one without.

Have you browsed through home-decor stores or catalogs and noticed the expensive prices on pillows? Here's a great, fun way to stretch your decorating dollars. Pillows can also be replaced or recovered to adjust to seasonal changes, new furniture, paint, or wallpaper. They are both decorative and useful and give your home a personal touch. Making your own gives you the advantage of customizing them to fit your individual needs.

Recommended Fabrics

Here's your chance to express yourself—your own personal style and tastes! First, decide on the location for your new creation. Which room and which piece of furniture will your accent pillow enhance? Will it be useful, helping to fill in the hollow of an easy chair, merely decorative and pretty to look at, or a little of both? The fabric for decorative pillows need not be as sturdy as fabric for pillows that will receive handling and wear. In general, select a fabric that is firmly woven and medium weight.

Consider the surface of the fabric. Do you want smooth, textured, shiny, or dull? Napped fabrics (refer to chapter 2) can work well in pillows; they add depth and character—just make sure the smooth direction runs from the top down.

Investigate theme fabrics that depict all manner of hobbies and sports from golfing, fishing, ballooning, and bicycling to dolls, dogs, cats, and more. Fabric has style just like paintings, whether it is romantic, modern, impressionistic, or avant-garde. The style of your pillow fabric should match the style of the room.

Materials

Fabric for one 17-inch square pillow: ½ yard exactly
 (I would get ⅝ yard or even more to allow for shrinkage or to adjust the pattern placement; see Layout and Cutting)
1 small spool of thread
1 18-inch square pillow form
For the fringed pillow only, 2 yards fringe. (An average width for fringe is 1½ inches and is the one I used for this project.)

Fringe Facts

- Fringe is available in endless colors and styles—select one that complements your fabric.

- The cut edge comes basted together to prevent tangling while sewing; the basting thread is easily removed afterward.

- Fringe stretches easily, so handle with care.

Time

Approximate cutting and sewing time: 1 hour without fringe; 1 hour, 30 minutes with fringe

New Skills

Positioning patterns on fabric to accommodate special designs
Trimming curved edges
Adding trim
Using a pillow form
Hand sewing—slipstitch

Fabric Preparation

Most home-decor experts agree that fabric for pillows should not be laundered prior to sewing because it can affect the hand (feel of the fabric) as well as the ability to remain durable and fresh looking over time. If you are concerned about cleaning your pillows in the future, there are some alternatives. To prevent soiling, you can

Profit Potential of Pillows

Accent pillows are probably the most popular and most sought-after home-decor accessory and are a basic to most people's decorating schemes. They are an item that can be made ahead of time in lush fabrics and vibrant colors to tempt would-be customers. If you live in a distinct region of the country, you may be able to capitalize on a regional theme such as Southwest or tropical, as I mentioned in the beginning of this chapter, and appeal to many people in your area. Gift shops, furniture stores, and home-decor shops are always looking for new and distinctive pillows for their customers, and you might be able to fill that need. We'll be talking more about consignment selling in the following business chapters.

Sewing individual custom-made pillows for customers is another good moneymaker. Many people who don't sew either have the fabric or would buy it if they knew someone could make it for them. Still others who sew don't realize how easy it is to make one or just don't have the time or interest to sew their own. These are some potentially profitable areas to explore in the future.

For now, I hope you enjoyed making your pillow. I can just imagine how striking it looks in that special place in your home!

spray pillows with a fabric protector such as Scotchguard. Some fabrics are pretreated with a similar finish that will be listed on the bolt end. For removing small stains, try spot remover; if the entire pillow needs to be cleaned, you must remove the cover and have it dry-cleaned.

If you have selected a washable fabric and want to wash the pillow cover in the future (it must be removed from the form and then resewn after laundering), preshrink the fabric and straighten the grain if necessary.

Layout and Cutting

For boldly patterned fabric, lay your fabric out in one flat piece, right side up, and look for predominant patterns or distinctive shapes and colors. These may need to be centered or placed at a certain position on the pillow top—I had to do this with the large rose on my sample fringed pillow. You may want to cut out an 18-inch square piece of tissue paper and place it over different areas on the fabric to see where you should cut. Just make sure the grain line (the square edge) of the pattern matches that of the fabric.

For plain fabric or patterned fabric that has no special layout requirements, fold the fabric in half on the lengthwise grain, right sides together, and cut an 18-inch square. This will yield two squares because the fabric is folded.

Mark the top of each section so you'll be able to distinguish it during sewing. If you are using a napped fabric, the smooth direction should run down the pillow.

Pillow Possibilities

Now that you've learned the basics for sewing pillows, you can really let your creativity flow. Here are some variations you may want to try:

- Use different fabric on each side for a reversible look.

- If you would like to make pillows that match your furniture exactly, check with the manufacturer to order fabric by the yard.

- Pillows are a wonderful way to display other needlecrafts such as quilting, embroidery, or appliqué.

- Decorate children's rooms with pillows made from a favorite sweatshirt, T-shirt, or old pair of Levi's, complete with pockets!

- Explore unconventional sources for fabric—flour sacks, towels, scarves, or lightweight throw rugs.

Sewing Instructions

Nonfringed Pillow

1. Pin the sections right sides together, matching the tops. Use a regular stitch length and sew ½-inch seams. Stitch leaving an 8-inch opening centered on the bottom (see step NP-1). Backstitch when you first start sewing and when you end the line of stitching. For a smoother look when done, rather than following the square edges of the fabric at the corners, sew gently curving lines around the corners (see step NP-2). Rather than "eyeballing it" as you sew, I recommend drawing a curved line with chalk or a marking pen first to follow as you sew. Trim close to the edge of the stitching line at the corners with pinking shears or pinking cutter, or clip with scissors (see step NP-3).

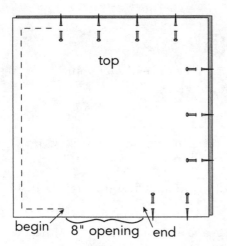

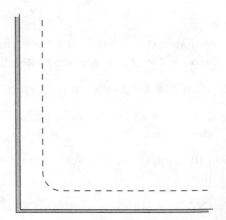

Step NP-1. Pin the sections right sides together, matching the tops. Use a regular stitch length and sew ½-inch seams. Stitch leaving an 8-inch opening centered on the bottom.

Step NP-2. For a smoother look when done, rather than following the square edges of the fabric at the corners, sew gently curving lines around the corners.

2. Turn right sides out and push the corners out with your fingers until the corners are smooth.

3. Lay the pillow cover on a table and squish the pillow form through the opening, working to get it straight and fill in the corners.

4. At the opening, let one side lay flat, fold the other under ½ inch, and pin together. Sew by hand using a slipstitch (see chapter 4). Try not to catch the pillow form in the stitching.

Fringed Pillow

1. Pin the fringe around the edge of one pillow section, fringed side to the inside, and then stitch it on by machine with a regular stitch at ½ inch. Some machines have a built-in walk-

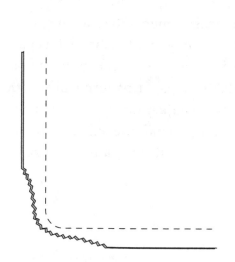

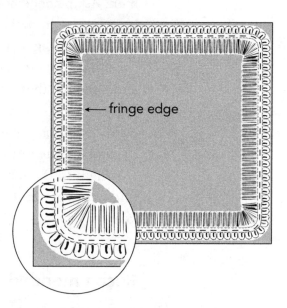

fringe edge

Step NP-3. Trim close to the edge of the stitching line at the corners with pinking shears or pinking cutter, or clip with scissors.

Step FP-1. Curve the fringe around the corners.

ing foot or an attachment that feeds the fabric evenly from the top and the bottom and prevents shifting of thick layers like this. If this is not an option, you may want to secure the fringe with hand basting prior to sewing it on the machine (see chapter 4). Be sure to curve the fringe around the corners (see step FP-1).

2. Follow steps 1–4 under Nonfringed Pillow.

 # Apron

Are we having fun yet? I hope so! I particularly liked designing and making this butcher-style apron for you, and I know you will have as much fun making one for yourself. It's unisex, and one size fits all, although I show how to add a little extra width and length for men. As an added bonus, there's enough extra fabric in the 54- to 60-inch layout to make a matching child's apron (fits children ages 4–12 depending on their build).

I am going to give you the measurements to draw the patterns, and although they can be drawn directly on the fabric with chalk or marking pen, I recommend drawing them out on newspaper, tissue paper, or butcher paper first. Making a paper pattern will allow you to see how the apron fits and make adjustments if needed before cutting into the fabric. If you plan to make the aprons more than once or ever want to sell them, you will want a paper pattern to keep.

Recommended Fabrics

Washable medium-weight cotton or cotton blends; denim, chambray, poplin, sailcloth, canvas

Materials

None of these yardages allow for shrinkage. I would add ⅛ yard if you think your fabric will shrink.

For one adult's apron: 1⅜ yards of 36- or 45-inch fabric
For one adult's apron and one child's apron: 1⅛ yards
   of 54- to 60-inch fabric
For one child's apron: ⅔ yard of any width fabric
1 large spool of thread
For adult's apron: 3 yards of 1-inch twill tape or
   other ribbon or trim suitable for making ties
For child's apron: 2½ yards of ¾-inch tape

Time

Approximate time for drawing the pattern and
   cutting for adult's apron: 45 minutes to 1 hour;
   for child's: 30 more minutes
Approximate sewing time for adult's apron: 1 to
   1½ hours; for child's: 45 more minutes

New Skills

Drawing a pattern
Fitting
Design details—placing pockets and adding ties
Topstitching

Drawing the Pattern

I have listed explicit instructions for drawing the pattern for the
adult's apron and the child's apron.

Handy Hint

If you're making both an adult's and a child's apron, make the child's first for practice— then the adult's will go quicker and easier.

For Adult's Apron

This pattern should fit a range of average sizes unless you are very small or very large. Draw the pattern to these measurements first and then hold it up to see whether you need to add or subtract from the side seams. Use a piece of paper at least 18 inches wide and 35 inches long. Follow these directions, and refer to figure 22 as you go:

1. On the right edge of the paper, mark off 35 inches and label it as a fold (line A).

2. At the bottom of line A, square a line 18 inches to the left (line B).

3. At the left end of line B, square a line 24 inches up (line C).

4. At the top of line A, square a line to the left, 5 inches for women or 6 inches for men (line D).

5. Draw a smoothly curving line from the end of line D to the end of line C (line E).

6. Now draw a 9 × 15-inch pocket pattern. Notice that the grain line on the pocket can go either direction depending on the look you want.

7. Draw pocket placement lines on the apron 10 inches up from the bottom for women and 9 inches up from the bottom for men. The pocket is 7 inches in from line A and 8 inches deep. Note: The placement lines are smaller than the pocket pattern because they are for placing the pockets after the seam allowances are folded in.

For Child's Apron

Use a piece of paper at least 9 inches wide and 22 inches long. Follow the directions for the adult apron, but substitute these measurements:

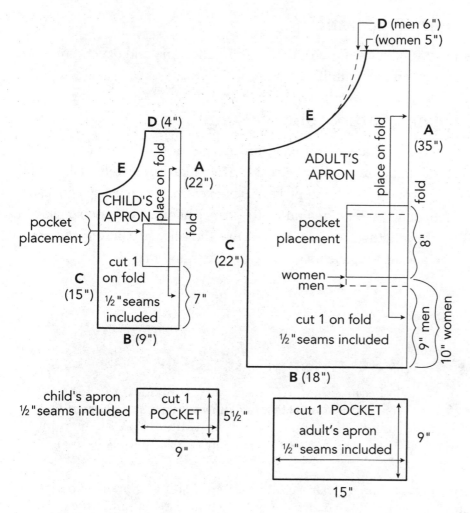

Figure 22. Patterns for the adult's apron and child's apron.

1. Line A = 22 inches, line B = 9 inches, line C = 15 inches, line D = 4 inches.

2. The pocket measures 5½ × 9 inches. Place it 7 inches up from the bottom; draw in 4 inches and up 4½ inches.

   After drawing the patterns, all directions are the same for both the adult's and the child's apron.

Fabric Preparation

Preshrink your fabric in the washing machine and dryer. Press and straighten the grain if necessary.

Layout, Cutting, and Marking

Lay out the fabric and position the pattern according to the diagrams in figure 23 and figure 24). If you have selected a fabric with lines, you may want to place the pocket on the crosswise grain as I have done in the blue-and-white striped sample; otherwise, place it on the lengthwise grain. Do not use the selvage. Cut out the apron and pocket with shears or a rotary cutter and mat.

Profit Potential of an Apron

Aprons are another perfect gift because they are unisex and accommodate a wide range of sizes. The child's apron in this project extends the age range and desirability factor. What parent or grandparent wouldn't love to dress their little "cook's helper" in this adorable creation? And, as I've said before, the perfect gift is the perfect item to sell.

A high-profile cooking event for men is barbecuing. Perhaps that's why many catalogs catering to men offer aprons. Here's a chance to save the shipping costs and time needed to order by mail—customers can order directly from you! What's more, they can purchase one-of-a-kind creations.

This type of apron never goes out of style, so you won't be limited by fashion trends. Besides serving a useful purpose, wearing aprons makes a statement. My neighbor told me she always wears hers when company comes. It makes her feel like her cooking is exceptional and her dinner a special occasion. I'm sure others feel the same way, and this point has contributed to the apron's popularity and profit potential.

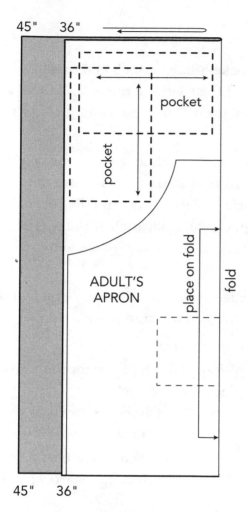

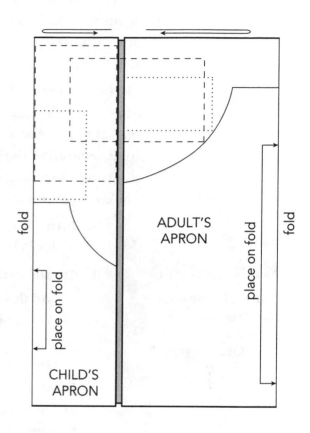

Figure 23. Layout for utilizing material (36-inch to 45-inch) for aprons.

Figure 24. Layout for utilizing material (54-inch to 60-inch) for aprons.

Mark the position of the pocket with chalk or a marking pen. Before sewing, pin the pocket to the apron to check the position. Adjust it accordingly depending on the length of your arms and personal preference. If you move the pocket, note these changes on the pattern for future use.

Sewing Instructions

1. Fold the top edge of the pocket under $\frac{1}{4}$ inch and under again $\frac{1}{4}$ inch. Stitch close to the edge and press. Fold the other three edges of the pocket under $\frac{1}{2}$ inch and press (see step SA-1).

2. Pin the pocket to the apron and topstitch it on in one continuous line following the arrows in step SA-2 (measure the pocket to find the appropriate place for the middle vertical lines separating the two pockets). Backstitch at the beginning and the end. (See figure 25 that shows placement of pocket on apron.)

3. Turn the entire edge of the apron under $\frac{1}{4}$ inch and under $\frac{1}{4}$ inch again, and pin into place.

4. Cut the twill tape into pieces:
   Adult's apron—two 30-inch pieces for the waist, two 24-inch pieces for the neck.
   Child's apron—two 24-inch pieces for the waist, two 20-inch pieces for the neck.

5. Insert the ties under the folded edges as in step SA-3, and stitch the entire edge of the apron starting at a bottom corner.

6. When done, flip the strap up and back over the fabric and topstitch close to the edge all the way around (see step SA-4). Be careful not to stretch the fabric when sewing the curved underarm seam. Press.

7. Press the apron, knot the ends of the ties, and you're ready to cook! (See figure 25 for a picture of the apron with pockets and straps in place.)

Handy Hint

To make pinning and sewing easier, press the edges under before you pin.

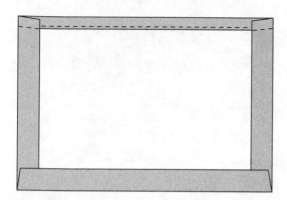

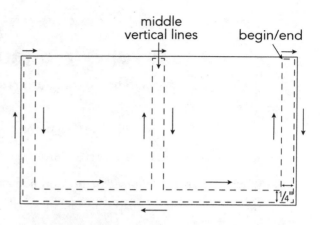

Step SA-1. Fold the top edge of the pocket under ¼ inch and under again ¼ inch. Stitch close to the edge and press. Fold the other three edges of the pocket under ½ inch and press.

Step SA-2. Pin the pocket to the apron and top-stitch it on in one continuous line following the arrows in the diagram.

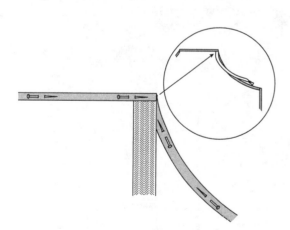

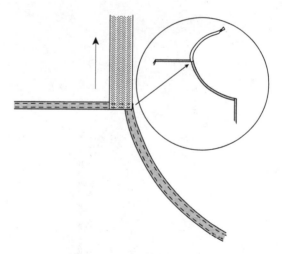

Step SA-3. Insert the ties under the folded edges as in the diagram, and stitch the entire edge of the apron starting at a bottom corner (illustration is showing the back of the apron).

Step SA-4. Flip the strap up and back over the fabric and topstitch close to the edge all the way around.

Ideas for Personalizing Your Apron

- Use iron-on initials to monogram, or letters to spell out names or words such as "Kiss the Cook."

- Make the pocket in a contrasting color or coordinating print.

- Sew ribbon, lace, or other trim across the apron and pocket tops.

- Decorate with purchased or homemade appliqués—get ideas from magazines, coloring books, and appliqué books.

- Cover purchased potholders with leftover fabric and include one in the apron pocket.

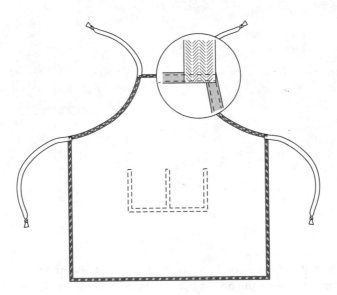

Figure 25. Back of finished apron showing pockets and straps in place.

Extra Sewing Hints

■ When changing to a new thread color, tie the new thread to the end of the old one and pull it through the machine to speed up threading. Be careful, though—the knot won't go through the needle.

■ Rotary cutters make quick work of cutting straight lines!

■ Before sewing on your project, use scraps of fabric to adjust stitch lengths and widths to see what is needed to hold the frayed edges securely.

■ Try basting glue instead of pins. Follow the bottle's directions!

■ Keep an eye on the spool of thread and stop sewing before it is entirely gone; otherwise, it can be drawn down into the bobbin case and jam the machine.

■ Fringe does not wash well, so do not make a fringed pillow if you want to wash it in the future.

■ When beginning a large project, fill two bobbins before you start so you won't have to stop and wind a new one partway through.

Your Crafts Vision

▼▼▼

NOW THAT YOU'VE HAD FUN learning to sew or perfecting some new techniques, you may want to think about selling your projects. I'm sure your family or friends have already admired your handiwork; perhaps some have asked to buy it. Sidebars about each project in chapter 5 briefly discuss the profit potential for the various items, but now I'd like to help you focus more closely on the prospect of selling your sewn crafts. This is a time for you to dream, visualize, and prioritize.

Dreams and Goals

Chances are you are reading this book because you have desired or fantasized about creating and selling handicrafts. Rarely during our hurried lives do we take time to actually let our dreams turn into concrete goals, so I suggest you schedule a dream session with yourself for at least 30 minutes. You'll want to be alone without interruptions and in a place that is comfortable and conducive to reflection and thoughtfulness. Bring a notepad and pencil so you can jot down ideas. Most important, bring the intent that you want to let your imagination run free regardless of seemingly impractical or unfeasible thoughts.

Curiosity

Try writing these open-ended sentences on your notepad, and then complete them with anything that comes to mind in regard to the curiosity you've had about selling your crafts:

> I wonder what it would be like to. . . .
> I wonder what would happen if. . . .
> Would I ever be able to . . . ?
> I've always wanted to. . . .

Handy Hint

Curiosity may have killed the cat, but it has certainly been the impetus for the realization of many dreams and goals.

Be as specific or as general as you want, and don't worry about whether you might actually be able to do what you write or how you would do it; the important part is just stating what you have been curious about. Seeing dreams in written form can be a powerful way to plant seeds that can later grow and flourish. You might be surprised to see what comes forth when you allow yourself to dream without restriction or preconceived ideas. The completion of these basic sentences will help disclose your true feelings, which always give direction to any goal. Two inspirational books that may further spur your imagination are *Do What You Love and the Money Will Follow: Discovering Your Right Livelihood* (Dell), by Marsha Sinetar, and *Starting Over: How to Change Careers or Start Your Own Business* (Warner Books), by Stephen Pollan.

Goals

Having goals and carrying them to fruition is the process by which we make our dreams come true. Try taking each one of your dreams and writing a goal that would lead the way to making it a reality.

Goals should be specific and provide measurable results so you'll know whether you have achieved them. For instance, you may have wondered whether you could actually make money selling a sewn handicraft. Your goal for this dream could be "I will design and produce one sewn item and sell it within 6 months." Or, maybe your dream was to earn some extra money doing something you love. This could produce several goals, such as "I will set aside 3 hours per week for crafting" or "I will make and sell two items within a year." Notice that the goals have time limits that will help you later when making detailed plans for carrying out your goals. You may want to read the rest of this chapter before you work on goals, and take a look at the sidebar, Goal-Setting Aid, on page 120.

Input from Others

If you are an experienced crafter or have even just tried your hand at crafting, how many times have people complimented you or even raved about something you have made? And how many times have you denied or minimized their comments by saying it was nothing or it really didn't take any talent or time? If you have entertained thoughts of selling your crafts, you have probably already received many compliments. Now is the time to start listening and take their admiration to heart. You are good, you do have talent, and you do have what it takes to make and sell something that others need and want.

On the other hand, how many times have you had an idea that seemed wonderful and exciting to you, and as soon as you told someone about it you received immediate criticism or negative comments? I don't know whether it is just human nature, but it seems people are always willing to give advice regardless of whether they know anything about a subject or not. I guess that's why I don't like to talk about my dreams with anyone other than my most trusted friends and relatives who always have my best interests in mind. I'm

Goal-Setting Aid

1. Check one:

   ☑ I need to support myself and others from my income.

   ☑ I need to support myself from my income.

   ❑ I need to partially support myself.

   ❑ I want to contribute to my family's income.

   ❑ I want to make money for a specific item (list it).

2. Check one:

   ☑ I want to craft full-time.

   ❑ I want to craft part-time.

   ❑ I want to craft _____ hours per week.

3. Do you want to be your own boss?

4. Will you work on weekends?

5. Do you have a creative mind, or are you willing to develop your creative abilities?

6. Do you have an aptitude for sewing and a desire to improve your skills?

7. Can you take reasonable risks, or must everything be a sure bet?

not saying you should never listen to criticism or negativity, but you should consider the advice and make your own decision without taking those types of comments personally.

Your Needs

Your actual needs—including income requirements and available time—will help you narrow down your goals and turn your dreams into realities.

Money Matters

Money, or the lack of it, will be a motivating force in some crafters' lives. You'll need to decide personally what role you'd like it to take in yours. Would you like to cover the cost of your materials and let it go at that? If so, you will have a wonderful free hobby, but you won't really be able to call your activity a business. We'll talk more about this in chapter 11, but according to the IRS, technically you must make a profit 3 out of 5 years or you aren't a business. Some crafters simply have no desire to develop their hobbies into businesses.

The smallest type of business and one that appeals to many crafters, particularly those who have another job or who don't necessarily need much extra income, is just to earn some extra money on the side, commonly called "pin" money. Perhaps you would like to subsidize a passion for shopping or want to save for a certain item like a new TV or a special vacation. Some people begin crafting for pin money and find that their business expands into much larger proportions.

Working at crafting part-time is the next logical step. If you have the time and desire to make crafting a major part of your life but don't want it as a full-time career, or if you want to see how it goes in anticipation of a major commitment, this might be for you. I have talked to many crafters who live for their hobbies and rush home from full-time jobs to craft at night and on weekends. Many have hopes of quitting their other employment as soon as they feel they are ready to transition to full-time crafting.

Full-time crafters need a substantial income to support themselves and possibly others. I know many husband-and-wife crafting teams who make a living traveling around the country to craft shows, fairs, and exhibitions. Other full-time crafters stay home and market their wares in other ways. If you want to make your living from crafting, you will need to commit your time, money, and energy and see yourself as a businessperson in addition to an artisan.

Margaret's Story

Margaret Metcalfe of Austin, Texas, is passionate about her sewing and spends almost every spare moment away from her full-time job crafting items for gifts and to sell. She makes her own special version of those popular Victorian bunny rabbits with floppy ears and appendages by dressing them in original and unique outfits.

Although she has sewn all her life, Margaret had never charged for her handiwork until a friend asked her to sew and stuff rabbits so the friend could make dresses for them. Margaret found that it was a lot of fun and started making dresses herself, but she wasn't content with plain old everyday dresses—she specialized in unique designs and colorful fabrics.

One of her favorites is a special rabbit she made for her 88-year-old mother who lives in a nursing home. She took it to work planning to visit her mother later, but when her coworker saw the adorable creation, she placed an order. At the nursing home, a woman who was totally bedridden with a brain tumor asked specifically for a rabbit dressed with a September theme. Margaret found lovely fabric with a back-to-school theme for the

Time Management

How much time do you want to devote to your crafts? This is a question that may take some time to answer. You'll need to analyze how much time you actually have by adding it up mentally or, better yet, keeping a record in writing. You may find that you need to make room in your life for your crafting pursuits, but don't get discouraged—you probably have more time than you think!

Last year I decided to discontinue my cable TV service because I seemed to be channel surfing continuously and not finding any-

project. The lady never let the treasured companion out of her sight until she died 3 weeks later with the bunny in her arms.

This gave Margaret the idea to create a different theme dress for each month of the year, complete with matching ear ribbons, for her mother's rabbit. Everyone in the nursing home looked forward to the beginning of the month to see how the rabbit would be dressed. After Margaret completed a year's worth of dresses, her mother, who loved the idea, now anticipates the fun of the monthly outfit change.

Margaret has expanded her business to include soft body dolls and sewing for clients. She especially enjoys making "Calendar Creations," dolls or rabbits with a wardrobe of theme dresses for each month of the year. Although Margaret's hobby provides occasional pin money now, she might expand her business after retirement when she'll have more time and energy to devote to her sewing.

thing I wanted to watch. I was shocked to realize how much time I had spent watching TV. Polls tell us that the average American spends 6 to 8 hours a day in front of the tube—that's enough time for a second career!

Talking on the phone, playing games on the computer, surfing the Internet, daydreaming, visiting with friends, and endless other activities can be curtailed or managed more effectively. If managing your time is a problem for you, you may have to schedule work times in writing on your calendar or day planner and then stick to them.

Your Talents

What are your particular talents, and how do you want to make use of them? We'll talk more in chapter 7 about zeroing in on specific products, but for now, I want to help you to start thinking in general terms about your skills and how they can best be used to produce items that you enjoy and that will bring joy to others.

Skills

Are you very artistic and do you enjoy immersing yourself in color, texture, and technique, or are you more practical and do you excel at figuring out how to put things together in a logical and fast way? Do you have the patience and desire to create unique, one-of-a-kind items, or would you rather spend less time on each piece and create a variety of handicrafts?

I felt for years that my handicrafts were somehow inferior to the stunning museum-quality ones I saw some other crafters produce. Yet my items, which were more varied but took less time to make, sold just as well. I finally realized that we all have different styles that will influence the type of craft we make and how we look at our business. Analyzing your own style will help you decide what type of product you want to produce.

> **Did you know???**
>
> According to a Hobby Industry Association report, the average crafter spends 7.5 hours per week on their hobby.

Product Preferences

Some people start out knowing exactly what they want to sew and sell, while others have no idea or a vague idea. Realizing that handicrafts can be classified in several different ways can aid decision making. If you're like me, you like to sew items that can actually be used instead of being totally aesthetic, or you may prefer a combination of both. Sewn crafts can also be separated by categories such as home decor, recreation or sports, toys, accessories, holiday decorations, and so on.

You may want to appeal to a specific sex or age group such as adults, teenagers, or babies. Demographic statistics tell us that the largest segment of our population is now over 55 years old. If you want to go by sheer numbers, senior citizens may be your target market. Perhaps you love children and have endless ideas for creating items for them. Personal preference, actual statistics, and your unique style will all contribute to what craft you choose to produce.

Part Two

For Profit

Profiting from Your Talent

▼▼

WHETHER YOU ARE MOTIVATED by a desire to be creative and original, a financial need, or simply the sheer fun of it, turning your hobby into a moneymaking endeavor will take some effort and planning. Luckily you have me—your personal business adviser and guide. After having graduated from the School of Hard Knocks, I feel immensely qualified to give you some pointers and help you start off in the right direction. In addition, many more resources are now available to aid would-be crafters than when I started, and I will be referring to some and listing many in the Resources section at the end of this book.

Transitioning from Giving to Selling

For anyone who might think transitioning from giving to selling sounds too mercenary, I'd like you to know that when you are selling, you are still giving, only now you're getting money for it. You can put the same love, creativity, and expertise into a salable item as you can a gift, so you are still benefiting humankind, but you are now getting paid for doing it. What a wonderful prospect! I'll talk more about valuing yourself as a businessperson in chapter 8, but you can take some specific actions now to start profiting from your talent.

Changing Your Attitude

Probably the biggest change that needs to take place when transitioning from giving your crafts away to selling them is a change in attitude. You are now going to be the boss, and you'll have to be organized and disciplined in how you spend your time and resources. You'll need to plan ahead; rather than thinking only about what you might like to create, you'll start anticipating what others might like to buy by becoming alert to market trends. You may become aware of competition, but you'll also develop business savvy to help you be more competitive. If you prepare yourself for possible failure or rejection from the start, you won't be as disappointed or let down if things don't go as planned. In general, you need a new mindset to make the transition.

Changing Your Workspace

Transitioning from hobby to business may necessitate some changes in your workspace. You might need to rearrange furniture to create a better work flow, invest in tools and equipment, buy a computer, or install a separate phone line. You might require additional storage for inventory and supplies, perhaps in a garage, basement, or rented storage unit if necessary. Sewing for profit will put more demands on your machine and other equipment, so here is a great way to justify spending money on upgrading or purchasing those special items you've been wanting.

Getting People on Your Side

One of the most difficult aspects of becoming a craftsperson for profit is letting friends and relatives, most of whom are used to receiving your creations as gifts, know that you are now going to sell them instead. I encountered this myself and have talked with hundreds of crafters who have gone through the same thing. The best resolution to this problem is to rally the support of those people to help you in your new cause of becoming a successful businessperson. You can do this in the form of an announcement by telling them that you have been receiving so much positive response to your crafts that you've decided to "go for it" and start selling them. Go on to state that you are going to have to start charging them in the future but that you appreciate their support and are going to give them a discount. (Don't make the discount more than 30%, or you will start to drastically reduce your profit.) Good friends and loving relatives will be proud of your efforts and willing to contribute to your success.

The Right Stuff

A recent nationwide study by the Hobby Industry Association indicated that 16% of crafters polled make items to sell. Do you have what it takes to operate your own business? Are you:

☐ Self-motivated?

☐ Self-disciplined?

☐ Able to plan ahead and make a commitment?

☐ In control of your time and money?

☐ Confident with a positive attitude?

☐ Supported and encouraged by those around you?

☐ Flexible and willing to admit mistakes?

☐ Not defeated by failure?

If you checked all of the above, you are well equipped to start a business. Good luck!

Letting People Know You're Serious

It's not enough to change your attitude and tell people that you are now sewing for profit. You will need to let them know you are serious by your actions. I talk to so many crafters who want to sell their creations but don't want to become involved in the business details. Then they wonder why people don't take them seriously, and they have a very difficult time with pricing and putting a value on both themselves and their products. Don't make this mistake if you truly want to make money selling your crafts. All of the basic business information is in this book, and it need not be an overwhelming part of the process. Chapter 11 gives you the nitty-gritty of choosing a business name, types of businesses, licensing, copyrights, insurance, and other details that will let people know you're serious.

Being Your Own Boss

Many people think that being your own boss means you won't have to do anything you don't want to do anymore. In reality, the truth about being self-employed is that you will probably work much harder than you have ever worked for someone else. On the other hand, you are the direct recipient of all the benefits that come from the effort you put in, which can be extremely gratifying.

The Benefits of Being Self-Employed

Have you ever wondered what it would be like to be in total control of your career or, if you're not thinking on that grand of a scale, to have the ability to generate some cash whenever you please? That's how I feel when I enter my workroom no matter what time of day. It is my domain, my control central, the place where I make things happen. I get to make all the decisions, and I get all the glory when something goes right. I have been self-employed for so long that I am addicted to the benefits and would do anything to not work for someone else again. If you have decided to do crafting part-time or occasionally, I know that you will also gain from the experience and find that it enhances your life in many ways.

Being able to make my own schedule and craft whenever I please in the comfort of my home is probably the biggest benefit for me. I am a night person, so I can sleep as long as I like in the morning and then work late at night. I like being able to run my errands when the stores aren't crowded, and I am able to avoid rush hour totally if I plan ahead.

The personal satisfaction of creating something unique and then getting paid for it is also very rewarding. I see direct results of my hard work, and in addition to the compliments and "strokes" I receive from customers who admire my wares, I get money to pay my bills and finance whatever adventure I have planned in the future.

Disadvantages

I hesitated including this section, because in my opinion the advantages of being self-employed obviously far outweigh the disadvantages, but I do want to mention a few potential drawbacks. Along with all the glory comes all the disappointment if a project doesn't go as planned. You will have to find a way to cope with an occasional failure. Martha Pullen, in her very inspirational book *You Can Make Money from Your Hobby* (Broadman & Holman), states, "If at first you don't succeed, join the club!" Successful self-employed people develop a thick skin and see failure as an obstacle, not as defeat. In fact, my many failures have all proved to be immense learning experiences that inevitably helped my progress toward bigger and better things.

Another potential disadvantage is actually an advantage to some people, depending on your personal style. Chances are you will be alone without much feedback from others if you are working in your home. This situation can make you feel isolated, or it can give you the solitude you need to create what you want. If you like input from others, you will need to find crafting comrades whether they be in clubs, organizations, newsletters, on the Internet, or simply from a support group of friends who can talk with you on the phone from time to time.

Developing a Plan

If you would like to start profiting from your sewing as quickly and easily as possible, you will need to develop a plan that will give all your actions and decisions direction. When I started, I had no plan and no direction. I literally floundered for years. It wasn't until I defined what I wanted (and didn't want) to do that my business took off. A plan will help you make decisions and enable you to go about things in a constructive rather than destructive way.

Simple but Effective

A business plan does not have to be involved to be effective. It simply entails listing your intentions and resources and seeing how you can make the most of both. A plan isn't the be-all and end-all in your business, and it can't be a substitute for learning as you go, but it can help you avoid many pitfalls that are common to most businesses and give you a jump start on your way. Business books, banks, loan institutions, and the Small Business Administration (see Resources) all have sample business plans that you can use, but I am going to give you a condensed and abridged version that will relate more directly to you as a sewing crafter.

Creative people are dreamers, not necessarily pragmatic businesspeople. We tend to want to do our craft and not bother with "the rest of it," as I have heard the business aspect referred to. You don't need to get bogged down—just try to put a simple response after each category, and you'll be well on your way to realizing your dream!

Sample Business Plan

Time to Devote to Crafting

- Full-time
- Part-time
- Less than part-time (list number of hours per week)

Income

- How much money do I want to make? (This can be in the form of a mission statement.)

Product

- What is it?
- How long does it take to make?
- How much does it cost to make?
- What will I charge for it? (See chapter 8 for pricing information.)

Target Market

- Who is going to use or want my product?
- How am I going to sell it? (See chapter 9 for ideas.)

  Fairs and festivals

  Malls

  Bazaars

Home parties

Retail, wholesale, or both

Other

Advertising and Publicity (see chapter 9)

■ How am I going to get the word out?

Newspapers

TV

Brochures or flyers

Other

Resources

■ What equipment and supplies do I own?

■ What do I need?

Financing

■ How much money do I need?

■ How much do I have?

■ How much do I need to borrow?

Plans for Growth

■ Am I prepared to expand?

■ Do I want to add new products?

■ Do I want to hire help?

Getting Help

Many places offer help, business counseling, and even financial support depending on your time and budget, and I list many of them in Resources. The library is free and accessible and holds a wealth of information, as does the Small Business Administration. One of the best things I did when starting my business was attend a free seminar put on by the IRS entitled "Tax Workshop for Small Businesses." I was able to ask questions and understand all about taxes without the fear or trepidation that is often associated with this subject. Community colleges continuously offer classes for new businesses. If your budget allows, you might talk with lawyers, accountants, or other business professionals. Local chambers of commerce cater to small businesses, as do various clubs and organizations. My bank publishes a free monthly newsletter aimed at business owners that I have found extremely helpful. Networking and talking with other crafters are invaluable also.

Important Criteria for Selecting a Salable Craft Item

- Does it appeal to a large number of people?
- Is it difficult enough to produce so that average people won't think they can just make it themselves?
- Is it different enough from other craft items to be considered unique?
- Is it cost-effective to produce?
- Does it have staying power, or will it go out of style quickly? If so, can it be easily modified or updated?
- Is it sturdy enough to withstand handling, packing and unpacking, and possibly shipping?
- Can you find a reliable source for materials to produce it?

Finding the Right Product

Deciding what kind of sewn crafts to produce will take some time, research, and a little bit of luck. Many who sew get their start simply by making something for themselves that they love and soon finding others want the same thing. This is how I started, but it is not how I succeeded or grew my business in the long run. I am going to give you some concrete suggestions for finding good craft ideas so you won't have to sit and wait for that special project to fall in your lap.

Potential Sale Items

To say that sewing offers unlimited potential items to sell is an understatement. In the Introduction I walked with you through my home and pointed out the sewn items in every room. Extend this journey to anywhere you go during your daily routine. This may include going to the car with its cup holders, map caddies, banners, and stick-on stuffed animals; to the grocery store decorated with banners, sewn and stuffed displays of food and other products, and the personnel who wear aprons and hats; and to the office where there are wall hangings, fabric picture frames, beanbag paperweights, and more. You will not be at a loss for ideas, but you will need to select the right ones for you.

Where to Get Additional Ideas

A recent report by the Hobby Industry Association listed magazines, books, and catalogs as the major sources from which crafters get their ideas. Family and friends were also found to be important sources. I recommend all of these, but you'll also have to do some footwork by becoming a supersleuth to get ideas for projects. Most of your investigating will be fun and enlightening. Begin by going to every craft fair, boutique, and mall that you can find. Take note of what other people are already producing and selling. The idea is not to copy what others have done but to get stimulation to develop a better mousetrap, fill a need that has not been met, or revive and adapt an old idea to modern times. You will be surprised at how creative you can become when you are in an atmosphere like this. Always carry a notepad so you won't forget those moments of inspiration.

After you have walked until your feet are sore, come home, put them up, and begin the next part of your research. Many of my ideas come from the multitude of catalogs that I receive in the mail each day. Browse through them with a new attitude even if you aren't particularly interested in the subjects. They are filled with sewn items, and one thing is for sure: The catalog has probably done a lot of market research before deciding to offer the items for sale, so there is a good chance these types of products are in demand.

Handy Hint

Other crafters have worked hard to get where they are, so don't stand and take notes right in front of their displays—do it discreetly after you have walked away. Remember, you are on a fact-finding mission, not being a copycat!

Graduate students in college always do a literature review to find out what has been written about a topic before starting their own research projects. They want to know what has already been done so they can come up with an original idea. I highly recommend going to your library and researching ideas you might have. Look through craft books and magazines on any subject. They all contain countless ideas for sewn items.

Subscribe to craft magazines and newsletters, and surf the Internet if possible for input on crafting (see Resources). Join craft clubs and organizations. Talk to people—your neighbors, friends, and family—to find out what they like and what they need. Listen to conversations that you're not involved in and be alert to clues for salable craft items. I try to find a new idea in almost every social situation by being aware of people's comments and how they can relate to my business ideas.

Keeping an Idea Notebook

- Use a three-ring binder filled with separate labeled pockets to keep track of ideas.

- Separate them into your chosen categories such as children, home decor, Victorian, kitchen, or anything else that seems appropriate.

- Save clippings from magazines, catalogs, advertisements, and craft flyers and file accordingly.

- Include self-generated sketches, notes, photos, and designs.

- Look through the notebook periodically to discard information that is no longer pertinent and to get ideas for future projects.

In the beginning of this section I stated that finding the right product also takes a little bit of luck. Who's to know if your idea won't become the next Cabbage Patch Kid or Beanie Baby! I'm sure their originators had hoped and planned for success, but no one could predict what huge moneymakers these would become. And they both started with someone sitting at a sewing machine, just like us!

Pricing Your Craft Sewing

▼▼▼

PRICING IS THE MOST IMPORTANT aspect of selling a craft. It doesn't matter how well you sew—if the item isn't priced right, it won't sell. Unfortunately, pricing is probably the biggest dilemma for anyone who wants to sell his or her handmade crafts. Sewing for ourselves, family, or friends is fun and easy, but when it comes to putting a price on our work, everything changes. I have been selling my sewn items for more than 30 years, so I am going to let you in on the secrets of pricing your sewing effectively.

Valuing Yourself

Just in case you're wondering what valuing yourself has to do with pricing a craft item, it has everything to do with it! Women in general are caregivers, and many find it difficult to ask for or even talk about money in a business setting. We give freely and most of the time don't ask for anything in return, so when it comes to putting a price on our sewing, we need to develop a completely new mind-set—one of receiving payment rather than doing it for free.

We are all multifaceted, multitalented individuals, and whatever we sew contains our own special touch of creativity. We are selling much more than handcrafted items; we are selling knowledge, skill, originality, expertise, and many times love and caring that went into each piece. Each handmade craft item is unique and valuable by its very nature.

During my last haircut, my hairdresser mentioned she was taking a sculpture class. She explained that cutting hair was like sculpting—each haircut was an individual work of art incorporating design, line, and texture. Cutting hair was secondary to what she was doing; she was expressing her creativity, her sense of proportion, her style, herself. What a wake-up call for me! The hairdresser looked upon herself as an artist, and although I have never thought of it in those terms, I am an artist too—I just have a different medium. How many times have I failed to see or appreciate the beauty in my own creations or even look at them as something aesthetic at all? Yet others see the beauty, realize the value, and even pay me for my efforts.

Pricing Basics

Many different formulas and types of pricing are possible. I am going to sort through the different factors and show you the formula that works best for me. I will be honest and tell you that I have had many failures in pricing my work, but I have persevered and gone on to operate a very successful business. My advice comes from simple research and hard-core experience.

Hourly Rate: A Crafter's Minimum Wage

The very simplest way to price a product is to multiply your hourly rate by the time it takes you to do something and then add in the cost of the materials. In equation form, it would look like this:

(hourly rate × number of hours) + cost of materials = price

Choosing a realistic and fair hourly rate depends on several variables: minimum wage, what you want to make, what you need to make, what you have made in the past, and/or what an average wage is for your area. These are all points to consider when deciding on an hourly rate, and if you've never done this before, it can be difficult.

The *easiest* way to arrive at an hourly rate is to ask someone who is already sewing the type of craft items you want to sell how much they charge, but it will be difficult to get anyone to tell you this information. How much someone makes is very personal, and besides, very few people will want to tell potential competition how to succeed. If more crafters remembered how difficult it was for them to start pricing, perhaps more would be willing to help the newcomers.

> ## Handy Hint
> Ads in craft magazines are the best place to find suppliers.

For those of you who have no idea where to start, I'm just going to tell you that based on my experience of talking to hundreds of crafters and having worked as a crafter for so long, you should be charging an absolute minimum of $8.00 per hour for your time. Remember, this is a minimum—you want to work your way up to much more per hour depending on your skill and expertise.

Cost of Materials

The cost of materials is how much you spent for all the items that went into making your craft, such as the fabric, thread, ribbon, trim, and so forth. People often ask me whether that means wholesale or retail; it doesn't matter—it just means how much you spent no matter what the price you paid for the materials. Of course, it would be advantageous to purchase everything at wholesale prices, but if you're just starting out, you probably won't need large quantities in the beginning. Besides, if you can price your product and make a profit buying your supplies retail, it will only be icing on the cake if and when you transition to wholesale buying.

Overhead

Overhead is anything other than the cost of the labor and materials, such as electricity, rent, equipment, maintenance, and tools. This is one area that many crafters overlook when pricing their products. It can be very difficult to designate a certain percentage or amount of overhead expense to an individual craft because overhead contains so many varied items. A very general rule for beginners is to add $2 to your basic hourly rate. So, if your hourly rate is $8, add $2 to that and figure the following basic pricing equation:

$$\text{labor (hourly rate} \times \text{number of hours)}$$
$$+ \text{ cost of materials } + \text{overhead} = \text{retail price}$$

Estimating and Tracking Your Time

The first time you make something will take longer than any other time you make it because you have to figure out how to do it and may experience some setbacks or roadblocks along the way. Remember, the more you do something, the faster you will get, but you'll need an idea or estimate of how long the project will take. Use an index card to keep track of your time when sewing an item. Remember that you can charge for only the time that you are actually working, not for taking breaks, making phone calls, tending to a child, and so forth. Clock in and out as needed and add up the total when you're done.

Sewing for profit requires a different attitude than hobby sewing. In other words, you have to "push" or constantly remind yourself that you need to do this task as quickly as possible. In general, you will not be able to leisurely sit and sew without regard to time, because the faster you sew, the more money you make.

Timesaving Tips

If speed is not your forte, there are many ways to get faster:

- ■ Take classes, read books, listen to tapes, and view videos to learn new skills.

- ■ Buy new tools that save time and increase efficiency.

- ■ Upgrade your machine, or purchase specialized attachments.

- ■ Put the item together in a different order, or eliminate some steps altogether.

- ■ Practice makes perfect—the more times you perform a task, the faster you will get!

Keeping Records

Keeping accurate records of your purchases is an absolute must for pricing, so develop a simple system from the start. Make out a separate pricing sheet for each item you sell by listing all the materials and their costs. Attach an envelope for saving receipts. You will not be able to memorize all this information, and you will want something for reference when shopping for lower prices. It will also give you a visual idea of where you might cut costs or try to do quantity buying.

The Psychology of Pricing

Believe it or not, you will need to become an amateur psychologist when pricing your product. It is not enough to calculate a realistic price; you may have to adjust it slightly to make it more appealing psychologically.

Odd Pricing

Odd pricing, or giving the illusion of a lower price, is a very common practice. For instance, instead of pricing an item at $20.00, you would charge $19.95 or $19.99. Personally, I like odd pricing and have had very favorable results with it. In general we are conditioned to odd pricing everywhere we look, so you can carry this concept into your pricing. You may have your own feelings about odd pricing now, or you may want to experiment with it and find what works for you.

Rounding Up

When pricing a product, you will sometimes arrive at an amount that is "neither here nor there" and will need to round up to a price that sounds more standard. For instance, if something priced out at $5.18, you should round it up to $5.25 or $5.50 ($5.49 if you are practicing odd pricing). Why don't we round down to the closest amount? Because we are here to make a profit! Many times I will price a product and simply feel that the amount sounds wrong. I'll try other prices that are in the same ballpark and see how I feel about them, selecting one I like better. This is purely subjective, but it has worked numerous times for me. You will develop a pricing sense the more you do it, too.

Competitive Pricing

Competitive pricing is just what it says—you find out what others are charging and you charge less. Doing this as a general practice is not good business, because you may not be able to make a profit at a lower price. You need to price the item out for yourself and then determine whether you can really sell it cheaper. Also, you should be reasonably sure that you are not selling exactly the same thing as someone else. One of your goals should be to produce a better mousetrap, and the best selling is done by offering more features, not lower prices.

Special Discounts

Giving special discounts takes extra pricing savvy but can lead to increased sales. You may want to make a package deal and offer several items together at a price that is lower than buying them individually, such as one for $4.99 or three for $12.00. (Notice that the individual price was odd pricing and the package deal was not— another pricing alternative.) This can be an effective selling technique; just be sure you are making a profit, although it may not be as much. Some people inflate the original price for an individual item and then do not make less profit when they discount a package deal.

Vanity Pricing

Vanity pricing is pricing a product higher than necessary to make it appear more valuable. It's hard to believe, but sometimes if a product is not priced high enough, it doesn't have perceived value, or people don't think it is worth very much. Your geographic location and target market will have a lot to do with vanity pricing. In general, people in urban, upscale areas with more discretionary income are used to paying higher prices than people pay in rural settings or in places where more people tend to be on a fixed income. However, many tourist areas use vanity pricing because people are more likely to spend more for items they buy on vacation or when traveling. It is very seldom that an item won't sell because it is priced too low, but if you are not getting the results you desire, you might try this tactic.

Ensuring Success

As crafters, most of us operate alone from our homes. We think our businesses are not significant enough to treat as seriously as large corporations and that we do not have to practice big-business principles. In fact, we crafters need big-business principles more than big businesses do because when we make a mistake, there is no one else to take up the slack, whereas when huge corporations make mistakes, they can absorb the loss in many ways. We need to use these principles but adjust them to our level to ensure success.

Test Marketing

One big-business principle that has helped me immensely is test marketing, or trying to sell a small quantity of crafts before producing a large amount to see how they are accepted by the public. We have all received coupons or seen advertisements for introductory

Making Policies

Here's another big-business principle that can really be useful for small businesses: policy making. How many times have you been in the position of being told that some practice is a business's policy and there are no alternatives? People are used to associating policies with something that cannot be changed, and you will need to capitalize on this in your business. Develop your own policies and write them down. Practice saying them out loud, and you will be surprised how they can help you achieve the results you want in your business.

Here are some examples of policies you may want to implement:

- Money-back guarantee
- No returns without receipt
- $15 fee for all returned checks
- Senior citizen discount

Table Linens—Placemats, Napkins, and Table Runner

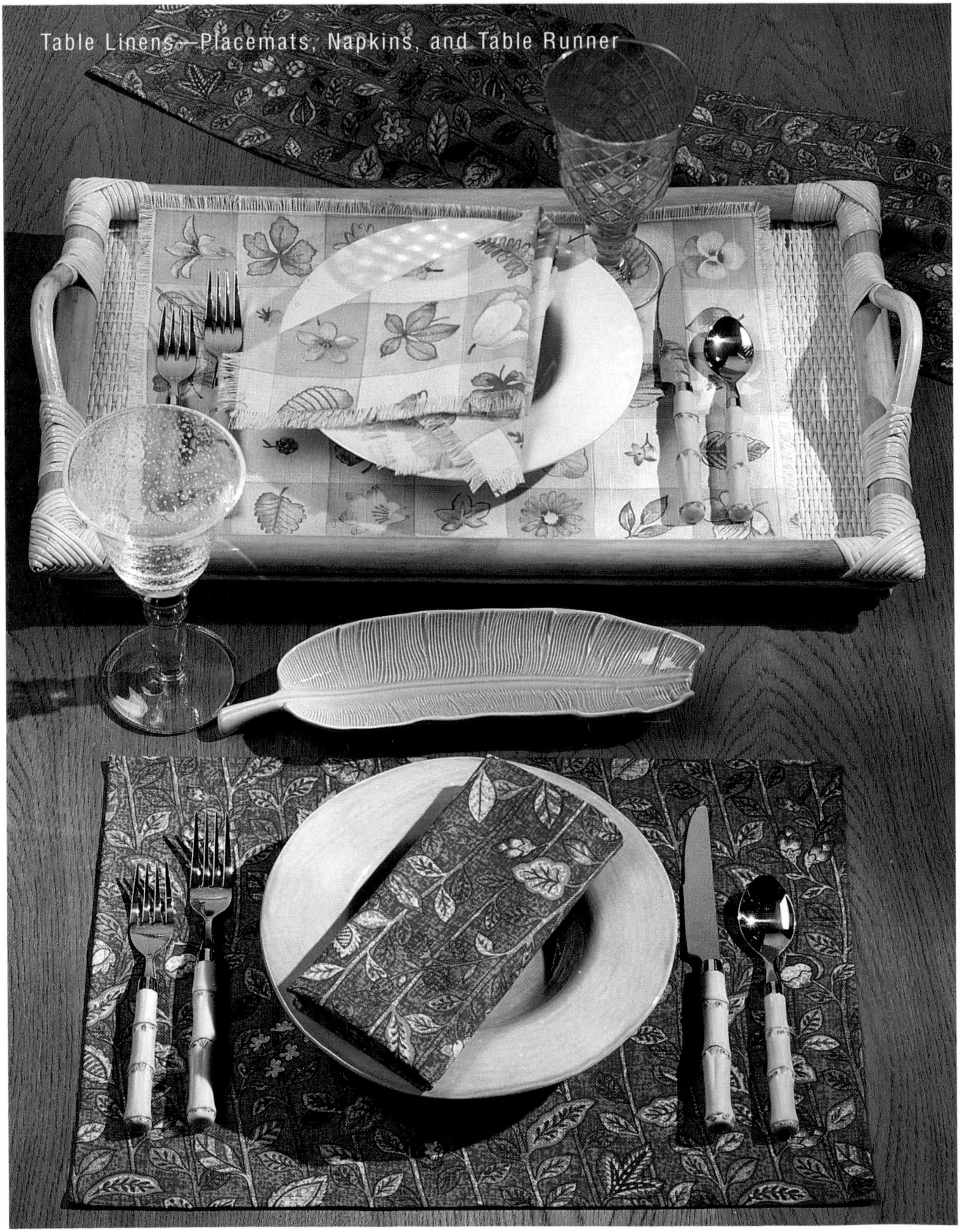

Aprons

offers in magazines, newspapers, the mail, or stores. Large corporations may do test markets in the tens of thousands, but we need to scale this down to fit our needs.

After you have priced your product and decided that you will be able to make a profit on it, you need to make a small quantity to perform your own test market. First make six. If they sell, make 12; if they sell, make 24; and increase in increments of 12. This is a relatively inexpensive way to test your craft and see whether producing it is really a feasible idea.

Being Flexible

Another way to ensure success is to always be flexible. Listen to what people say about your craft. Is it too expensive or too cheap, or would it work better if it had some additional feature? Could it be modified to appeal to a broader market? Be aware of trends or seasonal color changes that would affect the desirability of your craft. It's very seldom you will be able to produce a certain item continuously without adapting it to fit consumer demands and needs.

Pricing Indicators

Certain circumstances indicate a need to adjust prices. These are subtle areas of discussion, but I have found them very important to the profitability of my business over the years.

Stress Level

The first several years of my business were very stressful and filled with long hours of work that never seemed to end. I couldn't catch up and thought if I just worked harder, I would make more money. I wish someone would have given me the advice that I am about to give you. *If you are very busy or always behind, it is an automatic indication that you need to raise your prices.* This is another one of those big-business principles that we can apply directly to our small businesses. When you are too busy, it means that you can't keep up with the demand for your product. If you will raise your prices (start and continue with increments of 10%), you will find that you are working less and making more money. We think that if we charge more we won't get any business, but the demand for what you are doing has already been demonstrated if you are on overload, so go ahead and increase your prices. This is one of the most valuable pricing tips I can give you. Act on faith, and I guarantee you will see the rewards!

Did you know???

When sales drop on previously popular items, large companies change the packaging to appear different or they change product features so they are able to advertise using the words *new* and/or *improved.*

Keeping Up with the Cost of Living

One big mistake I made in the first several years of my business was that I never raised my prices. I was still selling my crafts and paying my bills, but I wasn't getting ahead or saving anything at all. Everyone else gets cost of living raises, and we need to, too, even if we are self-employed and at home. You can go to the library and find out what the standard rate per year is, develop your own percentage, or ask an accountant's advice, but you must increase your prices a little each year. Customers won't notice a small price increase, but they will be shocked if you raise your prices a lot at one time.

Market Saturation

Sometimes an item sells wonderfully for months or even years, and, all of a sudden, sales begin to drop. If you have kept up on trends in the field and are fairly sure you don't have serious competitors, you may have reached market saturation, or sold as many of the item that you are likely to sell at that price. You may increase sales by lowering the price if that is feasible; but if that doesn't work, it may be time to discontinue that item or find some way to modify it or add more features.

Additional Help

Many books contain information on pricing crafts and they are listed in the Resources section. I particularly like *The Crafter's Guide to Pricing Your Work* by Dan Ramsey (Betterway Books). In addition, "QuickBooks" offers an easy-to-use computer software program that calculates whether you are making a profit. Pricing takes practice, but if you use the basic formula I have provided and always do a test market, you'll be well on your way to success.

Selling Your Craft Sewing

▼▼▼

PEOPLE HAVE SOLD THEIR SEWING since money was invented, and they were probably trading hand-sewn items for other goods long before that. If you've reached this point in the book, you're ready to see exactly what selling your crafts is all about and to take your place in history with the countless others who made and are making money from their hobbies. Even though I have sold my handcrafts for almost 30 years, you have the advantage over me in that you have someone to tell you how to do it. In addition, there are many more venues for selling crafts now than when I started, so you'll have more choices and more chances to find success quickly and easily.

Having a Vision and a Plan

In chapters 6 and 7, we talked about your crafts vision and wrote a basic business plan. We then made certain specific goals. If you are serious about selling your handicrafts, I hope you have written these items in a notebook so you can use them as a guide when making business decisions. Referring to them will give you direction.

Home Sales and Shows

Retail selling is selling your crafts directly to consumers at full price. You, the manufacturer, do all the actual selling. Many outlets and opportunities exist for you to sell your crafts retail, and this is how most crafters start. Following is a discussion of many retail selling opportunities.

Selling to Friends

Selling crafts from your home can be one of the easiest and least expensive methods. Your first sales will undoubtedly be to family or friends who have seen and admired your crafts and want one for themselves or for a gift. You don't need to advertise, display, or promote—you just sell to customers who are already asking for your product! This is the ultimate situation, but soon you will want to expand and reach a larger audience of prospective buyers.

Did you know???

Some cities limit the number of yard sales held at one house per year. Check with your local chamber of commerce if you plan on sponsoring multiple sales.

Garage Sales

Having a garage sale is a great way to test market new products without making a large investment. You can take all the time and space you need to display and arrange merchandise. You'll have the option of devoting the whole sale to crafts or combining crafts and household items usually found at garage sales. Over the years before and after my many moves, I have been successful including one table of craft items along with my regular garage sale items. People enjoy finding and are drawn to attractive handmade crafts during their usual garage sale circuits around town.

Parties and Home Shows

Many people have hosted Tupperware or similar parties where guests are served refreshments and possibly entertained with games or activities, and then offered a sales presentation of products that they can order. A home craft party can be run in exactly the same way except that you are supplying the products instead of an outside company. You can hold the party yourself or combine with other crafters to reach more people and increase your visibility. Just make sure the various crafts are complementary rather than competitive.

Running a Successful Home Show

- Plan ahead—at least a year in advance.

- Make sure your dates don't conflict with major sports, cultural, or social events in the community.

- Combine your efforts with other crafters who have quality items that complement rather than compete with yours.

- Make out a schedule and clearly define everyone's duties.

- Prepare advertising, flyers, and press releases well ahead of time so people can schedule your event on their calendars.

- Make sure there is plenty of available parking, or work out a shuttle system.

- Have plenty of change, bags, and brochures on hand.

- Let customers sign a guest book so you can do a mailing next time.

- Plan ahead and tell customers your dates for the following year so they can anticipate your sale and tell their friends about it.

Kiddy Creations

Susan Boslough Adams teaches high school Spanish in the Beaverton School District near Portland, Oregon. Back in the early 1980s during a lunch break, the art teacher showed her a baby shower gift she had just made—a cute bib decorated with an appliquéd carrot. The art teacher related how the recipients appreciated not only a handmade gift but also something that was very useful and much needed. Susan was so impressed that she decided to sew some bibs herself.

Although she had sewn before, she didn't know how to appliqué and had to put her enthusiasm on hold. Later in the year she visited her college roommate, an avid seamstress, who taught Susan how to appliqué, and then her hobby really took off. At first she just gave the bibs for gifts, but other shower guests admired them and called her to make some for them. She soon found that everyone wants bibs—parents, grandparents, aunts and uncles, friends—virtually anyone who knows a child!

Susan improved on commercial bibs by designing larger ones with extra length on the bottoms to fit onto high-chair tables and prevent "dropsies." She made them much easier for moms by using Velcro instead of tie closures. She sews them from quilted ging-

Home shows take more effort and planning, but they can be extremely lucrative. Years ago, a *Family Circle* magazine article titled "Beyond Garage Sales: The Home Boutique" told how a group of women in a Chicago suburb had a Christmas sale at home called "The Stocking Stuffer." They pooled their time, money, and expertise for a year in advance and then sold crafts for several days during the holiday season. Women are still selling the same way today. Home shows require much planning, advertising, and actual time to make the crafts, but they can pay off with huge returns. Obvious security precautions must be taken when opening your home to the public, but many entrepreneurs throughout the country have done it successfully. This type of endeavor is best accomplished when the efforts of several crafters are combined and can lead to a popular and anticipated annual event.

ham fabric backed with heavy cotton flannel or rubberized terry cloth (available in fabric stores), and, of course, the individualized appliqués are the crowning touch. Inspiration for appliqué designs comes from coloring books, children's books, appliqué books, juvenile fabrics, and wrapping paper. Her most original was a seal for her niece who lives in Alaska, but others include ladybugs, ducks, pigs, and countless other motifs.

Susan charges $10 to $12 per bib and is delighted to make some money from her hobby, but her biggest motivation comes from the fun she has making them. Teaching is an intense, full-time profession, but designing and sewing bibs in the evenings and on weekends have greatly reduced her stress. Her three nieces have received more than 30 bibs that have all become treasured keepsakes. Their mom, Trix, says that the bibs "have seen better days," but no matter how tattered, stained, and worn they are, she still uses them.

Babies grow up and don't need bibs forever, but Susan has anticipated the changing needs of her customers and friends—she plans to start making appliquéd smocks that can be worn for play or school. She has also expanded her sewing to accommodate every age group by appliquéing sweatshirts with holiday or other custom designs

Barbara Brabec, in her book *Handmade for Profit* (Evans), has written an extensive and very informative section on home parties and boutiques. Among her many useful tips is to check zoning requirements before planning an open house event. It would be a shame to spend months preparing only to find you can't sell from your home. She does explain ways to get around this situation if necessary.

Flea Markets and Bazaars

Flea markets and bazaars are a relatively inexpensive way to test your ideas with the general public and get a feel for what larger craft festivals and fairs are like. Generally you rent a table, display your wares, and sell them. Flea markets are usually run by one owner or partners, while bazaars can be sponsored by groups or clubs. You can rent tables for as low as $10 and usually under $100. Keep in mind that both flea markets and bazaars attract a wide range of people with all kinds of new and used merchandise, so if your item doesn't have universal appeal, you may be discouraged if you participate in these events.

Selling on the Internet

The Internet is still in its infancy in regard to craft selling. Colorful and effective Web pages are expensive to produce and expensive to update, usually too costly for the average crafter. Potential customers need to be computer literate with access to the Internet and willing to search for crafts in order to find you. If they do find you, they can't touch or see items, which are usually essential parts of craft buying. Furthermore, because the average price of individual crafts is relatively inexpensive, the high and increasing cost of shipping could discourage craft buyers.

Yet, some crafters are experiencing success in this venue, and the Internet offers several options if you feel your crafts would sell well on the Web. Many people, myself included, pay a monthly rental fee for having a home page on someone else's Web site. This approach allows me to be part of the Internet craze without all the expense. The drawback is that customers can only find me if they first find the general Web site and then search me out within it. Customers need to call or write me to place an order; they can't order directly on the Internet with a credit card.

Other crafters are profiting from renting a page on what I would call Internet craft malls. A very popular one, www.coomers.com (of Coomers Craft Malls) features beautiful color photos of hundreds of crafts, all organized by specific categories. Customers can type in keywords—I tried "kitchen" and instantly re-

Succeeding in a Craft Mall

Back in 1988, Rufus Coomer of Springtown, Texas, opened what was probably the first craft mall in America. He noticed the abundance of crafters in his area and decided to bring them all together under one roof. The idea was an immediate success, and after opening several other stores across Texas, Coomers Craft Malls now total more than 30 stores nationwide. Their new concept stores also sell craft supplies. In addition, Coomers offers many items from its stores on the Internet—a wonderful opportunity for crafters who may not be able to afford or manage their own Web page. Rufus shares some of his best tips for selling in a craft mall:

- Get signed up—you can't sell if you don't take that first step!

- Fill your space as much as possible—the more items you have, the more chance someone will find something they want.

- Have something for everyone from inexpensive items to more expensive ones—this stimulates impulse buying.

- Arrange and display crafts attractively—the mall manager can offer suggestions for this.

- Price your items properly according to the mall's rules—this will make record keeping easier and speed payment.

- Keep enough inventory on hand to replenish your space when needed.

ceived numerous options for crafts that pertain to the kitchen. This type of Web page does allow consumers to order with credit cards. I noticed that the average craft price is more than $10, making them more cost-effective to purchase when there are shipping charges to consider. Again, the major disadvantage is that you don't actually get to touch and examine the craft, but you also don't have to spend hours on your feet walking through a mall or a fair.

Craft Fairs and Festivals

Craft fairs and festivals are by far the most popular way to sell hand-made crafts, so I am devoting a major portion of this chapter to this topic. Even though I am providing detailed information, keep in mind that starting small with the previously mentioned methods is always recommended before "taking the plunge" to a large craft fair. There's no substitute for experience, and you'll do better working your way up learning as you go.

Finding the Right Show for You

If you are into crafting, you've probably been to many fairs or festivals in your area as an attendee, but now you may want to become an exhibitor. Visit the show office at these fairs or ask any exhibitor for contact information and you're on your way. For expanding beyond your immediate geographic area, consider attending some of the literally thousands of craft fairs and festivals nationwide; some excellent sources list them (see Resources).

Craft Fair Checklist

- ☐ Dates and times
- ☐ What is provided
- ☐ Setup and teardown times
- ☐ Location with map if needed
- ☐ Parking pass
- ☐ Booth size, number, and location

- ☐ Equipment ordered
- ☐ Equipment taken from home
- ☐ Passes and nametags
- ☐ Sales permit
- ☐ Tax amount

Show promoters have a tendency to always tell you that they have the best show and that it is going to be a huge success, but the real scoop about shows comes from talking with exhibitors themselves. Before shows, while setting up, during shows, and after shows each day, the main topic of conversation among exhibitors is usually about what shows are good and what shows aren't. If you have never exhibited at a show before, trust your instincts and go with a show that you yourself love to attend. As soon as you participate in your first show, you will be privy to the show gossip and soon able to evaluate what shows are best for you.

> ## Did you know???
> Show promoters usually require 50% down and 50% due 30 or 60 days prior to the show opening. Luckily most promoters take credit cards!

Better yet, volunteer to work in someone's booth and learn firsthand what shows are like and where the best ones are located. Exhibitors are always looking for help, especially if they have come from out of town, and they are usually delighted have a fellow crafter assist them. If you have attended shows and collected promotional material from various vendors, call or write them to see whether they need help, or contact show promoters and let them know you're available. They'll pass the word along. You might get paid in addition to garnering valuable information and experience.

Booth Fees, Size, and Location

In general, you will need to sign up 6 months to a year in advance to participate in a craft show. Rates range anywhere from about $100 to thousands of dollars depending on the location and size of the show and the size of your booth. Promoters usually require 50% at the time of application and the balance sometime before the show starts.

Booths generally measure 10 × 10 feet, and you can rent more than one booth, although some shows accommodate new crafters or people with only a few products and sell booths that are 6 × 8 feet.

Over the years I have learned that the more space you have, the more you will sell. I started with one table and one craft and 20 years later have expanded to a 10 × 20-foot booth with more than 50 items.

Location, location, location—it is important in real estate and also very important at craft shows. Some promoters allow you to select your booth; others merely assign your booth depending on the demand for space at their show. If you cannot physically visit the show before you exhibit at it, request a floor plan to get an idea of traffic flow, entrance, exit, and restroom and food stand locations. All of these will influence the number of people who walk by your booth. In general, a corner booth near the front of the show is considered an optimum location. If you are a newcomer to a show, you may not get the first booth location you request. Some shows give priority to repeat exhibitors and allow them to keep the same location year after year.

Making a Dazzling Debut

According to the publishers of *Craftmaster News,* a common mistake made by novice crafters is that they think paying their money for a booth and showing up is all they have to do to ensure success. A show promoter is responsible for getting prospective buyers to the show, but after that, the individual crafter is in control. Here are some tips that may help your first-time craft show experience go more smoothly.

- An attractive and inviting booth display is extremely important. You want to draw and maintain customers' interest.

- Find some way to interact with customers—you need to become a salesperson in addition to being a craftsperson.

- Prior to signing up for your first show, visit as many craft shows as possible to get ideas and input.

Applying for Booth Space

You will need to fill in a simple application stating the exact nature of your business and what you intend to sell at the show. Be sure to present yourself and your application as professionally as possible—type it or use a computer and make sure nothing is misspelled. Fill in all the blanks and answer questions as thoroughly as possible. Competition can be stiff at popular shows, so you want to give yourself every advantage. Some shows are juried, and you will be asked to supply a sample of your handicraft and/or slides prior to acceptance. Plan ahead by taking good color photos and slides of your crafts so that you are not running around at the last minute trying to prepare them. Every time you produce a new craft you should photograph it and get extra copies to have on hand. You will need them in the future for promotional materials as well as for show applications.

Once in a while your application may get turned down. Some shows simply don't have room for newcomers (there is usually a waiting list), or you may have applied too late. A promoter once told me that my type of product simply wasn't right for his show, and he would rather not have me do the show than be disappointed when my crafts didn't sell. That forthright tip saved me hundreds of dollars in booth fees and made me much more discriminating before applying to shows in the future. I have always been grateful for the advice even though I was rejected.

Designing Your Booth

Arranging and setting up a booth take time and creativity. The best place to get inspiration is to look at other exhibitors' booths at craft fairs. Of course, you don't want to copy anything exactly, but this tactic will start your creative juices flowing and help you come up with original and new ideas of your own. Also browse through regular stores or shopping malls and notice how products are displayed. Magazines are also a good source for ideas. The options are endless. Keep a folder and take notes of your favorites, and then build on what you've seen to create something truly individual.

Creativity Is the Key

I have participated in several hundred craft shows with thousands of exhibitors, and I have never seen two booths that look exactly alike. Booth designs are as individual as the people who set them up, and all contain a special flair of creativity. Booths can be as simple as a decorated table or as elaborate as an individual tent. Tables, draping, and other display furniture are usually available for rent at shows but are extremely expensive, so if you are planning on exhibiting at several shows a year, you will probably want to invest in your own booth equipment.

Look in the Yellow Pages of your phone book to find display or fixture stores. If you live in a rural area, you may have to travel to the big city for a day to do this. Walk through them to see what is available. Used display and fixture stores offer items at huge discounts. You may have to dust, clean, or repaint equipment, but the savings are worth it.

If you're going to exhibit at shows held outdoors, you will need some sort of protection from the elements ranging from awnings to three-sided tents like the ones made by Fred's Studio Tents & Canopies in Stillwater, New York. Many companies supply fixtures and display equipment that are freestanding or attach to shelving or walls. (See Resources for details.) Use graph paper to sketch out areas for displaying products, allowing room for customers to browse. Make sure they can get in and out with ease rather than becoming trapped if the booth gets crowded.

Some of the most unique and attractive booths I've seen have also been the cheapest. One exhibitor simply rummaged through her attic to find the oldest and most worn items she could. She

Tips for Effective Signs

- Never make signs by hand unless you are a talented calligrapher! Some shows do not allow hand-drawn signs.

- Use a computer or commercial sign maker for professional-looking signs.

- National chains such as Fast Signs or American Sign Centers make professional signs and banners quickly and inexpensively.

- All signs should be clear and easy to read in one glance. Avoid fancy or intricate fonts that make certain letters indistinguishable from others.

- Use concise and descriptive words.

- Limit printing to one or two lines.

- Make major points and use color to accent important parts.

- Place signs in strategic places that can be seen from many angles.

salvaged an old hat, a camera, musical instrument cases, suitcases, drawers, washbowls, and even a bedpan, all of which she filled with her crafts. People stop to admire the display, and most buy her items. Another exhibitor who sells children's hats, backpacks, and fanny packs drapes and displays them on children's furniture including a school desk, small swing set, toy chests, and a chest of drawers with the drawers pulled out. The idea is not so much the money you spend but the individuality and personality of your display.

Making an Eye-Appealing Display

While arranging your booth, keep in mind that you want to make it as easy as possible for customers to see, admire, and buy your crafts. Place items in related groups or logical order so others understand immediately what type of product you have and how it can be of use to them. Don't crowd items so much that they can't be distinguished or spread them out so sparsely that they look lonely. You may need to install extra lighting or highlight areas to dramatically set off your crafts. Your goal is to get customers to stop, look, and eventually buy. Try to think what makes your craft different and how you can distinguish it and your booth from all the others.

Take some time to childproof your booth. Children naturally want to touch everything they see, and you'll be smart if you prepare for this in advance. Some adults seem oblivious to the actions of their children, and some will be so interested in your handicrafts that they do not notice what their children are doing. Keep some small colorful toys on hand for them. Sometimes you might even have to explain that merchandise is not to be played with and that you need to keep items neat and in their places.

Dust and clean all merchandise and label it with easy-to-read prices. I try to make my labels large enough so people won't have to use their glasses to read them. I have found that customers like to have the price labels on the front where they are easy to find rather than having to search the item for them. You may only have a few seconds to impress your customers, so don't make them ask for the price—they may decide it isn't worth the effort, especially if you're busy with someone else.

Stock your booth with bags or packaging, and get change in advance from the bank. Nothing is worse than losing a sale because you didn't have the right change! Stock up on receipt pads and pens. I buy pens in bulk because they have a way of vanishing no matter how careful I am.

Carrying Out a Theme

Even though you know your crafts inside and out, potential customers may have no idea what you have to offer or how they can use your items in their lives. You may only have a few moments to grab someone's attention, so you need to make the most of it. Developing a theme and carrying it out throughout your booth will help communicate exactly who you are and what you have to offer.

Designing a logo and picturing it on signs, labels, receipts, hangtags, boxes, bags, and anything else you can think of will show people immediately what you are selling and items they take with them will remind them of you and your products in the future. Your logo should also be printed on your brochures, pamphlets, flyers, business checks, shipping labels, and anywhere else you can appropriately use it. This makes it easier for people to identify and remember you (see chapter 10 for more information on logos).

My friend Julie sells teddy bears as well as all the materials to make them. It was easy for her to pick a logo made of several cute teddy bears sitting together in a row. A wife-and-husband team who sell all kinds of decorated gardening pots and tools call themselves

Using Color Effectively

Good use of color can distinguish you from other exhibitors and enable repeat customers to identify you in a crowd. It also helps undecided customers to find your booth if they want to return and make purchases later.

Jane, an exhibitor from Miami, sells beautiful hand-painted cloth masks. Her first and most popular mask is red, black, and white, and even though she has expanded her line to many more brightly colored masks, she has carried this original color theme throughout her booth. The table drapes, side walls, and display cases are all red, black, or white, as are her signs and promotional materials.

Debra, from a small town in Minnesota, sets a romantic mood for selling her hand-sewn Victorian dolls by decorating with pinks, creams, and rose tones. Potential customers understand immediately that her product is soft, frilly, and feminine.

the "Gardening Angels," and their logo features an angel holding one of their flower pots and a trowel.

Many new business owners can't afford to pay graphic designers or printers for custom signs, brochures, hangtags, or stationery. Later in this chapter I discuss how computers can be used to generate many if not all of the printed materials you need. I have used rubber stamps for years instead of getting custom-made receipt forms or preprinted envelopes. Rubber stamps come in many sizes and shapes and can even be made with elaborate drawings or designs. Shop at stationery or paper wholesalers for bargains on paper products, and review the Resources in the back of this book for mail-order sources and for companies that specialize in custom-printed supplies.

Batten Down the Hatches!

Make sure all equipment and display materials are sturdy, tied or taped down, and in good working condition. Shows can become very crowded, and people will brush against displays with their bodies, packages, or purses and can disrupt anything that is not securely in place. If your booth contains furniture, especially chairs or benches, customers will sit on them regardless of how delicate or decorative they look, so anticipate this and either cover them entirely with merchandise, or don't make them part of your display.

If you don't want a particular item touched, it is better to put it out of reach than label it with a sign. People usually reach for items before they read signs. There is almost always a way to display fragile items so they can be seen without potential damage. I have seen beautiful heirloom quilts hung and covered with clear plastic and intricate lace work protected in glass cases.

Setup Day

Allow as much time as possible for setting up your booth. Even though I almost always rent the same-sized space, usually some variable such as lighting, traffic flow, a post, a fan or blower, or a neighboring display changes the way I have to set up. Always wear comfortable clothes in layers because even if the show is inside, they may not run the heating or cooling system before the show starts. Take food and water and any other creature comforts you might need so you won't have to run out to get them.

Know Where You're Going

Some shows are so large that you need to make an appointment at a certain time to unload your car. Others have no loading or unloading requirements at all. One thing is for sure—finding where to unload and getting unloaded can be one of the most difficult aspects of exhibiting at craft fairs. In the ideal situation, you would drive right up to your booth and unload at your leisure (some indoor shows let you drive right inside the building!), but this is the exception rather than the rule. Try to find out in advance exactly where and when you can unload your vehicle and get a map and directions if possible. I have wasted hours driving up and down country roads or around city blocks with one-way streets just trying to find the right exhibitor entrance location.

Handy Hint

Running a booth is like playing store when you were a child, only now the merchandise and money are real! Keeping this in mind will help you relax and maintain a playful attitude. If it's fun for you, it will be fun for customers—and that's the best atmosphere for selling.

Be Prepared and Have a System

Luggage carriers or dollies are essential for transporting items from your vehicle to the booth as well as a step stool for reaching high areas. I carry a trunk of essential items to each show that contains scissors, Scotch tape, packing tape, duct tape, pins, paper, an electric screwdriver, manual screwdrivers (slotted and Phillips), hammer, staples, pens, and many other items that I may need while setting up or during the show. Be organized with a general plan of how you are going to lay everything out, and proceed in a systematic way. I have certain boxes that I always use to carry certain items so I always know what's inside without having to rummage through them.

Don't Get Sidetracked

Avoid the temptation to stop and talk to fellow exhibitors until you're done setting up. A lot of valuable time can be wasted this way. Simply ask whether you can talk later, or make a date for dinner some night during the show. You will want to get together with other exhibitors—some of these people will become lifelong friends—but save your socializing until your work is done.

Selling Basics

Many crafters who are very creative by nature experience difficulty when the time comes to actually sell their products. Remember that you have taken the time to research your special niche, you have done your best to make a quality craft, you have probably already had much positive feedback from family and friends, so now you simply need to let everyone else know how wonderful your items are. Try not to pounce on or overwhelm prospective customers, but look interested and pleased that they are visiting your booth. Greet them and be attentive, but give them time to explore and discover on their own.

Educate Your Customers

Doing some activity or demonstration always generates interest and gives people a reason to linger at your booth. Just make sure it has to do with your craft so questions and comments will stay on track. If your craft can be used in one or more ways, explain the uses and let customers try themselves. Nothing sells like education and actually holding and using the item. (Nancy Ingerson, who you'll read about in the sidebar on page 187, makes fabric-covered boxes—she

Booth Worker No-No's

- Don't read a book, balance your checkbook, or do other unrelated activities that make it appear you would rather be somewhere else.

- Don't eat or leave drinks sitting out—most shows prohibit food in booths.

- Don't talk on a cell phone or watch miniature TVs.

- Leave small children with a sitter—they can distract customers or take too much of your attention.

- Don't bring pets—they may be adorable, but some people are allergic to them.

- Don't gossip or carry on long conversations with friends or other exhibitors.

got customers so interested they wanted to make their own, and she developed a completely new business.) Pretend the customers are your best friends and you are helping them discover a wonderful new product.

What to Say

Always greet people cordially and learn to sense which customers want to talk, which need help intermittently, and which just want to be left alone to browse on their own. Ask talkative customers about themselves, their likes and dislikes, and be genuinely interested, but try to keep the subject on crafts and your crafts specifically. Gossiping or making conversations too personal will only waste time and take attention away from other customers who need your help. Avoid high-pressure sales techniques altogether—no sales situation warrants them, and especially not a craft show.

Some people will buy your craft items right away, some will need to think about it, and some will simply be interested. Learn to distinguish between the different types and treat each accordingly. Of course, you should always give priority to people who want to buy, so make sales quickly, thank the customers, and attend to potential customers who may need more information. If they want to think about it, always give them a brochure, flyer, or some printed information that they can carry with them for future reference. Make sure it contains your name, phone number, address, or booth number so they can easily find you when they are ready. If you are reasonably sure that someone is not interested in your product, be polite, thank them for stopping by, offer them a brochure, and turn your attention to helping or attracting other potential customers.

Getting Help

Many general business books have been written on the subject of salesmanship, and you might benefit from reading some if you feel selling is not your forte. I felt so inadequate when it came to selling that I took a community college course on sales techniques. Although most were geared for high-powered executives, I have remembered and used some of the general principles many times. For sound advice specifically about selling at craft shows, I recommend Kathryn Caputo's book *How to Show and Sell Your Crafts* (Betterway Books). She guides you through an entire chapter on what to say and what not to say to customers in your booth. If you're a novice, do role playing with family and friends before the show—the more you practice, the better you'll get!

Financial Management

Your goal is to sell your craft items, so you'll need to plan what methods of payment you'll accept and how you'll store them. Many crafters who sell small items limit their sales to cash only and find it the simplest way to handle finances.

Accepting Checks

If you're going to accept checks, you'll need to develop a policy for returned checks. Even though this is not a major problem, it can happen, and it is better to anticipate it rather than to be caught unprepared. You may decide to charge $10 or $15 for each returned check as some stores do and post this somewhere in your booth. The best deterrent is to record proper identification such as address, phone number, and driver's license. Always ask for two pieces of identification and make sure the information on both is the same. If this is a concern for you, I recommend talking with your banker about it.

What about Credit Cards?

I personally want to offer my customers as many ways to buy as possible, so I also take credit cards. I have found people will have a tendency to buy more quickly and to buy larger quantities if they can use credit cards. Merchant credit card accounts are usually set up with your bank, but some banks won't approve credit card accounts if you don't have a storefront or if you are a new business and haven't established a financial history. Independent businesses can help but are usually more expensive than banks. Two well-known ones are Pacific Card Services (888-255-3515) and Moseley Bankcard Services (888-248-3232). You will be expected to give your business name and address, telephone number, and social security number; list the type of products you sell; give trade references; and possibly fill out a financial statement. This service is not free no matter where you do business, so be prepared to pay a percentage of each sale (usually 2% to 6%) to the credit card company. Percentages are based on the volume of business you do and the average sale amount. Some vendors allow credit card sales only on amounts over $10 because of the fee involved.

> **Did you know???**
>
> Debit cards can be used exactly like credit cards if they contain the Visa or Mastercard logos. The only difference is, the money is taken directly out of your account—and there is no interest!

Each credit card sale must have authorization from the bank, which can be done in several ways. The easiest but most expensive way to do this is to rent or buy a credit card machine that gives immediate authorization and prints a receipt as soon as you swipe the card. This type of machine requires electricity and a phone line, both of which can be very expensive to rent or unavailable at some shows. Because of this, I take a manual machine to swipe the customers' cards and then type in the numbers and receive authorization on my electronic machine later at home or in the hotel room. The only disadvantage of this is that you don't know until later if the card is declined. Credit card companies are becoming so efficient and have so many safeguards against credit card fraud nowadays, however, that this is almost never a problem, but I always get another form of identification and a phone number for this reason. Your bank or credit card company will explain all the options when you apply for a merchant account (see also chapter 11).

Security at Craft Shows

- Package small items in larger containers.

- Don't have small or obscure areas in your booth that you can't see at all times.

- Keep money out of sight and remove cash periodically so you don't have large amounts on hand.

- Store extra stock and personal items out of sight, or lock them in your vehicle.

- Security is usually provided during shows and throughout the night, but after hours place all items under the tables or cover them with opaque fabric.

- Never leave valuable or expensive items in your booth when you're not there.

- Don't be overly distracted by individuals who seem to need a lot of attention— shoplifters sometimes work in pairs.

Operating Out of a Shoe Box

I'll never forget my first craft show when I was located next to a veteran exhibitor. She was setting up her cash register and made a comment about remembering when she used to operate out of a shoe box. She must have seen me blushing, and we both laughed as I pulled my shoe box out from under the counter! I still don't use a cash register, but I have a much more professional cash box.

Where you store cash, checks, and credit card vouchers at a show is largely up to personal preference. You may use a locking metal cash box, a Tupperware container, a moneybag, a shoe box, or a cash register. I know many crafters who simply keep their money in a fanny pack on the front side of their bodies and unzip it when they are making a sale. You may want to start small and simple and work your way up to a cash drawer or cash register, keeping in mind that these take up more room and can require electricity, which is sometimes not readily available or may be expensive to rent.

What to Do after Show Hours

Most shows provide 24-hour security, but I recommend always taking all money and valuables with you when you leave for the night. In addition, bring some lightweight but opaque pieces of fabric to drape over and completely cover everything in your booth. Show promoters never accept liability for lost or stolen merchandise, and it is always better to be safe than sorry.

Working at craft shows can be exhausting, but you won't want to miss the opportunity to socialize with other vendors when the day is over. If you're a newcomer, you will quickly become acquainted with your neighbors or other exhibitors during setup and the show. Don't be afraid to ask them if they have plans for dinner and take advantage of the opportunity to talk shop. It's also a chance to meet new friends with common interests.

Tearing Down and Packing Up

A pet peeve common to all show promoters is when exhibitors start dismantling and tearing down their booths before shows are over. Some are so adamant about this that they fine exhibitors or refuse to let them enter future shows. Their reasoning is that when people start packing and try to beat the rush to the loading dock, it hurts the whole show and makes it look like there's nothing left worth staying around for.

I have never understood why people want to start closing up shop before the allotted time. It takes weeks if not months to prepare for a show, and I want to take advantage of every opportunity to make sales. What about customers who are trying to find your booth at the end of the day to make one last purchase, or people who could only attend the last few hours and need to make use of all available time? I have made some fabulous sales during the last few minutes of shows. My advice is to hang in there, honor your commitment, and give yourself the maximum selling time. Packing isn't fun anyway, so why rush?

After you've made your last sale and the show is officially over, always store your money, receipts, and valuable items in a secure place before doing anything else. This is a busy time with people running everywhere, and it is easy to become distracted. If possible, enlist the help of a friend or hire someone reliable to help pack and keep an eye on things during the process. I usually group all items of one kind together for counting and packing.

Disassemble, fold, or wrap display items and fixtures in logical order so they will be ready for the next show. Remove all signs, placards, and banners, and store them so they won't get bent or torn. Check inside every empty box and under all tables and other display equipment to make sure you haven't overlooked anything. I

Handy Hint

When packing up your items at the end of the day, avoid the inclination to throw things in boxes with the idea of sorting through them later—you'll regret the added time and effort it takes.

usually pack everything and consolidate the boxes and trunks into one large pile and then ask someone to watch my things while I get the car. Crafters in general are wonderful, honest people, but you never know who might be around in all the confusion, so relock your car every time you make a trip until it is completely loaded.

Was the Show Worth It?

Years ago—it has been almost 20 now—when I started exhibiting at craft shows, you could almost estimate making a dollar for every consumer who came to the show. In other words, if the show attendance was 5,000, you would probably take in $5,000 gross. That hasn't held true for a long time for several reasons. Now so many shows are held, consumers have many more choices. Competition is keen, and craft shoppers have many places to spend their money. It is also increasingly difficult to get promoters to give you an accurate idea of how many attended the show—if it was poorly attended, they don't want to admit the low numbers.

Keeping Records

After attending a show, take some time to evaluate whether the time, effort, and cost were worth it. I made up a simple expense sheet on my computer with spaces that allow me to fill in amounts such as booth cost, advertising, gas, food, lodging, parking, electricity, equipment rental, license fees, insurance, and anything else that may have cost money. I add up the total costs and subtract them from my income to get a gross profit amount. I also keep an inventory sheet to record how many of each item I took to the show and how many I sold. I then must subtract the cost of the goods sold from the gross profit to get my net or real profit.

Keeping my own records for each show and filing them together each year helps me decide whether shows were really worth my time and whether I want to return in the future. The inventory sheet lets me know how many items I will need to prepare and helps me schedule my time. I can also see trends in which crafts consumers are buying in which areas and adjust accordingly. Some shows are good consistently year after year, and some shows seem to peak and then decline. I eliminate the unprofitable ones from my schedule in the future.

Selling through Craft Malls, Shops, and Galleries

If you're not ready or inclined to sell your handicrafts at fairs and festivals, there are other outlets. Craft malls, consignment shops, and galleries are all popular venues for sewn items.

Selling at Craft Malls

The popularity of craft malls is increasing across the country because they offer a clean, pleasant, temperature-controlled setting for both buyers and sellers. Consumers don't have to walk in the hot sunlight, dusty fields, or muddy parking lots, and crafters don't have to set up and man booths under the same inclement conditions that can be present at craft fairs. You'll be able to devote all your time to making your crafts, rather than trying to sell them.

Craft malls rent space on a monthly basis and offer everything from a single shelf up to a large floor space or entire room. In addition, a service fee of between 5% and 10% is usually charged on all sales in exchange for all the services that the mall provides, including advertising, merchandising, licensing, bookkeeping, and actually selling items and collecting sales tax. Most craft malls take responsibility for bad checks and also accept credit cards, two very large benefits for new crafters. In addition, good craft malls offer assistance and help in setting up attractive displays.

Even though craft malls rent space on a monthly basis, most mall owners agree that crafters need to rent for 3 to 6 months to realize the most benefit. It takes time for customers to notice and recognize new items, and if they see them over and over, they have

Finding the Right Consignment Shop for You

Consult the phone book for shops in your area, and visit them to find out what types of merchandise they sell. Some shops sell crafts in general, and some have themes such as home decor, children's crafts, or Southwest items. You may need to travel some distance or even out of your state to find just the right outlet for your crafts. When you're ready to do business, always call to set up an appointment to show your crafts. Here are some important questions to ask:

■ How long have you been in business? (Generally good consignment shops have been in operation at least 2 years.)

■ What are the terms of your contract? (If the shop does not have contracts, absolutely refuse to do business with them!)

■ How long will the items be displayed, and how much will I get paid when they sell?

■ How long after the sale will I receive a check?

■ Will I be notified if the supply is running low, or must I check to see whether restocking is necessary?

■ Can I help make a display, or will the store take care of all merchandising?

■ Whose insurance covers damaged, lost, or stolen items?

Streamlining the Crafting Process

Great American Crafts magazine is dedicated to crafters of every type, whether they are interested in trying crafting for the first time, craft occasionally, or are veteran crafters. Subscription to the magazine automatically makes you a member of the Great American Crafts Club and entitles you to receive a newsletter and project sheets. The club also hosts a new show on PBS. The magazine itself is filled with ideas and projects that range from easy to advanced and also lists many sources for supplies. Julie Stephani, the editor, shared these ideas for producing a craft efficiently:

- Use materials that are readily available and will remain so. You won't be able to keep producing the craft if the materials can't be found.

- Use quality tools—they may be a larger initial investment, but they will last longer and give years of service.

- Organize your workspace so you aren't running back and forth across the room to complete the steps of a project.

- Hire inexpensive help—family members or friends are a great place to start.

- Break the project down into steps, and complete the same step on several pieces before proceeding to the next.

- Do things in multiples—cut more than one at a time, sew everything you can with one color thread before changing to another color, and so forth.

more of a tendency to buy. Also, after your reputation grows, customers will return to make other purchases, which may take several months to occur. You'll have to decide whether you can afford the monthly rent and the percentage taken from your profits at craft malls. The extra time you have to make your crafts may be worth the expense.

Selling through Consignment Shops

Consignment shops provide a retail space for your crafts and in exchange usually split the price 50/50 or 60/40 with you (the shop receives the higher percentage), so in effect, you are selling to them wholesale. You do not receive payment until the items are sold.

Advantages

Many new crafters find consignment shops a good outlet when they are just starting out and have no idea how to market their crafts. Consignment shops can be a good way to reach the general public without having to set up a booth or have a sale of your own. You'll also be able to find out how your new ideas will be accepted. Another advantage is that you can devote all your time to producing the craft without the effort of marketing it.

Disadvantages

Probably the biggest disadvantage of selling on consignment is that you must bear the cost of producing the craft and then not receiving payment until it sells, if it ever does. Many consignment shops have a policy of marking down items after a certain time period, so you will receive less money the longer the item is in the store. Also, items may become shopworn or damaged, and you may be stuck with merchandise that can't be sold in less than perfect condition.

Selling to Galleries

Selling to art galleries can be a prestigious and profitable way to market crafts, especially if they are elaborate, one-of-a-kind, or relatively expensive items. Galleries usually operate on a consignment basis

MICHELE'S STORY

Michele Cokl Naylor grew up watching her mom sew dresses, and as soon as she was old enough, she began making dresses for her dolls. When she outgrew playing with dolls, she made clothes for her sister's dolls and for herself. Her hobby escalated when she participated in a Salvation Army Women's Auxiliary event where the members dressed new dolls and gave them to needy children. She loved sewing the dresses and took part in the event for several years in a row. She started designing dolls in her spare time, but these weren't normal baby dolls to play with—they were unique works of art that could be displayed or hung on a wall to be admired. By that time Michele was working as a computer programmer, and when she took some of her dolls to work, her coworkers told her she was in the wrong business.

A friend suggested that Michele exhibit at a psychic fair in the area, but it was a dismal failure. Not to be discouraged, she applied to enter a juried neighborhood art fair and was accepted. This provided a better venue for selling her dolls and was the beginning of her new career as a doll maker and designer. She attended more shows, and as her reputation grew, she helped form and manage a co-op gallery in Cincinnati, Ohio, where she worked for 4 years. In addition to her dolls, she sold items made by other crafters, and her business grew even more.

for large or more expensive crafts and may buy smaller or less expensive items outright at wholesale pricing. Some galleries are organized as co-ops and offer the work of many artists, displaying items of each crafter's work in a specific area. Co-ops are run strictly on consignment. As with consignment shops, you must wait until an

Michele has always felt that she "had dolls in her" and was thrilled that her hobby developed into a full-time business. She finds inspiration from color, nature, or simply a stroll through a fabric store. Her dolls represent people she's known, seen, or made up. They are whimsical or serious, and each one is a symbol of the feminine spirit. Her husband, Roger, a writer, contributes little poems to go with some of the dolls.

Since Michele and her husband both have careers that allow them to live anywhere, they realized a lifetime dream in 1996 and moved to Arizona, where they love to hike and enjoy nature. Now her dolls, which she sells at galleries, often contain small pebbles, feathers, or other treasures she has found along the many paths she walks. In addition, Michele makes smaller dolls that can be worn as pins. A favorite design is her "Mended Heart Pin," which is fabric shaped into a heart that has been mended with a small patch and embellished with beads and decorative stitching. She plans to investigate the Internet for marketing her dolls in the future.

item is sold before you receive payment, so you have to be able to produce the item and wait possibly several months before it is sold. You also take the chance that your products can become shopworn or damaged. One crafter told me she was thrilled when a gallery featured her craft item front and center in the gallery's display window, but her enthusiasm turned to disappointment when the item didn't sell and the gallery returned it bleached from sunlight.

How to Approach Galleries

Never drop by galleries unannounced with your crafts, but call for an appointment to show your work to the owner or manager. This approach is much more professional, and you will be assured that the buyer is available and willing to give full attention to you and your work. When selling on consignment to galleries, be sure to sign a contract outlining the same conditions as one from consignment shops.

How to Handle Wholesale Orders

It is the dream of many crafters to be approached by wholesale clients, and craft shows provide a good venue for these buyers who are looking for new products. Analyze the craft or crafts you sell and decide in advance whether you could sell them wholesale. There are several points to consider.

Be Prepared

The first craft item I sold wholesale was a sewn angel Christmas tree ornament. When I was approached by a wholesale client (usually called a buyer) at my booth, I was caught totally off guard. I didn't know what to do or say, but luckily I kept my cool long enough to ask for a card so I could call her later and work out the details. I'd like to give you a few pointers that will help your first encounter go smoothly.

Print out a simple list of wholesale policies on your letterhead, or make up a brochure so you will have something useful to give the buyer. Include retail and wholesale prices, minimum orders, and payment and return policies. I usually require companies to pay in advance for first-time orders (I do accept credit cards for this purchase, or you can ask for a check) and then for repeat orders give them terms of "net 30," which means they must pay in full 30 days after I ship the products and invoice them.

If the item you are selling is relatively inexpensive—say, under $10 retail—I recommend giving the buyer a free sample. If your products are more expensive or you don't want to give away free samples, you must have a color picture or a very clear drawing to accompany your policy sheet. Ask for a business card so you can follow up with a phone call at a later time.

Crafting and Selling— A Balancing Act

Sewing crafts and selling them can be wonderfully fulfilling as well as a lot of work. Managing a business and scheduling creative time for craft sewing can be a real balancing act, so I'd like to devote the remainder of this chapter to helping you to make the most of your time and resources. You'll be able to accomplish much more if you're organized from the start, and you will actually find that you work less and make more money with a little planning and discipline.

The Crafting Side

Our love for crafting is what started us toward a moneymaking venture, so we don't want to lose sight of the fun and enjoyment it offers us. We also need quality time in our workrooms to design and make new crafts to keep up with new demands. Producing the best product in the least amount of time for the least amount of money is the name of the game.

Becoming an Efficiency Expert

Examining all the processes used in making each item and deciding whether you can combine some, change some to make them go faster, or eliminate some altogether will help you to become as efficient as possible. Large companies hire experts trained to do this with commercially made products, and we can do it ourselves with our own products no matter how small or simple. Jot down the various steps required to make individual crafts, and go over each one in this analytical way.

In addition, seek out ways to improve your personal skills and possibly apply a new twist to your projects. I am constantly taking classes, reading magazines and books, and surfing the Internet for ideas, products, or tools that can help me sew faster and stimulate my thinking so I can design new items.

Time Management

Scheduling regular work times for sewing is very important. Time has a way of slipping away if we don't actively try to make use of it. A lot can be accomplished in an hour here and an hour there, but I have found that I am much more productive if I set aside blocks of time in 2- to 4-hour increments. Your train of thought is not interrupted, and you are much more likely to complete projects when you have longer blocks of time. I can still be spontaneous when friends call about a fun outing or I decide I simply have to take off and see the leaves in the peak of their fall colors, but I need to reschedule that missed block of time somewhere during the week if I want to remain on track. This might be late at night or in the early morning hours, but at least I have the flexibility to do this, and I am grateful for that.

Many crafters, as well as other busy people, find that turning on an answering machine during work periods allows them to get more done. Others screen their calls and answer only when necessary. I personally like to answer each call and make my conversations short and to the point. Then I don't have to spend time later returning calls, and I don't offend people if they know I am screening and don't pick up for them. Whatever your telephone style, find a way to limit personal calls during business hours and handle business calls as quickly as possible.

Time-Out

One of the biggest mistakes I made in the early years of my business was to never schedule breaks or vacations for myself. I had become a workaholic and built up a successful business, but I was

Tips for Success

Nancy Ingerson, who lives in Salem, Oregon, started sewing and selling beautifully embellished fabric-covered boxes at craft fairs. Her delightful samples enticed customers to try making their own, so she responded to the demand: In addition to decorated boxes, she now sells plain boxes, fabric, patterns, and kits. She has a make-it, take-it table in her booth where customers can sit down and cover a simple box. They can then buy extra supplies at the booth or order them by mail. She found that using the new fusibles allows her or her customers to complete boxes much faster without actually sewing on the machine, and she calls her technique "sewing with an iron." Here are some tips from this veteran craft show exhibitor:

- The higher the quality of materials used, the higher the quality of the craft.

- Display your crafts as they will be used—fill them with baubles or group them with other items so customers can visualize the item in their homes.

- Never use solid colors for fabric items—they soil easily and every smudge shows.

- Let people touch and hold items—the magic is in the movement.

stressed out and tired. I found that even taking 1 day a month for a special trip or fun event gave me a rest and a needed change from my routine. Now I make sure to schedule at least 2 days off a week (most people get 2-day weekends, so why can't I?), as well as an additional morning, afternoon, or evening out during the week. I actually accomplish much more now that I am rested, and looking forward to my off times is great for my mental attitude. Please note that you do need to write these times in on your calendar to make sure you don't miss them!

The Business Side

As crafters, many of us would love to spend our entire time crafting rather than handling the everyday details of running a business, but we all must do a certain amount of desk work if we want to keep selling and making a profit. Here are some tips for minimizing the business work and maximizing the returns.

Basic Business Supplies

Purchase some basic business supplies to prevent making numerous trips when the individual needs arise. Staples, rubber bands, Scotch tape, glue and rubber cement, and paper clips are standard supplies for any office. All of these can be purchased at discount office supply stores, through mail order (see Resources), and at discounters from time to time. Buy as many items in bulk as you can—these are all things that you can use around the house even if you decide to discontinue business later.

In addition, stock up on extra stamps to eliminate waiting in long post office lines. My business includes a lot of mail order, and I finally decided to get a postage meter. Postage meters don't save you money—in fact, you have to pay monthly to rent a meter—but they save time, which can translate into money along the way. Check with your local post office for details on postage meters.

Time Efficiency

Desk work isn't fun, but it can be streamlined for better efficiency. I find it extremely helpful to delegate certain tasks to certain days during the week and then I am not repeating the same tasks every day. For instance, I have a file marked "Invoices," and whenever I receive a bill from a supplier or even household bills for utilities, mortgage, and so forth, they go straight into this folder. I pay them all on Wednesday of each week. This is much more efficient than sitting down every day when the mail comes and addressing envelopes and getting out my checkbook to write checks. It is also a lot better than saving a big stack of bills for the end of the month and taking the chance of missing or making late payments. The same type of system can be used for ordering supplies, recording receipts, or tallying expenditures, and some of these tasks need only be done every several weeks or every month. This way I never have to worry about these "unfun" aspects of my business, and I can free my mind for more creative endeavors.

Computers Can Help

If you're like me and many others who are part of the "over-40 majority," you may have resisted computer technology because of the cost and the learning curve or both. If you've grown up using computers, you're one step ahead of the game. The fact is that computers can save a lot of time, effort, and expense in the long run.

I create all my own business cards, stationery, hangtags, signs, and banners on the computer. In addition, I manage my inventory and make purchase orders, mailing labels, packing slips, invoices, and sales receipts. I have saved hundreds, if not thousands, of dollars designing my own ads, flyers, and brochures, not to mention drastically reducing my phone bill by using e-mail whenever possible instead of phone calls. I also fill out craft show applications and do my scheduling and travel planning on the computer.

Computers take some getting used to—I still hate it when I make a mistake and mine beeps at me—but in the long run they are worth it. Community colleges as well as libraries and computer stores offer classes. There are hundreds of books written in plain language that are easily understandable. However, there is no substitute for sitting down and taking the time to experiment and see what works. You will learn quickly when you have the incentive to find quicker and easier ways to run your business.

What if you live in the boonies far from a metropolitan area? A computer can be even more valuable because it can enable you to do things yourself if services are not available in your area and can be your link to the rest of the world via e-mail and the World Wide Web. Popular computer companies such as Gateway offer wonderful programs by supplying you with the latest technology, helping you learn to use it, and allowing you to trade it in after 2 to 4 years to keep up with changing needs and/or technology. You can call them or visit their Web site (800-846-2000 or www.gateway.com), and they will literally talk with you until the cows come home to set you up with a system that fits your needs and budget.

Marketing Your Craft Sewing

Advertising and Publicity

▼▼

AFTER YOU'VE DECIDED WHAT craft or crafts to make and you've priced them out realistically, you'll need to get the word out about yourself and your work to all your prospective customers. This is an area that many crafters don't understand and sometimes feel uncomfortable with, but it is very important to the success of your business. It doesn't matter how beautifully you sew your handicrafts—if you don't find effective ways to let the general public know about them, you'll never sell anything.

Marketing Your Creations: Presenting Yourself and Your Crafts Effectively

Many people, myself included, start out thinking marketing and selling are synonymous. In reality, marketing comes before selling, and how much you sell can be directly related to how well you do your marketing. Marketing is all about presenting a favorable image of yourself and your product to others. I'm going to break this down into several helpful topics, but if this concept seems difficult, think back to your target market and pick an imaginary customer or even a friend or relative who fits the profile. Keeping them in mind as you are speaking, writing, or composing artwork or visuals will make your task much easier and more fun.

Choosing a Business Name or Logo

One of the best ways to start developing your professional image and identity is to adopt a business name or logo. A business name and/or logo helps to carry a distinctive theme and voice through all areas of your work.

Consider first whether you want to use your own name or create a separate business name. In general, using your own name won't let people know what you do unless you add a descriptive sentence after it. This requires extra space and expense on printed forms or ads and extra time for potential customers to find out what your business is all about. If your name is so unusual that it is difficult to pronounce or spell, you'd do better concentrating on a

Getting People to Remember You

Giving away small, entertaining, or useful items imprinted with your business name, address, and phone number is a way to get people to remember you and your products. We've all received pens, notepads, key chains, or refrigerator magnets from businesses, and every time we use them we are reminded who gave them to us. I own an imprinted decorative thimble that was given to me more than 20 years ago by a craft supplier I still order from today. The Drawing Board (800-210-4431) produces a free promotional idea book that shows hundreds of advertising specialties including the aforementioned items as well as balloons, letter openers, shirts, caps, coffee cups, golf balls, calendars, and much more, at prices from $0.25 up.

catchy business name that does not include your real name. I also advise not using initials unless they have some catchy meaning like Busy B Designs (Beatrice is the crafter's first name), because initials alone (e.g., K & L Enterprises) don't portray anything about you or your crafts.

It would be better to incorporate all or part of your name into a business name, such as Kemper's Kritters (stuffed animals) or Munchkins by Marinucci (children's clothes and accessories) so customers can associate your name with a type of craft. Using part of your own name can also make your business name sound more personal or endearing, such as Carol's Crafts, Ann's Artistries, Tina's Crafting Shop, Deb-Kins (the crafter's first name is Debbie), or Golden Threads (the crafter's last name is Golden). There are exceptions to every rule, and I know a crafter who has very successfully broken this one. Her business name is Charlene!, and although it doesn't tell customers a thing about what she does, she has developed an exclusive identity for the wide variety of crafts she produces. I think customers like the mystique that she has developed and seek her out to buy another one of her creations just so they can say they own a Charlene!

Possibilities for business names that do not include your own name are endless. Ask relatives and close friends to help you brainstorm to come up with ideas. Have fun and be creative, but don't go so overboard that people need to consult a dictionary to figure it out or groan when they hear it because it is so corny. Keep it simple and to the point—The Lace Lady, Stitch 'n Stuff, The Leathermaid, French Handsewing—or jazz it up—Knittin' in the Woods, Homespun Specialties, Slight Indulgence (custom-painted silk scarves), Soft Shells (hand-sewn shawls). Sewn crafts open the door to all kinds of plays on words, such as Sew Nice, Sew Fine, Seams Sensational, Sew Selective, and Sew Smart. Don't forget that humor and rhymes always attract attention and can really help develop a friendly identity—Fit to Be Tied, Unique Technique, Having a Fit, Crazy Daisy.

Remember, above all, that a business name is meant to attract business, not deter it. Stay away from words or phrases that could have a detrimental or double meaning such as "rags"—this is a slang word for clothes and may sound chic, but it is also a derogatory description for worn-out clothing. Did your mother ever tell you never to mention politics or religion in public gatherings? Although you may feel strongly about your personal beliefs, this warning should also be applied to a business name unless you are producing some craft that targets a specific group. You don't want to take the chance of turning off potential customers in any way.

Your Business Card—An Effective Marketing Tool

One of the most important things you can do to promote your new image is to get business cards. These can be as simple or as elabo-

Tips for an Effective Business Card

- Include all pertinent information—name, address, phone number, fax, e-mail, and so forth, in print that is easy to read.

- Make use of clip art, logo, or business name to further enhance the message.

- Color or textured paper or finishes make your card stand out.

- Office supply stores as well as many computer programs can assist you in designing your cards. Graphic artists can be very helpful but are usually expensive.

- Give everyone two cards—one for themselves and one for a friend.

- Don't go anywhere without your card—it can be your most valuable marketing tool!

rate as you want. If you're not sure which direction your crafting will take, simply list your name, address, and phone number, and use some small piece of clip art to give the general idea like a sewing machine, spool of thread, or other sewing tools. You can get more specific after you decide on a specific craft.

Brochures or Flyers

Along with a distinctive business card, many crafters produce a brochure or pamphlet to give more details about themselves and their businesses. This can be as simple as a single piece of paper or as elaborate as a folded shiny brochure. Almost all computers come with a simple brochure program that offers several differ-ent styles. Office supply stores and graphic artists often design business cards and brochures as a package deal. Brochures and flyers can contain a brief biography, pic-tures or drawings of your crafts, prices, ordering informa-tion, a schedule of shows or list of businesses where they can be purchased, and a coupon, if appropriate. Examine and critique promotional materials from other crafters to get ideas, but take care not to copy anything directly.

Developing a Portfolio

Depending on the type of craft you decide to produce, you may profit from developing a portfolio to show prospective customers. Make the photos as clear and pro-fessional as possible, and remember, color sells. Along with a good close-up shot of the craft with an uncluttered background, include a picture of someone using or holding the item in a fun and upbeat setting. Some craft shows are juried and require color slides of your crafts to determine whether you'll be admitted, so if you anticipate applying to them, you'll need slides in addition to photographs.

> ### Handy Hint
> Always proofread your writing at least five times to make sure the spelling and grammar are correct. I learned this valuable tip from my sister who is a journalist, and it is a necessity for a professional look.

Advertising

Advertising can lead to new opportunities for selling your crafts and allow you to reach customers you may not normally come into contact with. In general, advertising costs money, so you'll have to do some research and have a firm idea of your audience before investing in it.

Word-of-mouth advertising is the only free method of advertising and also by far the most desirable and effective. It has been estimated that everyone has at least 200 people they can influence, so the potential for this type of advertising is enormous. Nothing compares to the testimonial of a satisfied customer, so you'll want to do everything to ensure customers speak well of you and your products. Be pleasant, cordial, and ethical in all your business dealings. Strive to give the best value for the best price, and take pride in every item you produce. Giving everyone two business cards as I mentioned earlier is the best way to increase word-of-mouth advertising.

Did you know???

Advertising experts agree that most consumers must see an ad several times before they actually notice it, so placing an ad only once and then tallying results will not accurately indicate effectiveness.

Newsletters and Bulletins

Schools, churches, clubs, and organizations all publish newsletters that can be inexpensive ways to advertise. These are grassroots ways to spread the word about your handicrafts and to reach many people you know personally or others who you don't have the time or desire to contact individually. Ads in programs for musical or theatrical performances also fall into this category and can serve to remind people who are already your customers that they need more of your products or stimulate them to do word-of-mouth advertising to their friends.

Newspapers and Magazines

Newspapers and magazines are not a cost-effective way to advertise crafts because of the relatively high cost. For your general information, classified ads are the least expensive, appearing all together in the same section of the publication, usually with text only. More costly display ads are positioned throughout the publication with artwork and text. If you feel you have a craft item that might sell this way, I recommend you start with an ad in a "pennysaver" type of publication to test this medium.

Direct Mail

As a crafter, you are more likely to profit from direct-mail advertising by using it as a means to let customers know where you will be selling your crafts than to actually sell them by mail. You can develop your own mailing list by having a sign-up list at shows or fairs. Direct mail can be a major investment, and a return of 1% (for a rented mailing list) is considered good for mailings, so research this method thoroughly before committing. The return can be much better (5% to 10%) if you're mailing to a list of preferred customers, and I would always advise this approach as a first choice.

Since I live in a small town and exhibit at shows nationwide, I have great success sending preshow announcements to customers or interested people who have signed up at my booth in the past. If you live in a large metropolitan area and don't need to travel far to shows, you can use a mailing list of customers in your area just as effectively.

I usually mail from 300 to 1,000 pieces and get a return of 10% to 20%, which is well above the average response. I track my mailings by adding a coupon that customers can redeem at my booth.

Handy Hint

If you are going to exhibit in an area more than once, you must develop at least one new craft to offer customers who have already bought everything you have.

During the last several years I have added line drawings of my new designs and included an order blank to appeal to customers who can't come to the shows. Understandably, customers don't respond as well to this because they can't actually see and touch the items, but I have had a response of about 5%, which compares favorably to national averages.

I have come a long way since my first mailing almost 20 years ago when my husband printed all the stick-on mailing labels on our computer and we, together with several family members, folded, stuffed, sorted, and licked envelopes. Now I pay a mailing service (look in the Yellow Pages to locate one in your area) to manage my database and do all my mailings. If you're just starting out, work your way up slowly and hedge your bets by mailing to customers or potential customers whose names you have gathered personally. I've prepared a sample letter (see page 199) to help you compose one of your own when the time is right. You can use it as a guide, discarding parts that aren't relevant and adding information that is pertinent to your business.

Publicity

Publicity is any free way you can get your name or information about your product out to the general public. It is all about building your image and your reputation and is a way to maximize your exposure. Crafters can take advantage of publicity in all kinds of creative ways, and I am going to describe the most popular ones.

Networking

Networking is a well-known and free way to promote your business, and if you have the gift of gab, it may work well for you. If you're proud of your handicrafts and enthusiastic about your business, it is a natural result to want to talk about them to others. Just remember

KAREN'S KREATIONS IS COMING YOUR WAY!

insert logo here

Dear _____ ,

It's hard to believe almost a year has flown by since we met at the Southeast Craft Show at the Tampa Fairgrounds. I just wanted to drop you a line to remind you of this year's upcoming dates _____ and to invite you to stop by my booth #107—KAREN'S KREATIONS—to see my new hand-sewn Christmas ornaments, all with an animal theme. I'm excited about these lovable pets and can't wait to show them to you. Please take advantage of the discount coupon I'm offering below. I hope to see you there!

Karen

10% OFF *any purchase at* KAREN'S KREATIONS BOOTH #107 (next to the yogurt stand)

SOUTHEAST CRAFT SHOW—TAMPA FAIRGROUNDS, JAN. 10–12, 10–5 PM

Unable to attend the show this year? Here's a sampling of my new kreations:

insert craft photo

Doggie Daze
_____
(# ordered)

insert craft photo

Horsing Around
_____
(# ordered)

insert craft photo

Kuddly Kittens
_____
(# ordered)

$9.95 EACH

ORDER BLANK

NAME
_____

ADDRESS
_____
_____
_____

PHONE NUMBER
_____

CREDIT CARD
_____

EXP. DATE _____

Total # × $9.95 =

$ _____

All ornaments $9.95 each; please include $2.50 postage for the first ornament and $0.50 for each additional.

TOTAL enclosed

$ _____

Thank You!

Checks, money orders, Visa, MasterCard, Novus, American Express accepted.
Send to or call: Karen's Kreations, 123 Kozy Kove, Keokuk, KS 32123, (123) 456-7890.

not to monopolize conversations or appear pushy as this will turn people off rather than impress them. Clubs, organizations, or similar groups of people are considered traditional venues for networking, but it can be done effectively virtually any time you talk to someone. I know a crafter who always carries a sample of her work with her in her purse, and when people ask what she does, she is ready to show them as well as talk about it. She has had wonderful response with this method.

Public Speaking

Clubs, guilds, and civic groups are always looking for speakers who can entertain members at their functions and meetings. Again, unless you are speaking to a business club that wants to know how you succeeded in yours, you must speak about a topic that is more general and tie your personal story in when appropriate. For instance, you could speak about the huge arts-and-crafts movement taking place in America, the personal benefits derived from crafting, and give stories about crafters who have found their niche. You can even suggest ways that people in the audience can get into crafting themselves. Bring samples of your crafts and pass them around or make an attractive display. Be prepared with cards, brochures, a schedule of craft shows where you'll be appearing, and have an accessible supply of your products if people want to purchase them after the talk. It is best to ask a friend or relative to take money and make change so you can answer questions and not appear to be there with the sole intent of selling.

One of my most successful events as a public speaker was to a Soroptimist Club whose members are mostly professional women. The topic was "Entrepreneurship—How to Start Your Own Business," and I was quite intimidated. What could I as a crafter working from my home tell this educated and savvy crowd? And how could I tie in my business and hopefully gain some new customers? I decided to be truthful and just explain how I literally stumbled into my business after friends and relatives admired my crafts and wanted to buy them. I told how I learned from my mistakes and advised how others could reach success more quickly by doing more research, testing out ideas, and mapping out a business plan. With each example I showed a different craft item and related what valuable business lesson I gained from producing it. I had set up a table in the back of the room with about six each of the eight items that I was making then, including Christmas tree skirts, placemats with matching napkins, aprons, and some other home-decor items. As soon as my talk ended, women rushed to the table and literally grabbed everything in sight, and I took orders for many more (this is when I learned you should have someone attend the table and do the actual selling for you). I went home with a mailing list of 75 new or prospective clients!

Why was this event so successful? The comments I heard after my presentation gave me some clues. Many of the women who had worked in traditional jobs their entire lives had wondered what it would be like to have their own businesses. They said they admired my courage and persistence and appreciated hearing the anecdotes that went with the crafts. Even though they may never start businesses of their own, they were inspired and entertained. Furthermore, few had the time or desire to do crafting and were delighted to find someone who sold these items.

This turned out to be a dream situation. Of course, all public speaking won't yield such impressive results, but I wanted to give you an example and let you know what is possible with this form of promotion. It probably wouldn't be worth your while to pursue this marketing venue until you have a variety of items to offer, and if public speaking just sounds too scary, it's better to promote your business in some way that would be more comfortable for you.

Getting over the Jitters

It is natural to feel nervous or experience some anxiety when making a public appearance for the first time. One lesson I've learned from both TV and radio appearances is to talk directly to the interviewer rather than to the camera or microphone. Talk to them like you are talking to your best friend, or even visualize your best friend listening to you—this will relax you instantly. Remember that you are being interviewed because people are interested in what you have to say and this is your opportunity to fulfill their curiosity, not a reason to withdraw and be fearful.

Newspapers and Magazines

Print media offers several opportunities for publicity. First, you may want to send a press release to the editor or reporter of your local publications about your craft-making activities. Make sure it is newsworthy rather than an ad for your product. Writing a good press release is an art that can take a lot of trial and error, and if you are going to do it yourself, you'll need to research the topic thoroughly. Libraries contain books on how to write press releases; for a discussion by a successful crafter turned author, I encourage you to read Barbara Brabec's book *Homemade Money* (Betterway Books).

An effective press release can result in a feature article in which you will be interviewed in depth, a critical review of your product, or a small blurb that tells the basic facts. Since publicity is free and you are not calling the shots, you can never be sure what direction it will take, but any form can help to advance your cause.

You may also increase recognition of your name by writing articles yourself. In general, you must send a proposal or query letter to the editor of the publication to give them an idea in outline form what you want to write about. You can call publications in advance

Tips for a Dynamic Press Release

Refer to the sample press release and see how it incorporates these essentials:

- ■ Use colored paper or a border to make the release stand out.

- ■ Make a header that says "FOR IMMEDIATE RELEASE" and includes the date, a contact person, and their phone number (also e-mail if appropriate).

- ■ Write a "lead" or title that explains clearly what news you are releasing.

- ■ Put the most important things first—who you are and what your product or service is; the first paragraph should grab your attention.

- ■ Speak in terms that anyone with a sixth grade education could understand— don't make the reader use a dictionary to figure out the meaning!

- ■ List the most appealing benefits for the reader of what you have to offer.

- ■ Include price and ordering information.

- ■ End with past accomplishments that can give credibility to your release.

- ■ Try to limit your release to one page and indicate the end by using three slashes centered at the bottom. If you must use more than one page, put "(continued on next page)" at the bottom of the first page and the slash lines on the bottom of the last page.

and ask for their writers' guidelines that tell how you must submit query letters, details on writing styles, and payment amounts, if there are any. Some newspapers and magazines accept unsolicited articles, but I always check first. You must write about a technique, a general area of crafting, or a human-interest story, not about your specific business. You can mention your business in a personal anecdote, introduction, or conclusion but not continuously throughout the text.

If you have never written an article before, don't risk embarrassing yourself and wasting an editor's time by submitting an

FOR IMMEDIATE RELEASE   Contact: Mary Roehr
April 10, 1995   Telephone: 520-282-4971

MARY ROEHR PUBLISHES ***SEW HILARIOUS,*** SEWING'S FIRST CARTOON BOOK

SEDONA, Arizona--In her 20 years as a crafter and sewing teacher,
Mary Roehr has witnessed plenty of seam-splitting situations, such
as the woman who buried her husband in the sand on their vacation so
she could be free to sew and the dressmaker who did mending with duct
tape, paper clips, and glue. Now she has gathered the best ones in
the just-published ***SEW HILARIOUS,*** sewing's first cartoon book.

"Whether you're cutting out your daughter's princess costume the
night before Halloween or ripping out a seam for the hundredth time,
sewing can be a pretty serious business," Roehr says. "But there's
also a lighter side, and that's what I've captured in ***SEW HILARIOUS.***
Anyone who sews will see themselves in this book."

The 64-page ***SEW HILARIOUS*** is bursting with rib-tickling cartoons
under headings such as "Learning to Sew," "Sewing for Others,"
"Sewing as Therapy," and more. Every sewer will be able to relate
to the antics and adventures of Roehr's imaginary character, Super
Sewer. The final chapter, "The Life of a Fabriholic," ties this
humorous yarn together.

SEW HILARIOUS is priced at $9.95 plus $2.50 for postage from
Mary Roehr Books & Video, 500 Saddlerock Circle, Sedona, AZ 86336,
(520) 282-4971, or ask for it at local fabric stores.

Roehr is the author of ***Sewing as a Home Business, Altering Women's
Ready-to-Wear,*** *and* ***Altering Men's Ready-to-Wear.*** She contributes to
Sew News, Threads, and *Vogue Patterns* and exhibits at craft fairs
nationwide where she sells her books and hand-sewn crafts.

///

unpolished manuscript. I took a 3-month course at our local community college on how to get published before I approached my first editor. The time and effort invested was definitely worth it—I realized a personal dream to write an article for my favorite magazine, and I have used the skills many times over the years.

In addition to getting paid for writing articles, I have been very successful in writing free articles for small newsletters in exchange for running my ad in the same issue. This has led to national recognition of my name and to mail-order business. The best way to open the door for writing is to read every publication about crafting you can so you know the general subjects, types of articles, and tone of articles that are needed. You also don't want to duplicate anything that has been written already (although you may write about an old topic if you have a new slant), so you need to research thoroughly beforehand.

Television and Radio Publicity

I have been on several TV talk shows across the country and even taped nine shows for PBS that have been aired continuously for several years. In most of these situations, I personally called the moderator of the talk show and presented him or her with my ideas. In one, where I was promoting my book, *Sewing as a Home Business,* I discussed which types of sewing businesses were the most profitable and was allowed to mention my book only once during the 8-minute show. I sold several hundred books just from that one instance and had calls for months afterward. Another time I talked about sewing as a lost art and was able to use various crafts I sold as examples of how people could enjoy this ancient art and make some money, too. On the air I showed how even a beginning sewer could make a simple pincushion from scraps of fabric. Television thrives on having something colorful and interesting to look at, so I set up an appealing display of my crafts behind the interview area. At the end of the show the camera panned the display, and I was able to plug the upcoming craft fair and booth where I would be exhibiting.

From my experience on television talk shows, I have learned that it is common for the interviewer to ask you to provide a list of questions for them to ask about your subject. Make sure the response to each isn't a simple yes or no but contains explanations that can lead the discussion in your favor. Just make sure they don't become sales pitches. Send ahead and bring samples of your best work with you. Television stations love colorful visuals, and these will help stimulate interest and conversation.

We've all watched television talk shows that highlight interesting personalities and their businesses. How do most of these "celebrities" get on TV? Unless they are a famous movie star or author, they have probably called the station and booked the engagement themselves. Television stations need a constant source of program ideas, and they'll love to hear from you if you have something that is truly newsworthy and appeals to their viewing audience. You'll have a better chance of succeeding if you call stations that present subjects that are similar in nature to what you are proposing. Rather than blatantly trying to sell your craft, you'll need to approach them with something of human interest that can eventually lead to a discussion of your business.

Radio is similar to television except you must rely entirely on speech, so you'll need to sound enthusiastic and lively. As with television, you'll probably be asked to supply questions in advance. Don't make your answers sound like a commercial, but give a personal touch by using anecdotes and amusing stories. Supply interesting facts about the craft industry, the nature and appeal of your area of expertise, why it is popular, and how it has personally enriched your life. As with television, send or bring samples. Although listeners obviously won't be able to see your work, the compliments from the announcer might be enough to stimulate sales.

The Pinecone Promotion

One of the best television talk shows I've ever seen was presented by a woman who made all kinds of crafts from pinecones. When the host introduced the guest and said she was there to talk about pinecones, I almost changed channels, but as the camera scanned a table laden with pinecones of various sizes and shapes, I immediately realized there was more to pinecones than I thought. The crafter related how her grandmother had taken her on walks through the woods to find the different varieties, what locations and altitudes contribute to the best cones, the peak times for harvesting, how to preserve them, and, of course, how they can be used to make beautiful and whimsical decorations with her own creations as examples. By the end of the show, I was ready to go on my own pinecone hunt, but I'm sure most of the viewers headed right for her booth at the next craft fair.

My first airwave encounter was at the radio station in my hometown, and it was pretty much of a flop. I was in high school and had made shirts for a local rock band. I wanted to promote my business to other bands in the area but knew I couldn't just talk about that, so I approached the station with the idea of talking about a fund-raiser the band was doing and somehow hoped to tie in the shirts. The station had allotted only 5 minutes for the interview, and even though I had taken the shirts to impress the announcer, his questions and comments did more to promote the fund-raiser and the band than it did my sewing.

Looking back and trying to learn from my mistakes, I can see that I possibly could have been more successful if I had approached a television station where viewers could at least have seen the shirts instead of just hearing about them. Using the upcoming fund-raiser and the appearance of the band as a hook was good, but I needed to focus my presentation on something that related to the shirts more, such as the importance of distinctive clothing for performers, current styles, comfort, and care qualities.

If you are serious about promoting your crafts on television or radio, I highly recommend John Wade's book, *Dealing Effectively with the Media* (Crisp Publications). It tells how to find stations, approach them, what to say during the interview, and even how to practice beforehand.

Teaching

If you are an expert at your craft and passionate about it, you would probably do well teaching others about it. While teaching is a good way to publicize yourself, you may well earn some extra income if you teach at a community college or store. Unless you want to actively pursue this as a significant part of your income, remember that you are doing it mainly to publicize your name and business.

You might be wondering why you would want to give away trade secrets and help train possible competition. First, if you have created a specific design, you should copyright it to prevent plagiarism. Second, you should teach techniques rather than how to do a specific design and use some generic item for the class to practice on. Third, no one will ever be you, and even if you were teaching them how to duplicate one of your craft items exactly, they probably wouldn't be able to do it with your flair and style anyway.

I prefer teaching free, short classes to clubs or church groups as a way to promote my name and business. I charge for materials and teach an easy technique that allows students to complete a simple craft. I show samples of the craft items I sell to inspire the students but also to promote future sales. I have done this very successfully at the Boys & Girls Clubs, 4-H, and Brownies. I feel good about showing children how they can get satisfaction from making something themselves, and I spread goodwill about my business to all the parents.

"Go Forth and Multiply"

Perhaps this quote from the Bible doesn't seem appropriate or relevant for a how-to book on sewing, but I can relate to this message in my business almost daily as I sit down at my machine. I start with a basic idea (which I often feel comes from divine inspiration) and turn it into a satisfying and profitable venture by producing hundreds of handicrafts. Whether you want to sew for fun or profit or both, I hope that sewing will provide you with a wonderful pastime and a creative outlet for many years to come. My final wish is that you build on your skills so sewing will bring you more and more pleasure.

Several years ago, the American Sewing Guild coined the phrase "Each one teach one," and that has been its motto ever since. If you've found success and fulfillment through sewing, perhaps in the future you can help others to start and enjoy sewing too. It's a new millennium and a perfect time to breathe new life into this ancient art that offers so much to its participants!

A Mini-Course in Crafts-Business Basics

by Barbara Brabec

▼▼

THIS SECTION OF THE BOOK will familiarize you with important areas of legal and financial concern and enable you to ask the right questions if and when it is necessary to consult with an attorney, accountant, or other business adviser. Although the tax and legal information included here has been carefully researched by the author and is accurate to the best of her knowledge, it is not the business of either the author or publisher to render professional services in the area of business law, taxes, or accounting. Readers should therefore use their own good judgment in determining when the services of a lawyer or other professional would be appropriate to their needs.

Information presented applies specifically to businesses in the United States. However, because many U.S. and Canadian laws are similar, Canadian readers can certainly use the following information as a start-up business plan and guide to questions they need to ask their own local, provincial, or federal authorities.

Contents

1. **Starting Right**

2. **Taxes and Record Keeping**

   Is Your Activity a "Hobby" or a "Business"?
   Self-Employment Taxes
   Sales Tax Is Serious Business

3. **The Legal Forms of Business**

   Sole Proprietorship
   Partnership
   LLC (Limited Liability Company)
   Corporation

4. **Local and State Laws and Regulations**

   Business Name Registration
   Licenses and Permits
   Use of Personal Phone for Business
   Zoning Regulations

5. **General Business and Financial Information**

   Making a Simple Business Plan
   When You Need an Attorney
   Why You Need a Business Checking Account
   Accepting Credit Cards

6. **Minimizing the Financial Risks of Selling**

   Selling to Consignment Shops
   Selling to Craft Malls
   Avoiding Bad Checks

7. Insurance Tips

Homeowner's or Renter's Insurance
Liability Insurance
Insurance on Crafts Merchandise
Auto Insurance

8. Important Regulations Affecting Artists and Craftspeople

Consumer Safety Laws
Labels Required by Law
The Bedding and Upholstered Furniture Law
FTC Rule for Mail-Order Sellers

9. Protecting Your Intellectual Property

Perspective on Patents
What a Trademark Protects
What Copyrights Protect
Copyright Registration Tips
Respecting the Copyrights of Others
Using Commercial Patterns and Designs

10. To Keep Growing, Keep Learning

Motivational Tips

A "Things to Do" Checklist with Related Resources

- Business Start-Up Checklist
- Government Agencies
- Craft and Home-Business Organizations
- Recommended Crafts-Business Periodicals
- Other Services and Suppliers
- Recommended Business Books
- Helpful Library Directories

1. Starting Right

In preceding chapters of this book, you learned the techniques of a particular art or craft and realized its potential for profit. You learned what kinds of products are likely to sell, how to price them, and how and where you might sell them.

Now that you've seen how much fun a crafts business can be (and how profitable it might be if you were to get serious about selling what you make!) you need to learn about some of the "nitty-gritty stuff" that goes hand in hand with even the smallest business based at home. It's easy to start selling what you make and it's satisfying when you earn enough money to make your hobby self-supporting. Many crafters go this far and no further, which is fine. But even a hobby seller must be concerned about taxes and local, state, and federal laws. And if your goal is to build a part- or full-time business at home, you must pay even greater attention to the topics discussed in this section of the book.

Everyone loves to make money . . . but actually starting a business frightens some people because they don't understand what's involved. It's easy to come up with excuses for why we don't do certain things in life; close inspection of those excuses usually boils down to fear of the unknown. We get the shivers when we step out of our comfort zone and try something we've never done before. The simple solution to this problem lies in having the right information at the right time. As someone once said, "Knowledge is the antidote to fear."

The quickest and surest way to dispel fear is to inform yourself about the topics that frighten you. With knowledge comes a sense of power, and that power enables you to move. Whether your goal is merely to earn extra income from your craft hobby or launch a genuine home-based business, reading the following information will help you get started on the right legal foot, avoid financial pitfalls, and move forward with confidence.

When you're ready to learn more about art or crafts marketing or the operation of a home-based crafts business, a visit to your library or bookstore will turn up many interesting titles. In addition to the special resources listed by this book's author, you will find my list of recommended business books, organizations, periodicals, and other helpful resources later in this chapter. This information is arranged in a checklist you can use as a plan to get your business up and running.

Before you read my Mini-Course in Crafts-Business Basics, be assured that I understand where you're coming from because I was once there myself.

For a while I sold my craft work, and this experience led me to write my first book, *Creative Cash*. Now, 20 years later, this crafts-business classic ("my baby") has reached its sixth edition. Few of those who are totally involved in a crafts business today started out with a business in mind. Like me, most began as hobbyists looking for something interesting to do in their spare time, and one thing naturally led to another. I never imagined those many years ago

Social Security Taxes

When your crafts-business earnings are more than $400 (net), you must file a Self-Employment Tax form (Schedule SE) and pay into your personal Social Security account. This could be quite beneficial for individuals who have some previous work experience but have been out of the workplace for a while. Your re-entry into the business world as a self-employed worker, and the additional contributions to your Social Security account, could result in increased benefits on retirement.

Because so many senior citizens are starting home-based businesses these days, it should be noted that there is a limit on the amount you can earn before losing Social Security benefits. The good news is that this dollar limit increases every year, and once you are past the age of 70, you can earn any amount of income and still receive full benefits. For more information, contact your nearest Social Security office.

when I got serious about my craft hobby that I was putting myself on the road to a full-time career as a crafts writer, publisher, author, and speaker. Because I and thousands of others have progressed from hobbyists to professionals, I won't be at all surprised if someday you, too, have a similar adventure.

2. Taxes and Record Keeping

"Ambition in America is still rewarded . . . with high taxes," the comics quip. Don't you long for the good old days when Uncle Sam lived within his income and without most of yours?

Seriously, taxes are one of the first things you must be concerned about as a new business owner, no matter how small your endeavor. This section offers a brief overview of your tax responsibilities as a sole proprietor.

Is Your Activity a "Hobby" or a "Business"?

Whether you are selling what you make only to get the cost of your supplies back or actually trying to build a profitable business, you need to understand the legal difference between a profitable hobby and a business, and how each is related to your annual tax return.

The IRS defines a hobby as "an activity engaged in primarily for pleasure, not for profit." Making a profit from a hobby does not automatically place you "in business" in the eyes of the Internal Revenue Service, but the activity will be *presumed* to have been engaged in for profit if it results in a profit in at least 3 out of 5 years. Or, to put it another way, a "hobby business" automatically becomes a "real business" in the eyes of the IRS at the point where you can state that you are (1) trying to make a profit, (2) making regular business transactions, and (3) have made a profit 3 out of 5 years.

As you know, all income must be reported on your annual tax return. How it's reported, however, has everything to do with the amount of taxes you must pay on this income. If hobby income is less than $400, it must be entered on the 1040 tax form, with taxes payable accordingly. If the amount is greater than this, you must file a Schedule C form with your 1040 tax form. This is to your advantage, however, because taxes are due only on your *net profit*. Because you can deduct expenses up to the amount of your hobby income, there may be little or no tax at all on your hobby income.

Self-Employment Taxes

Whereas a hobby cannot show a loss on a Schedule C form, a business can. Business owners must pay not only state and federal income taxes on their profits, but self-employment taxes as well. (See sidebar, Social Security Taxes, page 215.) Because self-employed people pay Social Security taxes at twice the level of regular, salaried workers, you should strive to lower your annual gross profit figure on the Schedule C form through every legal means possible. One way to do this is through careful record keeping of all expenses related to the operation of your business. To quote IRS publications, expenses are deductible if they are "ordinary, necessary, and somehow connected with the operation and potential profit of your business." In addition to being able to deduct all expenses related to the making and selling of their products, business owners can also depreciate the cost of tools and equipment, deduct the overhead costs of operating a home-based office or studio (called the Home Office Deduction), and hire their spouse or children.

> *Avoid this pitfall:* Many new businesses that end up with a nice net profit on their first year's Schedule C tax form find themselves in financial trouble when tax time rolls around because they did not make estimated quarterly tax payments throughout the year. Aside from the penalties for underpayment of taxes, it's

a terrible blow to suddenly realize that you've spent all your business profits and now have no money left for taxes. Be sure to discuss this matter with a tax advisor or accountant when you begin your business.

Given the complexity of our tax laws and the fact that they are changing all the time, a detailed discussion of all the tax deductions currently available to small-business owners cannot be included in a book of this nature. Learning, however, is as easy as reading a book such as *Small Time Operator* by Bernard Kamoroff (my favorite tax and accounting guide), visiting the IRS Web site, or consulting your regular tax adviser.

You can also get answers to specific tax questions 24 hours a day by calling the National Association of Enrolled Agents (NAEA). Enrolled agents (EAs) are licensed by the Treasury Department to represent taxpayers before the IRS. Their rates for doing tax returns are often less than those you would for an accountant or CPA.

Keeping Tax Records

Once you're in business, you must keep accurate records of all income and expenses, but the IRS does not require any special kind of bookkeeping system. Its primary concern is that you use a system that clearly and accurately shows true income and expenses. For the sole proprietor, a simple system consisting of a checkbook, a cash receipts journal, a cash disbursements ledger, and a petty cash fund is quite adequate. Post expenses and income regularly to avoid year-end pile-up and panic.

If you plan to keep manual records, check your local office supply store or catalogs for the *Dome* series of record-keeping books, or use the handy ledger sheets and worksheets included in *Small Time Operator*. (This classic tax and accounting guide by CPA Bernard Kamoroff includes details on how to keep good records and prepare financial reports.) If you have a computer, there are a number of accounting software programs available, such as Intuit Quicken, MYOB (Mind Your Own Business) Accounting, and Intuit Quick-

An important concept to remember is that even the smallest business is entitled to deduct expenses related to its business, and the same tax-saving strategies used by "the big guys" can be used by small-business owners. Your business may be small now or still in the dreaming stage, but it could be larger next year and surprisingly profitable a few years from now. Therefore it is in your best interest to always prepare for growth, profit, and taxes by learning all you can about the tax laws and deductions applicable to your business. (See also sidebar, Keeping Tax Records.)

Sales Tax Is Serious Business

If you live in a state that has a sales tax (all but five states do), and sell products directly to consumers, you are required by law to register with your state's Department of Revenue (Sales Tax division) for a resale tax number. The fee for this in most states ranges from $5 to $25, with some states requiring a bond or deposit of up to $150.

Books, the latter of which is one of the most popular and best bookkeeping systems for small businesses. The great advantage of computerized accounting is that financial statements can be created at the press of a key after accounting entries have been made.

Regardless of which system you use, always get a receipt for everything and file receipts in a monthly envelope. If you don't want to establish a petty cash fund, spindle all of your cash receipts, tally them at month's end, and reimburse your personal outlay of cash with a check written on your business account. On your checkbook stub, document the individual purchases covered by this check.

At year's end, bundle your monthly tax receipt envelopes and file them for future reference, if needed. Because the IRS can audit a return for up to 3 years after a tax return has been filed, all accounting and tax records should be kept at least this long, but 6 years is better. Personally, I believe you should keep all your tax returns, journals, and ledgers throughout the life of your business.

Depending on where you live, this tax number may also be called a Retailer's Occupation Tax Registration Number, resale license, or use tax permit. Also, depending on where you live, the place you must call to obtain this number will have different names. In California, for example, you would contact the State Board of Equalization; in Texas, it's called the State Comptroller's Office. Within your state's revenue department, the tax division may have a name such as sales and use tax division or department of taxation and finance. Generally speaking, if you check your telephone book under "Government," and look for whatever listing comes closest to "Revenue," you can find the right office.

If your state has no sales tax, you will still need a reseller's permit or tax exemption certificate to buy supplies and materials at wholesale prices from manufacturers, wholesalers, or distributors. Note that this tax number is only for supplies and materials used to make your products, not for things purchased at the retail level or for general office supplies.

Once registered with the state, you will begin to collect and remit sales and use tax (monthly, quarterly, or annually, as determined by your state) on all *taxable sales*. This does not mean *all* of your gross income. Different states tax different things. Some states put a sales tax on certain services, but generally you will never have to pay sales tax on income from articles sold to magazines, on teaching or consulting fees, or subscription income (if you happen to publish a newsletter). In addition, sales taxes are not applicable to:

- **Items sold on consignment through a charitable organization, shop, or other retail outlet, including craft malls and rent-a-space shops (because the party who sells directly to the consumer is the one who must collect and pay sales tax).**

- **Products you wholesale to others who will be reselling them to consumers. (Be sure to get their tax-exemption ID number for your own files, however, in case you are ever questioned as to why you did not collect taxes on those sales.)**

As you sell throughout the year, your record-keeping system must be set up so you can tell which income is taxable and which is tax-exempt for reporting on your sales tax return.

Collecting Sales Tax at Craft Shows

States are getting very aggressive about collecting sales tax, and agents are showing up everywhere these day, especially at the larger craft fairs, festivals, and small-business conferences. As I was writing this chapter, a posting on the Internet stated that in New Jersey the sales tax department is routinely contacting show promoters about a month before the show date to get the names and addresses of exhibitors. It is expected that other states will soon be following suit. For this reason, you should always take your resale or tax collection certificate with you to shows.

Although you must always collect sales tax at a show when you sell in a state that has a sales tax, how and when the tax is paid to the state can vary. When selling at shows in other states, you may find that the show promoter has obtained an umbrella sales tax certificate, in which case vendors would be asked to give management a check for sales tax at the end of the show for turning over to a tax agent. Or you may have to obtain a temporary sales tax certificate for a show, as advised by the show promoter. Some sellers who regularly do shows in two or three states say it's easier to get a tax ID number from each state and file an annual return instead of doing taxes on a show-by-show basis. (See sidebar, Including Tax in the Retail Price, page 222.)

Collecting Sales Tax at a Holiday Boutique

If you're involved in a holiday boutique where several sellers are offering goods to the public, each individual seller will be responsible for collecting and remitting his or her own sales tax. (This means someone has to keep very good records during the sale so each seller receives a record of the sale and the amount of tax on that sale.) A reader who regularly has home boutiques told me that in her community she must also post a sign at her "cash station" stating that sales tax is being collected on all sales, just as craft fair sellers must do in some states. Again, it's important that you get complete details from your own state about its sales tax policies.

> *Avoid this pitfall:* Individuals who are selling "just for the fun of it" may think they don't have to collect sales taxes, but this is not true. As an official in my state's Department of Revenue told me, "Everyone who sells anything to consumers must collect sales tax. If you hold yourself out as a seller of merchandise, then you're subject to tax, even if you sell only a couple of times a year." The financial penalties for violating this state law can be severe. In Illinois, for example, lawbreakers are subject to a penalty of 20% over and above any normal tax obligation, and could receive for each offense (meaning each return not filed)

Including Tax in the Retail Price

Is it okay to incorporate the amount of sales tax into the retail price of items being sold directly to consumers? I don't know for sure because each state's sales tax law is different.

Crafters like to use round-figure prices at fairs because this encourages cash sales and eliminates the need for taking coins to make change. Some crafters tell their customers that sales tax has been included in their rounded-off prices, but you should not do this until you check with your state. In some states, this is illegal; in others, you may find that you are required to inform your customers, by means of a sign, that sales tax has been included in your price. You may also have to print this information on customer receipts as well.

If you make such a statement and collect taxes on cash sales, be sure to report those cash sales as taxable income and remit the tax money to the state accordingly. Failure

from 1 to 6 months in prison and a fine of $5,000. As you can see, the collection of sales tax is serious business.

Collecting Tax on Internet Sales

Anything you sell that is taxable in your state is also taxable on the Internet. This is simply another method of selling, like craft fairs or mail-order sales. You don't have to break out Internet sales separately; simply include them in your total taxable sales.

3. The Legal Forms of Business

Every business must take one of four legal forms:

Sole Proprietorship
Partnership
LLC (Limited Liability Company)
Corporation

to do this would be a violation of the law, and it's easy to get caught these days when sales tax agents are showing up at craft fairs across the country.

Even if rounding off the price and including the tax within that figure turns out to be legal in your state, it will definitely complicate your bookkeeping. For example, if you normally sell an item for $5 or some other round figure, you must have a firm retail price on which to calculate sales tax to begin with. Adding tax to a round figure makes it uneven. Then you must either raise or lower the price, and if you lower it, what you're really doing is paying the sales tax for your customer out of your profits. This is no way to do business.

I suggest that you set your retail prices based on the pricing formulas given in this book, calculate the sales tax accordingly, and give your customers change if they pay in cash. You will be perceived as a professional when you operate this way, whereas crafters who insist always on "cash only" sales are sending signals to buyers that they don't intend to report this income to tax authorities.

As a hobby seller, you automatically become a sole proprietor when you start selling what you make. Although most professional crafters remain sole proprietors throughout the life of their business, some do form craft partnerships or corporations when their business begins to generate serious money, or if it happens to involve other members of their family. You don't need a lawyer to start a sole proprietorship, but it would be folly to enter into a partnership, LLC or corporation, without legal guidance. Here is a brief look at the main advantages and disadvantages of each type of legal business structure.

Sole Proprietorship

No legal formalities are involved in starting or ending a sole proprietorship. You're your own boss here, and the business starts when you say it does and ends automatically when you stop running it. As discussed earlier, income is reported annually on a Schedule C form and taxed at the personal level. The sole proprietor is fully liable for all business debts and actions. In the event of a lawsuit, personal assets are not protected.

Partnership

There are two kinds of partnerships: general and limited.

A *general partnership* is easy to start, with no federal requirements involved. Income is taxed at the personal level and the partnership ends as soon as either partner withdraws from the business. Liability is unlimited. The most financially dangerous thing about a partnership is that the debts incurred by one partner must be assumed by all other partners. Before signing a partnership agreement, make sure the tax obligations of your partner are current.

In a *limited partnership,* the business is run by general partners and financed by silent (limited) partners who have no liability beyond an investment of money in the business. This kind of partnership is more complicated to establish, has special tax withholding regulations, and requires the filing of a legal contract with the state.

> *Avoid this pitfall:* Partnerships between friends often end the friendship when disagreements over business policies occur. Don't form a partnership with anyone without planning in advance how the partnership will eventually be dissolved, and spell out all the details in a written agreement. What will happen if either partner dies, wants out of the business, or wants to buy out the other partner? Also ask your attorney about the advisability of having partnership insurance, to protect against the complications that would arise if one of the partners becomes ill, incapacitated, or dies. For additional perspective on the pros and cons of partnerships, read the book *The Perils of Partners*.

The Limited Legal Protection of a Corporation

Business novices often think that by incorporating their business they can protect their personal assets in the event of a lawsuit. This is true if you have employees who do something wrong and cause your business to be sued. As the business owner, however, if you personally do something wrong and are sued as a result, you might in some cases be held legally responsible, and the "corporation door" will offer no legal protection for your personal assets.

Or, as CPA Bernard Kamoroff explains in *Small Time Operator,* "A corporation will not shield you from personal liability that you normally should be responsible for, such as not having car insurance or acting with gross negligence. If you plan to incorporate solely or primarily with the intention of limiting your legal liability, I suggest you find out first exactly how limited the liability really is for your particular venture. Hire a knowledgeable lawyer to give you a written opinion." (See section 7, Insurance Tips.)

LLC (Limited Liability Company)

This legal form of business reportedly combines the best attributes of other small-business forms while offering a better tax advantage than a limited partnership. It also affords personal liability protection similar to that of a corporation. To date, few craft businesses appear to be using this business form.

Corporation

A corporation is the most complicated and expensive legal form of business and not recommended for any business whose earnings are less than $25,000 a year. If and when your business reaches this point, you should study some books on this topic to fully understand the pros and cons of a corporation. Also consult an accountant or attorney for guidance on the type of corporation you should select—a "C" (general corporation) or an "S" (subchapter S corporation). One book that offers good perspective on this topic is *INC Yourself—How to Profit by Setting Up Your Own Corporation*.

The main disadvantage of incorporation for the small-business owner is that profits are taxed twice: first as corporate income and again when they are distributed to the owner-shareholders as dividends. For this reason, many small businesses elect to incorporate as subchapter S corporations, which allows profits to be taxed at owners' regular individual rates. (See sidebar, The Limited Legal Protection of a Corporation, on page 225.)

4. Local and State Laws and Regulations

This section will acquaint you with laws and regulations that affect the average art or crafts business based at home. If you've unknowingly broken one of these laws, don't panic. It may not be as bad as you think. It is often possible to get back on the straight and narrow merely by filling out a required form or by paying a small fee of some kind. What's important is that you take steps now to comply with the laws that pertain to your particular business. Often, the fear of being caught when you're breaking a law is much worse than doing whatever needs to be done to set the matter straight. In the end, it's usually what you don't know that is most likely to cause legal or financial problems, so never hesitate to ask questions about things you don't understand.

Even when you think you know the answers, it can pay to "act dumb." It is said that Napoleon used to attend meetings and pretend to know nothing about a topic, asking many probing questions. By feigning ignorance, he was able to draw valuable information and insight out of everyone around him. This strategy is often used by today's small-business owners, too.

Business Name Registration

If you're a sole proprietor doing business under any name other than your own full name, you are required by law to register it on both the local and state level. In this case, you are said to be using an "assumed," "fictitious," or "trade" name. Registration enables authorities to connect an assumed name to an individual who can be held responsible for the actions of a business. If you're doing business under your own name, such as Kay Jones, you don't have to register your business name on either the local or state level. If your name is part of a longer name, however (for example, Kay Jones Designs), you should check to see if your county or state requires registration.

Local Registration

To register your name, contact your city or county clerk, who will explain what you need to do to officially register your business on

Picking a Good Business Name

If you haven't done it already, think up a great name for your new business. You want something that will be memorable—catchy, but not too cute. Many crafters select a simple name that is attached to their first name, such as "Mary's Quilts" or "Tom's Woodcrafts." This is fine for a hobby business, but if your goal is to build a full-time business at home, you may wish to choose a more professional-sounding name that omits your personal name. If a name sounds like a hobby business, you may have difficulty getting wholesale suppliers to take you seriously. A more professional name may also enable you to get higher prices for your products. For example, the above names might be changed to "Quilted Treasures" or "Wooden Wonders."

Don't print business cards or stationery until you find out if someone else is already using the name you've chosen. To find out if the name has already been registered, you

the local level. At the same time, ask if you need any special municipal or county licenses or permits to operate within the law. (See the next section, Licenses and Permits.) This office can also tell you how and where to write to register your name at the state level. If you've been operating under an assumed name for a while and are worried because you didn't register the name earlier, just register it now, as if the business were new.

Registration involves filling out a simple form and paying a small fee, usually around $10 to $25. At the time you register, you will get details about a classified ad you must run in a general-circulation newspaper in your county. This will notify the public at large that you are now operating a business under an assumed name. (If you don't want your neighbors to know what you're doing, simply run the ad in a newspaper somewhere else in the county.) After publication of this ad, you will receive a Fictitious Name Statement that you must send to the county clerk, who in turn will file it with your registration form to make your business completely legit-

can perform a trademark search through a search company or hire an attorney who specializes in trademark law to conduct the search for you. And if you are planning to eventually set up a Web site, you might want to do a search to see if that domain name is still available on the Internet. Go to www.networksolutions.com to do this search. Business names have to be registered on the Internet, too, and they can be "parked" for a fee until you're ready to design your Web site.

It's great if your business name and Web site name can be the same, but this is not always possible. A crafter told me recently she had to come up with 25 names before she found a domain name that hadn't already been taken. (Web entrepreneurs are grabbing every good name they can find. Imagine my surprise when I did a search and found that two different individuals had set up Web sites using the titles of my two best-known books, *Creative Cash* and *Homemade Money*.)

imate. This name statement or certificate may also be referred to as your DBA ("doing business as") form. In some areas, you cannot open a business checking account if you don't have this form to show your bank.

> *Avoid this pitfall:* Failure to register your business name may result in your losing it—after you've spent a considerable amount of money on business cards, stationery, advertising, and so on. If someone sees your name, likes it, and finds on checking that it hasn't been registered, they can simply register the name and force you to stop using it.

State Registration

Once you've registered locally, contact your secretary of state to register your business name with the state. This will prevent its use by a corporate entity. At the same time, find out if you must obtain any kind of state license. Generally, home-based crafts businesses will not need a license from the state, but there are always exceptions. An artist who built an open-to-the-public art studio on his property reported that the fine in his state for operating this kind of business without a license was $50 a day. In short, it always pays to ask questions to make sure you're operating legally and safely.

Federal Registration

The only way to protect a name on the federal level is with a trademark, discussed in section 9.

Licenses and Permits

A "license" is a certificate granted by a municipal or county agency that gives you permission to engage in a business occupation. A "permit" is similar, except that it is granted by local authorities. Until recently, few crafts businesses had to have a license or permit of any kind, but a growing number of communities now have new laws on their books that require home-based business owners to obtain a "home occupation permit." Annual fees for such permits may range from $15 to $200 a year. For details about the law in your particular community or county, call your city or county clerk (depending on whether you live within or outside city limits).

Use of Personal Phone for Business

Although every business writer stresses the importance of having a business telephone number, craftspeople generally ignore this advice and do business on their home telephone. Although it's okay to use a home phone to make outgoing business calls, you cannot advertise a home telephone number as your business phone number without being in violation of local telephone regulations. That means you cannot legally put your home telephone number on a business card or business stationery or advertise it on your Web site.

That said, let me also state that most craftspeople totally ignore this law and do it anyway. (I don't know what the penalty for breaking this law is in your state; you'll have to call your telephone company for that information and decide if this is something you want to do.) Some phone companies might give you a slap on the wrist and tell you to stop, while others might start charging you business line telephone rates if they discover you are advertising your personal phone number.

The primary reason to have a separate phone line for your business is that it enables you to freely advertise your telephone number to solicit new business and invite credit card sales, custom order inquiries, and the like. Further, you can deduct 100% of the costs of a business telephone line on your Schedule C tax form, while deductions for the business use of a home phone are severely limited. (Discuss this with your accountant.)

If you plan to connect to the Internet or install a fax machine, you will definitely need a second line to handle the load, but most crafters simply add an additional personal line instead of a business line. Once on the Internet, you may have even less need for a business phone than before because you can simply invite contact from buyers by advertising your e-mail address. (Always include your e-mail and Internet addresses on your business cards and stationery.)

If your primary selling methods are going to be consignment shops, craft fairs, or craft malls, a business phone number would be necessary only if you are inviting orders by phone. If you present a holiday boutique or open house once or twice a year, there should be no problem with putting your home phone number on promotional fliers because you are, in fact, inviting people to your home and not your business (similar to running a classified ad for a garage sale).

If and when you decide a separate line for your business is necessary, you may find it is not as costly as you think. Telephone companies today are very aware of the number of people who are working at home, and they have come up with a variety of affordable packages and second-line options, any one of which might be perfect for your crafts-business needs. Give your telephone company a call and see what's available.

Zoning Regulations

Before you start any kind of home-based business, check your home's zoning regulations. You can find a copy at your library or at city hall. Find out what zone you're in and then read the information under "Home Occupations." Be sure to read the fine print and note the penalty for violating a zoning ordinance. In most cases, someone who is caught violating zoning laws will be asked to cease and desist and a penalty is incurred only if this order is ignored. In other cases, however, willful violation could incur a hefty fine.

Zoning laws differ from one community to another, with some of them being terribly outdated (actually written back in horse-and-buggy days). In some communities, zoning officials simply "look the other way" where zoning violations are concerned because it's easier to do this than change the law. In other places, however, zoning regulations have recently been revised in light of the growing number of individuals working at home, and these changes have not always been to the benefit of home-based workers or self-employed individuals. Often there are restrictions as to (1) the amount of space in one's home a business may occupy (impossible to enforce, in my opinion), (2) the number of people (customers, students) who can come to your home each day, (3) the use of non-family employees, and so on. If you find you cannot advertise your home as a place of business, this problem can be easily solved by renting a PO box or using a commercial mailbox service as your business address.

Although I'm not suggesting that you violate your zoning law, I will tell you that many individuals who have found zoning to be a problem do ignore this law, particularly when they have a quiet business that is unlikely to create problems in their community.

Zoning officials don't go around checking for people who are violating the law; rather, they tend to act on complaints they have received about a certain activity that is creating problems for others. Thus, the best way to avoid zoning problems is to keep a low profile by not broadcasting your home-based business to neighbors. More important, never annoy them with activities that emit fumes or odors, create parking problems, or make noise of any kind.

Although neighbors may grudgingly put up with a noisy hobby activity (such as sawing in the garage), they are not likely to tolerate the same noise or disturbance if they know it's related to a home-based business. Likewise, they won't mind if you have a garage sale every year, but if people are coming to your home every year to buy from your home shop, open house, home parties, or holiday boutiques, you could be asking for trouble if the zoning laws don't favor this kind of activity.

> *Avoid this pitfall:* If you're planning to hold a holiday boutique or home party, check with zoning officials first. (If they don't know what a holiday boutique is, tell them it's a temporary sales event, like a garage sale.) Generally, the main concerns will be that you do not post illegal signs, tie up traffic, or otherwise annoy your neighbors. In some areas, however, zoning regulations strictly prohibit (1) traffic into one's home for any commercial reason; (2) the exchange of money in a home for business reasons; or (3) the transfer of merchandise within the home (affecting party plan sellers, in particular). Some sellers have found the solution to all three of these problems as simple as letting people place orders for merchandise that will be delivered later, with payment collected at time of delivery.

5. General Business and Financial Information

This section offers introductory guidelines on essential business basics for beginners. Once your business is up and running, however, you need to read other crafts-business books to get detailed information on the following topics and many others related to the successful growth and development of a home-based art or crafts business.

Making a Simple Business Plan

As baseball star Yogi Berra once said, "If you don't know where you are going, you might not get there." That's why you need a plan.

Like a road map, a business plan helps you get from here to there. It doesn't have to be fancy, but it does have to be in written form. A good business plan will save you time and money while helping you stay focused and on track to meet your goals. The kind of business plan a craftsperson makes will naturally be less complicated than the business plan of a major manufacturing company, but the elements are basically the same and should include:

- *History*—how and why you started your business
- *Business description*—what you do, what products you make, why they are special
- *Management information*—your business background or experience and the legal form your business will take
- *Manufacturing and production*—how and where products will be produced and who will make them; how and where supplies and materials will be obtained, and their estimated costs; labor costs (yours or other helpers); and overhead costs involved in the making of products
- *Financial plan*—estimated sales and expense figures for 1 year
- *Market research findings*—a description of your market (fairs, shops, mail order, Internet, and so on), your customers, and your competition
- *Marketing plan*—how you are going to sell your products and the anticipated cost of your marketing (commissions, advertising, craft fair displays, and so on)

If this all seems a bit much for a small crafts business, start managing your time by using a daily calendar/planner and start a

Get a Safety Deposit Box

The longer you are in business, the more important it will be to safeguard your most valuable business records. When you work at home, there is always the possibility of fire or damage from some natural disaster, be it a tornado, earthquake, hurricane, or flood. You will worry less if you keep your most valuable business papers, records, computer disks, and so forth off-premises, along with other items that would be difficult or impossible to replace. Some particulars I have always kept in my business safety deposit box include master software disks and computer back-up disks; original copies of my designs and patterns, business contracts, copyrights, insurance policies, and a photographic record of all items insured on our homeowner's policy. Remember: Insurance is worthless if you cannot prove what you owned in the first place.

notebook you can fill with your creative and marketing ideas, plans, and business goals. In it, write a simple mission statement that answers the following questions:

- What is my primary mission or goal in starting a business?
- What is my financial goal for this year?
- What am I going to do to get the sales I need this year to meet my financial goal?

The most important thing is that you start putting your dreams, goals, and business plans on paper so you can review them regularly. It's always easier to see where you're going if you know where you've been.

When You Need an Attorney

Many business beginners think they have to hire a lawyer the minute they start a business, but that would be a terrible waste of money if you're just starting a simple art or crafts business at home, operating as a sole proprietor. Sure, a lawyer will be delighted to hold your hand and give you the same advice I'm giving you here (while charging you $150 an hour or more for his or her time). With this book in hand, you can easily take care of all the "legal details" of a small-business start-up. The day may come, however, when you do need legal counsel, such as when you:

Form a Partnership or Corporation

As stated earlier, an attorney's guidance is necessary in the formation of a partnership. Although many people have incorporated without a lawyer using a good how-to book on the topic, I wouldn't recommend doing this because there are so many details involved, not to mention different types of corporate entities.

Defend an Infringement of a Copyright or Trademark

You don't need an attorney to get a simple copyright, but if someone infringes on one of your copyrights, you will probably need legal help to stop the infringer from profiting from your creativity. You can file your own trademark application (if you are exceedingly careful about following instructions), but it would be difficult to protect your trademark without legal help if someone tries to steal it. In both cases, you would need an attorney who specializes in copyright, patent, and trademark law. (If you ever need a good attorney who understands the plight of artists and crafters, contact me by e-mail at barbara@crafter.com and I'll refer you to the attorney who has been helpful to me in protecting my common-law trademark to *Homemade Money*, my home-business classic. The sixth edition of this book includes the details of my trademark infringement story.)

Negotiate a Contract

Many craft hobbyists of my acquaintance have gone on to write books and sell their original designs to manufacturers, suddenly finding themselves with a contract in hand that contains a lot of confusing legal jargon. When hiring an attorney to check any kind of contract, make sure he or she has experience in the particular field involved. For example, a lawyer specializing in real estate isn't going to know a thing about the inner workings of a book publishing company and how the omission or inclusion of a particular clause or phrase might impact the author's royalties or make it difficult to get publishing rights back when the book goes out of print. Although I have no experience in the licensing industry, I presume the same thing holds true here. What I do know for sure is that the problem with most contracts is not so much what's *in* them, as what *isn't*. Thus you need to be sure the attorney you hire for specialized contract work has done this kind of work for other clients.

Hire Independent Contractors

If you ever grow your business to the point where you need to hire workers and are wondering whether you have to hire employees or can use independent contractors instead, I suggest you seek counsel from an attorney who specializes in labor law. This topic is very complex and beyond the scope of this beginner's guide, but I do want you to know that the IRS has been on a campaign for the past several years to abolish independent contractors altogether. Many small businesses have suffered great financial loss in back taxes and penalties because they followed the advice of an accountant or regular attorney who didn't fully understand the technicalities of this matter.

If and when you do need a lawyer for general business purposes, ask friends for a reference, and check with your bank, too, because it will probably know most of the attorneys with private practices in your area. Note that membership in some small-business organizations will also give you access to affordable prepaid legal services. If you ever need serious legal help but have no funds to pay for it, contact the Volunteer Lawyers for the Arts.

Why You Need a Business Checking Account

Many business beginners use their personal checking account to conduct the transactions of their business, *but you must not do this* because the IRS does not allow commingling of business and personal income. If you are operating as a business, reporting income on a Schedule C form and taking deductions accordingly, the lack of a separate checking account for your business would surely result in an IRS ruling that your endeavor was a hobby and not a business. That, in turn, would cost you all the deductions previously taken on earlier tax returns and you'd end up with a very large tax bill. Don't you agree that the cost of a separate checking account is a small price to pay to protect all your tax deductions?

You do not necessarily need one of the more expensive business checking accounts; just a *separate account* through which you run all business income and expenditures. Your business name does not have to be on these checks so long as only your name (not your spouse's) is listed as account holder. You can save money on your checking account by first calling several banks and savings and loan institutions and comparing the charges they set for imprinted checks, deposits, checks written, bounced checks, and other services. Before you open your account, be sure to ask if the bank can set you up to take credit cards (merchant account) at some point in the future.

Avoid this pitfall: Some banks charge extra for each out-of-state check that is deposited, an expense that is prohibitively expensive for active mail-order businesses. For that reason, I have always maintained a business checking account in a savings and loan association, which has no service charges of any kind (except for bad checks). S&L's also pay interest on the amount in a checking account, whereas a bank may not. The main disadvantage of doing your business checking through an S&L is that they do not offer credit card services or give business loans. At the point where I found I needed the latter two services for my publishing business, I had to open a second account with a local bank.

Accepting Credit Cards

Most of us today take credit cards for granted and expect to be able to use them for most everything we buy. It's nice to be able to offer credit card services to your craft fair customers, but it is costly and thus not recommended for beginning craft sellers. If you get into selling at craft fairs on a regular basis, however, at some point you may find you are losing sales because you don't have "merchant status" (the ability to accept credit cards as payment).

Some craftspeople have reported a considerable jump in sales once they started taking credit cards. That's because some people who buy with plastic may buy two or three items instead of one, or may be willing to pay a higher price for something if they can charge it. Thus, the higher your prices, the more likely you are to lose sales if you can't accept credit cards. As one jewelry maker told me, "I always seem to get the customers who have run out of cash and left their checkbook at home. But even when they have a check, I feel uncomfortable taking a check for $100 or more."

This section discusses the various routes you can travel to get merchant status. You will have to do considerable research to find out which method is best for you. All will be costly, and you must have sufficient sales, or the expectation of increased sales, to consider taking credit cards in the first place. Understand, too, that taking credit cards in person (called face-to-face transactions where you have the card in front of you) is different from accepting credit cards by phone, by mail, or through a Web site (called non–face-to-face transactions). Each method of selling is treated differently by bankcard providers.

Avoid this pitfall: If you are relatively new at selling, and uncertain about whether you will be taking credit cards for a long time, do not sign a leasing arrangement for credit card processing equipment. Instead, leave yourself an escape route by opting for a rental agreement you can get out of with a month's notice, such as that offered by some banks and organizations discussed below.

Merchant Status from Your Bank

When you're ready to accept credit cards, start with the bank where you have your business checking account. Where you bank, and where you live, has everything to do with whether you can get merchant status from your bank. Home-business owners in small towns often have less trouble than do those in large cities. One crafter told me Bank of America gave her merchant status with no problem, but some banks simply refuse to deal with anyone who doesn't operate out of a storefront. Most banks now insist that credit card sales be transmitted electronically, but a few still offer manual printers and allow merchants to send in their sales slips by mail. You will be given details about this at the time you apply for merchant status. All banks will require proof that you have a going business and will want to see your financial statements.

Merchant Status through a Crafts Organization

If you are refused by your bank because your business is home based or just too new, getting bankcard services through a crafts or home-business organization is the next best way to go. Because such organizations have a large membership, they have some negotiating power with the credit card companies and often get special deals for their members. As a member of such an organization, the chances are about 95% that you will automatically be accepted into its bankcard program, even if you are a brand-new business owner.

One organization I can recommend to beginning sellers is the National Craft Association. Managing Director Barbara Arena tells me that 60% of all new NCA members now take the

MasterCard/VISA services offered by her organization. "Crafters who are unsure about whether they want to take credit cards over a long period of time have the option of renting equipment," says Barbara. "This enables them to get out of the program with a month's notice. NCA members can operate on a software basis through their personal computer (taking their laptop computer to shows and calling in sales on their cell phone) or use a swipe machine. Under NCA's program, crafters can also accept credit card sales on their Internet site."

For more information from NCA and other organizations offering merchant services, see Craft and Home Business Organizations on page 284.

Merchant Status from Credit Card Companies

If you've been in business for a while, you may find you can get merchant status directly from American Express or Novus Services, Inc., the umbrella company that handles the Discover, Bravo, and Private Issue credit cards. American Express says that in some cases it can grant merchant status immediately on receipt of some key information given on the phone. As for Novus, many crafters have told me how easy it was to get merchant status from this company. Novus says it needs only your Social Security number and information to check your credit rating. If Novus accepts you, it can also get you set up to take VISA and MasterCard as well, if you meet the special acceptance qualifications of these two credit card companies. (Usually, they require you to be in business for at least 2 years.)

Merchant Status from an Independent Service Organization Provider (ISO)

ISOs act as agents for banks that authorize credit cards, promoting their services by direct mail, through magazine advertising, telemarketing, and on the Internet. Most of these bankcard providers are operating under a network marketing program (one agent representing one agent representing another, and so on). They are everywhere on the Internet, sending unsolicited e-mail messages to Web site owners. In addition to offering the merchant account service itself, many are also trying to get other Web site owners to promote the same service in exchange for some kind of referral fee. I do not recommend that you get merchant status through an ISO because I've heard too many horror stories about them. If you want to explore this option on the Internet, however, use your browser's search button and type "credit cards + merchant" to get a list of such sellers.

In general, ISOs may offer a low discount rate but will sock it to you with inflated equipment costs, a high application fee, and extra fees for installation, programming, and site inspection. You will also have to sign an unbreakable 3- or 4-year lease for the electronic equipment.

> ***Avoid this pitfall:*** Some people on the Internet may offer to process your credit card sales through their individual merchant account, but this is illegal as it violates credit card company rules. And if you were to offer to do this for someone else, your account would be terminated. In short, if you do not ship the goods, you can't process the sale.

As you can see, you must really do your homework where bankcard services are concerned. In checking out the services offered by any of the providers noted here, ask plenty of questions. Make up a chart that lets you compare what each one charges for application and service fees, monthly charges, equipment costs, software, discount rates, and transaction fees.

Transaction fees can range from $0.20 to $0.80 per ticket, with discount rates running anywhere from 1.67 to 5%. Higher rates are usually attached to non–face-to-face credit card transactions, paper transaction systems, or a low volume of sales. Any rate higher than

5% should be a danger signal because you could be dealing with an unscrupulous seller or some kind of illegal third-party processing program.

I'm told that a good credit card processor today may cost around $800, yet some card service providers are charging two or three times that amount in their leasing arrangements. I once got a quote from a major ISO and found it would have cost me $40 a month to lease the terminal—$1,920 over a period of 4 years—or I could buy it for just $1,000. In checking with my bank, I learned I could get the same equipment and the software to run it for just $350!

In summary, if you're a nervous beginner, the safest way to break into taking credit cards is to work with a bank or organization that offers equipment on a month-by-month rental arrangement. Once you've had some experience in taking credit card payments, you can review your situation and decide whether you want to move into a leasing arrangement or buy equipment outright.

6. Minimizing the Financial Risks of Selling

This book contains a good chapter on how and where to sell your crafts, but I thought it would be helpful for you to have added perspective on the business management end of selling through various outlets, and some things you can do to protect yourself from financial loss and legal hassles.

You must accept the fact that all businesses occasionally suffer financial losses of one kind or another. That's simply the nature of business. Selling automatically carries a certain degree of risk in that we can never be absolutely sure that we're going to be paid for anything until we actually have payment in hand. Checks may bounce, wholesale buyers may refuse to pay their invoices, and consignment shops can close unexpectedly without returning merchandise to crafters. In the past few years, a surprising number of craft mall owners have stolen out of town in the middle of the night, taking with them all the money due their vendors, and sometimes the vendors' merchandise as well. (This topic is beyond the scope of this book, but if you'd like more information on it, see my *Creative Cash* book and back issues of my *Craftsbiz Chat* newsletter on the Internet at www.crafter.com/brabec.)

Now, I don't want you to feel uneasy about selling or be suspicious of every buyer who comes your way, because that would take all the fun out of selling. But I *do* want you to know that bad things sometimes happen to good craftspeople who have not done their homework (by reading this book, you are doing *your* homework). If you will follow the cautionary guidelines discussed in this section, you can avoid some common selling pitfalls and minimize your financial risk to the point where it will be negligible.

Selling to Consignment Shops

Never consign more merchandise to one shop than you can afford to lose, and do not send new items to a shop until you see that payments are being made regularly according to your written consignment agreement. It should cover the topics of:

- Insurance (see Insurance Tips, section 7)
- Pricing (make sure the shop cannot raise or lower your retail price without your permission)
- Sales commission (40% is standard; don't work with shop owners who ask for more than this. It makes more sense to wholesale products at 50% and get payment in 30 days)
- Payment dates
- Display of merchandise

■ Return of unsold merchandise (some shops have a clause stating that if unsold merchandise is not claimed within 30 to 60 days after a notice has been sent, the shop can dispose of it any way it wishes)

Above all, make sure your agreement includes the name and phone number of the shop's owner (not just the manager). If a shop fails and you decide to take legal action, you want to be sure your lawyer can track down the owner. (See sidebar, State Consignment Laws, below.)

Selling to Craft Malls

Shortly after the craft mall concept was introduced to the crafts community in 1988 by Rufus Coomer, entrepreneurs who understood the profit potential of such a business began to open malls all over the country. But there were no guidebooks and everyone was flying by the seat of his or her pants, making up operating rules along the way. Many mall owners, inexperienced in retailing, have

State Consignment Laws

Technically, consigned goods remain the property of the seller until they are sold. When a shop goes out of business, however, consigned merchandise may be seized by creditors in spite of what your consignment agreement may state. You may have some legal protection here, however, if you live in a state that has a consignment law designed to protect artists and craftspeople in such instances. I believe such laws exist in the states of CA, CO, CT, IL, IA, KY, MA, NH, NM, NY, OR, TX, WA, and WI. Call your secretary of state to confirm this or, if your state isn't listed here, ask whether this law is now on the books. Be sure to get full details about the kind of protection afforded by this law because some states have different definitions for what constitutes "art" or "crafts."

since gone out of business, often leaving crafters holding the bag. The risks of selling through such well-known chain stores as Coomers or American Craft Malls are minimal, and many independently owned malls have also established excellent reputations in the industry. What you need to be especially concerned about here are new malls opened by individuals who have no track record in this industry.

I'm not telling you *not* to set up a booth in a new mall in your area—it might prove to be a terrific outlet for you—but I am cautioning you to keep a sharp eye on the mall and how it's being operated. Warning signs of a mall in trouble include:

- less than 75% occupancy
- little or no ongoing advertising
- not many shoppers
- crafters pulling out (usually a sign of too few sales)
- poor accounting of sales
- late payments

If a mall is in trouble, it stands to reason that the logical time for it to close is right after the biggest selling season of the year, namely Christmas. Interestingly, this is when most of the shady mall owners have stolen out of town with crafters' Christmas sales in their pockets. As stated in my *Creative Cash* book:

> If it's nearing Christmastime, and you're getting uncomfortable vibes about the financial condition of a mall you're in, it might be smart to remove the bulk of your merchandise— especially expensive items—just before it closes for the holidays. You can always restock after the first of the year if everything looks rosy.

Avoiding Bad Checks

At a craft fair or other event where you're selling directly to the public, if the buyer doesn't have cash and you don't accept credit cards, your only option is to accept a check. Few crafters have bad check problems for sales held in the home (holiday boutique, open house, party plan, and such), but bad checks at craft fairs are always possible. Here are several things you can do to avoid accepting a bad check:

- Always ask to see a driver's license and look carefully at the picture on it. Write the license number on the check.

- If the sale is for a large amount, you can ask to see a credit card for added identification, but writing down the number will do no good because you cannot legally cover a bad check with a customer's credit card. (The customer has a legal right to refuse to let you copy the number as well.)

- Look closely at the check itself. Is there a name and address printed on it? If not, ask the customer to write in this information by hand, along with his or her phone number.

- Look at the sides of the check. If at least one side is not perforated, it could be a phony check.

- Look at the check number in the upper right-hand corner. Most banks who issue personalized checks begin the numbering system with 101 when a customer reorders new checks. The Small Business Administration says to be more cautious with low sequence numbers because there seems to be a higher number of these checks that are returned.

- Check the routing number in the lower left-hand corner and note the ink. If it looks shiny, wet your finger and see if the ink rubs off. That's a sure sign of a phony check because good checks are printed with magnetic ink that does not reflect light.

Collecting on a Bad Check

No matter how careful you are, sooner or later, you will get stuck with a bad check. It may bounce for one of three reasons:

> **nonsufficient funds (NSF)**
> **account closed**
> **no account (evidence of fraud)**

I've accepted tens of thousands of checks from mail-order buyers through the years and have rarely had a bad check I couldn't collect with a simple phone call asking the party to honor his or her obligation to me. People often move and close out accounts before all checks have cleared, or they add or subtract wrong, causing their account to be overdrawn. Typically, they are embarrassed to have caused a problem like this.

When the problem is more difficult than this, your bank can help. Check to learn its policy regarding bounced checks. Some automatically put checks through a second time. If a check bounces at this point, you may ask the bank to collect the check for you. The check needs to be substantial, however, because the bank fee may be $15 or more if they are successful in collecting the money.

If you have accepted a check for a substantial amount of money and believe there is evidence of fraud, you may wish to do one of the following:

- **Notify your district attorney's office**
- **Contact your sheriff or police department (because it is a crime to write a bad check)**
- **Try to collect through small claims court**

For more detailed information on all of these topics, see *The Crafts Business Answer Book*.

7. Insurance Tips

As soon as you start even the smallest business at home, you need to give special attention to insurance. This section offers an introductory overview of insurance concerns of primary interest to crafts-business owners.

Homeowner's or Renter's Insurance

Anything in the home being used to generate income is considered to be business-related and thus exempt from coverage on a personal policy. Thus your homeowner's or renter's insurance policy will not cover business equipment, office furniture, supplies, or inventory of finished goods unless you obtain a special rider. Such riders, called a "Business Pursuits Endorsement" by some companies, are inexpensive and offer considerable protection. Your insurance agent will be happy to give you details.

As your business grows and you have an ever-larger inventory of supplies, materials, tools, and finished merchandise, you may find it necessary to buy a special in-home business policy that offers broader protection. Such policies may be purchased directly from insurance companies or through craft and home-business organizations that offer special insurance programs to their members.

Avoid this pitfall: If you have an expensive computer system, costly tools, equipment, or office furnishings, the coverage

Insuring Your Art or Crafts Collection

The replacement cost insurance you may have on your personal household posses-sions does not extend to "fine art," which includes such things as paintings, antiques, pictures, tapestries, statuary, and other articles that cannot be replaced with new arti-cles. If you have a large collection of art, crafts, memorabilia, or collector's items, and its value is more than $1,500, you may wish to have your collection appraised so it can be protected with a separate all-risk endorsement to your homeowner's policy called a "fine arts floater."

afforded by a simple business rider to your homeowner's policy may be insufficient for your needs. Although you may have replacement-value insurance on all your personal possessions, anything used for business purposes would be exempt from such coverage. In other words, the value of everything covered by the rider would be figured on a depreciable basis instead of what it would cost to replace it. (See also sidebar, Insuring Your Art or Crafts Collection, on page 249.)

Liability Insurance

There are two kinds of liability insurance. *Product* liability insurance protects you against lawsuits by consumers who have been injured while using one of your products. *Personal* liability insurance protects you against claims made by individuals who have suffered bodily injury while on your premises (either your home or the place where you are doing business, such as in your booth at a craft fair).

Your homeowner's or renter's insurance policy will include some personal liability protection, but if someone were to suffer bodily injury while on your premises for *business* reasons, that coverage might not apply. Your need for personal liability insurance will be greater if you plan to regularly present home parties, holiday boutiques, or open house sales in your home where many people might be coming and going throughout the year. If you sell at craft fairs, you would also be liable for damages if someone were to fall and be injured in your booth or if something in your booth falls and injures another person. For this reason, some craft fair promoters now require all vendors to have personal liability insurance.

As for product liability insurance, whether you need it depends largely on the type of products you make for sale, how careful you are to make sure those products are safe, and how and where you sell them. Examples of some crafts that have caused injury to consumers and resulted in court claims in the past are stuffed toys with wire or pins that children have swallowed; items made of yarn or fiber that burned rapidly; handmade furniture that collapsed when someone put an ordinary amount of weight on it; jewelry with sharp points or other features that cut the wearer, and so on. Clearly, the best way to avoid injury to consumers is to make certain your products have no health hazards and are safe to use. (See discussion of consumer safety laws in section 8.)

Few artists and craftspeople who sell on a part-time basis feel they can afford product liability insurance, but many full-time craft professionals, particularly those who sell their work wholesale, find it a necessary expense. In fact, many wholesale buyers refuse to buy from suppliers that do not carry product liability insurance.

I believe the least expensive way to obtain both personal and product liability insurance is with one of the comprehensive in-home or crafts-business policies offered by a crafts- or home-business organization. Such policies generally offer $1 million of both personal and product liability coverage. (See A "Things to Do" Checklist with Related Resources on page 278 and the Resources section for some organizations you can contact for more information. Also check with your insurance agent about the benefits of an umbrella policy for extra liability insurance.)

Insurance on Crafts Merchandise

As a seller of art or crafts merchandise, you are responsible for insuring your own products against loss. If you plan to sell at craft fairs, in craft malls, rent-a-space shops, or consignment shops, you may want to buy an insurance policy that protects your merchandise both at home or away. Note that while craft shops and malls generally have fire insurance covering the building and its fixtures, this coverage cannot be extended to merchandise offered for sale because it is not the property of the shop owner. (Exception: Shops and malls in shopping centers are mandated by law to buy fire insurance on their contents whether they own the merchandise or not.)

This kind of insurance is usually part of the home- or crafts-business insurance policies mentioned earlier.

Auto Insurance

Be sure to talk to the agent who handles your car insurance and explain that you may occasionally use your car for business purposes. Normally, a policy issued for a car that's used only for pleasure or driving to and from work may not provide complete coverage for an accident that occurs during business use of the car, particularly if the insured is to blame for the accident. For example, if you were delivering a load of crafts to a shop or on your way to a craft fair and had an accident, would your business destination and the "commercial merchandise" in your car negate your coverage in any way? Where insurance is concerned, the more questions you ask, the better you'll feel about the policies you have.

8. Important Regulations Affecting Artists and Craftspeople

Government agencies have a number of regulations that artists and craftspeople must know about. Generally, they relate to consumer safety, the labeling of certain products, and trade practices. Following are regulations of primary interest to readers of books in Prima's FOR FUN & PROFIT series. If you find a law or regulation related to your particular art or craft interest, be sure to request additional information from the government agency named there.

Consumer Safety Laws

All product sellers must pay attention to the Consumer Product Safety Act, which protects the public against unreasonable risks of injury associated with consumer products. The Consumer Product

Safety Commission (CPSC) is particularly active in the area of toys and consumer goods designed for children. All sellers of handmade products must be doubly careful about the materials they use for children's products because consumer lawsuits are common where products for children are concerned. To avoid this problem, simply comply with the consumer safety laws applicable to your specific art or craft.

Toy Safety Concerns

To meet CPSC's guidelines for safety, make sure any toys you make for sale are:

■ Too large to be swallowed

■ Not apt to break easily or leave jagged edges

■ Free of sharp edges or points

■ Not put together with easily exposed pins, wires, or nails

■ Nontoxic, nonflammable, and nonpoisonous

The Use of Paints, Varnishes, and Other Finishes

Since all paint sold for household use must meet the Consumer Product Safety Act's requirement for minimum amounts of lead, these paints are deemed to be safe for use on products made for children, such as toys and furniture. Always check, however, to make sure the label bears a nontoxic notation. Specialty paints must carry a warning on the label about lead count, but "artist's paints" are curiously exempt from CPS's lead-in-paint ban and are not required to bear a warning label of any kind. Thus you should *never* use such paints on products intended for use by children unless the label specifically states they are *nontoxic* (lead-free). Acrylics and other water-based paints, of course, are nontoxic and completely safe for use on toys and other products made for children. If you plan to use a finishing coat, make sure it is nontoxic as well.

Fabric Flammability Concerns

The Flammable Fabrics Act is applicable only to those who sell products made of fabric, particularly products for children. It prohibits the movement in interstate commerce of articles of wearing apparel and fabrics that are so highly flammable as to be dangerous when worn by individuals, and for other purposes. Most fabrics comply with this act, but if you plan to sell children's clothes or toys, you may wish to take an extra step to be doubly sure the fabric you are using is safe. This is particularly important if you plan to wholesale your products. What you should do is ask your fabric supplier for a *guarantee of compliance with the Flammability Act*. This guarantee is generally passed along to the buyer by a statement on the invoice that reads "continuing guaranty under the Flammable Fabrics Act." If you do not find such a statement on your invoice, you should ask the fabric manufacturer, wholesaler, or distributor to furnish you with their "statement of compliance" with the flammability standards. The CPSC can also tell you if a particular manufacturer has filed a continuing guarantee under The Flammable Fabrics Act.

Labels Required by Law

The following information applies only to crafters who use textiles, fabrics, fibers, or yarn products to make wearing apparel, decorative accessories, household furnishings, soft toys, or any product made of wool.

Different government agencies require the attachment of certain tags or labels to products sold in the consumer marketplace, whether manufactured in quantity or handmade for limited sale. You don't have to be too concerned about these laws if you sell only at local fairs, church bazaars, and home boutiques. As soon as you get out into the general consumer marketplace, however—doing large craft fairs, selling through consignment shops, craft malls, or wholesaling to shops—it would be wise to comply with all the federal labeling laws. Actually, these laws are quite easy to comply with because the required labels are readily available at inexpensive prices, and you can even make your own if you wish. Here is what the federal government wants you to tell your buyers in a tag or label:

- *What's in a product, and who has made it.* The Textile Fiber Products Identification Act (monitored both by the Bureau of Consumer Protection and the Federal Trade Commission) requires that a special label or hangtag be attached to all textile wearing apparel and household furnishings, with the exception of wall hangings. "Textiles" include products made of any fiber, yarn, or fabric, including garments and decorative accessories, quilts, pillows, placemats, stuffed toys, rugs, and so on. The tag or label must include (1) the name of the manufacturer and (2) the generic names and percentages of all fibers in the product in amounts of 5 percent or more, listed in order of predominance by weight.

- *How to take care of products.* Care Labeling Laws are part of the Textile Fiber Products Identification Act, details about which are available from the FTC. If you make wearing apparel or household furnishings of any kind using textiles, suede, or leather, you must attach a permanent label that explains how to take care of the item. This label must indicate whether the item is to be dry-cleaned or washed. If it is washable, you must indicate whether in hot or cold water, whether bleach may or may not be used, and the temperature at which it may be ironed.

- *Details about products made of wool.* If a product contains wool, the FTC requires additional identification under a separate law known as the Wool Products Labeling Act of 1939. FTC rules require that the labels of all wool or textile products clearly indicate when imported ingredients are used. Thus, the label for a skirt knitted in the United States from wool yarn imported from England would read, "Made in the USA from imported products" or similar wordage.

If the wool yarn was spun in the United States, a product made from that yarn would simply need a tag or label stating it was "Made in the USA" or "Crafted in USA" or some similarly clear terminology.

The Bedding and Upholstered Furniture Law

This is a peculiar state labeling law that affects sellers of items that have a concealed filling. It requires the purchase of a license, and products must have a tag that bears the manufacturer's registry number.

A Proper Copyright Notice

Although a copyright notice is not required by law, you are encouraged to put a copyright notice on every original thing you create. Adding the copyright notice does not obligate you to formally register your copyright, but it does serve to warn others that your work is legally protected and makes it difficult for anyone to claim they have "accidentally stolen" your work. (Those who actually do violate a copyright because they don't understand the law are called "innocent infringers" by the Copyright Office.)

A proper copyright notice includes three things:

1. The word *copyright,* its abbreviation *copr.,* or the copyright symbol, ©

2. The year of first publication of the work (when it was first shown or sold to the public)

3. The name of the copyright owner. Example: © 2000 by Barbara Brabec. (When the words *All Rights Reserved* are added to the copyright notation, it means that copyright protection has been extended to include all of the Western Hemisphere.)

The copyright notice should be positioned in a place where it can easily be seen. It can be stamped, cast, engraved, painted, printed, wood-burned, or simply written by hand in permanent ink. In the case of fiber crafts, you can attach an inexpensive label with the copyright notice and your business name and logo (or any other information you wish to put on the label).

Bedding laws have long been a thorn in the side of crafters because they make no distinction between the large manufacturing company that makes mattresses and pillows, and the individual craft producer who sells only handmade items. "Concealed filling" items include not just bedding and upholstery, but handmade pillows and quilts. In some states, dolls, teddy bears, and stuffed soft sculpture items are also required to have a tag.

Fortunately, only 29 states now have this law on the books, and even if your state is one of them, the law may be arbitrarily enforced. (One exception is the state of Pennsylvania, which is reportedly sending officials to craft shows to inspect merchandise to see if it is properly labeled.) The only penalty that appears to be connected with a violation of this law in any state is removal of merchandise from store shelves or craft fair exhibits. That being the case, many crafters choose to ignore this law until they are challenged. If you learn you must comply with this law, you will be required to obtain a state license that will cost between $25 and $100, and you will have to order special "bedding stamps" that can be attached to your products. For more information on this complex topic, see *The Crafts Business Answer Book*.

FTC Rule for Mail-Order Sellers

Even the smallest home-based business needs to be familiar with Federal Trade Commission (FTC) rules and regulations. A variety of free booklets are available to business owners on topics related to advertising, mail-order marketing, and product labeling (as discussed earlier). In particular, crafters who sell by mail need to pay attention to the FTC's Thirty-Day Mail-Order Rule, which states that one must ship customer orders within 30 days of receiving payment for the order. This rule is strictly enforced, with severe financial penalties for each violation.

Unless you specifically state in your advertising literature how long delivery will take, customers will expect to receive the product within 30 days after you get their order. If you cannot meet this ship-ping date, you must notify the customer accordingly, enclosing a postage-paid reply card or envelope, and giving them the option to cancel the order if they wish. Now you know why so many catalog sellers state, "Allow 6 weeks for delivery." This lets them off the hook in case there are unforeseen delays in getting the order delivered.

9. Protecting Your Intellectual Property

"Intellectual property," says Attorney Stephen Elias in his book, *Patent, Copyright & Trademark*, "is a product of the human intellect that has commercial value."

This section offers a brief overview of how to protect your intel-lectual property through patents and trademarks, with a longer discus-sion of copyright law, which is of the greatest concern to individuals who sell what they make. Because it is easy to get patents, trademarks, and copyrights mixed up, let me briefly define them for you:

- A *patent* is a grant issued by the government that gives an inventor the right to exclude all others from making, using, or selling an invention within the United States and its territories and possessions.

- A *trademark* is used by a manufacturer or merchant to identify his or her goods and distinguish them from those manufactured or sold by others.

- A *copyright* protects the rights of creators of intellectual property in five main categories (described in this section).

Perspective on Patents

A patent may be granted to anyone who invents or discovers a new and useful process, machine, manufacture or composition of matter, or any new and useful improvement thereof. Any new, original, and ornamental design for an article of manufacture can also be patented. The problem with patents is that they can cost as much as $5,000 or more to obtain, and, once you've got one, they still require periodic maintenance through the U.S. Patent and Trademark Office. To contact this office, you can use the following Web sites: www.uspto.com or www.lcweb.loc.gov.

Ironically, a patent doesn't even give one the right to sell a product. It merely excludes anyone else from making, using, or selling your invention. Many business novices who have gone to the trouble to patent a product end up wasting a lot of time and money because a patent is useless if it isn't backed with the right manufacturing, distribution, and advertising programs. As inventor Jeremy Gorman states in *Homemade Money,* "Ninety-seven percent of the U.S. patents issued never earn enough money to pay the patenting fee. They just go on a plaque on the wall or in a desk drawer to impress the grandchildren 50 years later."

What a Trademark Protects

Trademarks were established to prevent one company from trading on the good name and reputation of another. The primary function of a trademark is to indicate origin, but in some cases it also serves as a guarantee of quality.

You cannot adopt any trademark that is so similar to another that it is likely to confuse buyers, nor can you trademark generic or descriptive names in the public domain. If, however, you come up with a particular word, name, symbol, or device to identify and distinguish your products from others, you may protect that mark by trademark provided another company is not already using a similar mark. Brand names, trade names, slogans, and phrases may also qualify for trademark protection.

Many individual crafters have successfully registered their own trademarks using a how-to book on the topic, but some would say never to try this without the help of a trademark attorney. It depends on how much you love detail and how well you can follow directions. Any mistake on the application form could cause it to be rejected, and you would lose the application fee in the process. If this is something you're interested in, and you have designed a mark you want to protect, you should first do a trademark search to see if someone else is already using it. Trademark searches can be done using library directories, an online computer service (check with your library), through private trademark search firms, or directly on the Internet through the Patent and Trademark Office's online search service (see A "Things to Do" Checklist with Related Resources). All of these searches together could still be inconclusive, however, because many companies have a stash of trademarks in reserve waiting for just the right product. As I understand it,

Selling How-To Projects to Magazines

If you want to sell an article, poem, or how-to project to a magazine, you need not copyright the material first because copyright protection exists from the moment you create that work. Your primary consideration here is whether you will sell "all rights" or only "first rights" to the magazine.

The sale of first rights means you are giving a publication permission to print your article, poem, or how-to project once, for a specific sum of money. After publication, you then have the right to resell that material or profit from it in other ways. Although it is always desirable to sell only "first rights," some magazines do not offer this choice.

If you sell all rights, you will automatically lose ownership of the copyright to your material and you can no longer profit from that work. Professional designers often refuse to work this way because they know they can realize greater profits by publishing their own pattern packets or design leaflets and wholesaling them to shops.

these "nonpublished" trademarks are in a special file that only an attorney or trademark search service could find for you.

Like copyrights, trademarks have their own symbol, which looks like this: ®. This symbol can be used only after the trademark has been formally registered through the U.S. Patent and Trademark Office. Business owners often use the superscript initials: ™ with a mark to indicate they've claimed a logo or some other mark, but this offers no legal protection. While this does not guarantee trademark protection, it does give notice to the public that you are claiming this name as your trademark. However, after you've used a mark for some time, you do gain a certain amount of common-law protection for that mark. I have, in fact, gained common-law protection for the name of my *Homemade Money* book and successfully defended it against use by another individual in my field because this title has become so closely associated with my name in the home-business community.

Whether you ever formally register a trademark or not will have much to do with your long-range business plans, how you feel about protecting your creativity, and what it would do to your business if someone stole your mark and registered it in his or her own name. Once you've designed a trademark you feel is worth protecting, get additional information from the Patent and Trademark Office and read a book or two on the topic to decide whether this is something you wish to pursue. (See A "Things to Do" Checklist with Related Resources.)

What Copyrights Protect

As a serious student of the copyright law, I've pored through the hard-to-interpret copyright manual, read dozens of related articles and books, and discussed this subject at length with designers, writers, teachers, editors, and publishers. I must emphasize, however, that I am no expert on this topic, and the following information does not constitute legal advice. It is merely offered as a general guide to a very complex legal topic you may wish to research further on your own at some point. In a book of this nature, addressed to hobbyists and beginning crafts-business owners, a discussion of copyrights must be limited to three basic topics:

- What copyrights do and do not protect
- How to register a copyright and protect your legal rights
- How to avoid infringing on the rights of other copyright holders

One of the first things you should do now is send for the free booklets offered by the Copyright Office (see A "Things to Do" Checklist with Related Resources). Various free circulars explain copyright basics, the forms involved in registering a copyright, and how to submit a copyright application and register a copyright.

Protecting Your Copyrights

If someone ever copies one of your copyrighted works, and you have registered that work with the Copyright Office, you should defend it as far as you are financially able to do so. If you think you're dealing with an innocent infringer—another crafter, perhaps, who has probably not profited much (if at all) from your work—a strongly worded letter on your business stationery (with a copy to an attorney, if you have one) might do the trick. Simply inform the copyright infringer that you are the legal owner of the work and the only one who has the right to profit from it. Tell the infringer that he or she must immediately cease using your copyrighted work, and ask for a confirmation by return mail.

If you think you have lost some money or incurred other damages, consult with a copyright attorney before contacting the infringer to see how you can best protect your rights and recoup any financial losses you may have suffered. This is particularly important if the infringer appears to be a successful business or corporation. Although you may have no intention of ever going to court on this matter, the copyright infringer won't know that, and one letter from a competent attorney might immediately resolve the matter at very little cost to you.

They also discuss what you cannot copyright. Rather than duplicate all the free information you can get from the Copyright Office with a letter or phone call, I will only briefly touch on these topics and focus instead on addressing some of the particular copyright questions crafters have asked me in the past.

Things You Can Copyright

Some people mistakenly believe that copyright protection extends only to printed works, but that is not true. The purpose of the copyright law is to protect any creator from anyone who would use the creator's work for his or her own profit. Under current copyright law, claims are now registered in seven classes, five of which pertain to crafts:

1. *Serials* (Form SE)—periodicals, newspapers, magazines, bulletins, newsletters, annuals, journals, and proceedings of societies.
2. *Text* (Form TX)—books, directories, and other written works, including the how-to instructions for a crafts project. (You could copyright a letter to your mother if you wanted to— or your best display ad copy, or any other written words that represent income potential.)
3. *Visual Arts* (Form VA)—pictorial, graphic, or sculptural works, including fine, graphic, and applied art; photographs, charts; technical drawings; diagrams; and models. (Also included in this category are "works of artistic craftsmanship insofar as their form but not their mechanical or utilitarian aspects are concerned.")
4. *Performing Arts* (Form PA)—musical works and accompanying words, dramatic works, pantomimes, choreographic works, motion pictures, and other audiovisual works.
5. *Sound Recordings* (Form SR)—musical, spoken, or other sounds, including any audio- or videotapes you might create.

Things You Cannot Copyright

You can't copyright ideas or procedures for doing, making, or build-ing things, but the *expression* of an idea fixed in a tangible medium may be copyrightable—such as a book explaining a new system or technique. Brand names, trade names, slogans, and phrases cannot be copyrighted, either, although they might be entitled to protection under trademark laws.

The design on a craft object can be copyrighted, but only if it can be identified separately from the object itself. Objects them-selves (a decorated coffee mug, a box, a tote bag) cannot be copy-righted.

Copyright Registration Tips

First, understand that you do not have to formally copyright any-thing because copyright protection exists from the moment a work is created, whether you add a copyright notice or not.

So why file at all? The answer is simple: If you don't file the form and pay the fee (currently $30), you'll never be able to take anyone to court for stealing your work. Therefore, in each instance where copy-right protection is considered, you need to decide how important your work is to you in terms of dollars and cents, and ask yourself whether you value it enough to pay to protect it. Would you actually be willing to pay court costs to defend your copyright, should some-one steal it from you? If you never intend to go to court, there's lit-tle use in officially registering a copyright; but because it costs you nothing to add a copyright notice to your work, you are foolish not to do this. (See sidebar, Protecting Your Copyrights, on page 262.)

If you do decide to file a copyright application, contact the Copyright Office and request the appropriate forms. When you file the copyright application form (which is easy to complete), you must include with it two copies of the work. Ordinarily, two actual copies of copyrighted items must be deposited, but certain items are exempt from deposit requirements, including all three-dimensional sculptural works and any works published only as reproduced in or on jewelry, dolls, toys, games, plaques, floor cover-ings, textile and other fabrics, packaging materials, or any useful article. In these cases, two photographs or drawings of the item are sufficient.

Note that the Copyright Office does not compare deposit copies to determine whether works submitted for registration are similar to any material already copyrighted. It is the sender's responsibility to determine the originality of what's being copyrighted. (See discussion of "original" in the next section, under Respecting the Copyrights of Others.)

Mandatory Deposit Requirements

Although you do not have to officially register a copyright claim, it *is* mandatory to deposit two copies of all "published works" for the collections of the Library of Congress within 3 months after publication. Failure to make the deposit may subject the copyright owner to fines and other monetary liabilities, but it does not affect copyright protection. No special form is required for this mandatory deposit.

Note that the term *published works* pertains not just to the publication of printed matter, but to the public display of any item. Thus you "publish" your originally designed craftwork when you first show it at a craft fair, in a shop, on your Web site, or any other public place.

Respecting the Copyrights of Others

Just as there are several things you must do to protect your "intellectual creations," there are several things you must not do if you wish to avoid legal problems with other copyright holders.

Copyright infringement occurs whenever anyone violates the exclusive rights covered by copyright. If and when a copyright case goes to court, the copyright holder who has been infringed on must

Changing Things

Many crafters have mistakenly been led to believe that they can copy the work of others if they simply change this or that so their creation doesn't look exactly like the one they have copied. But many copyright court cases have hinged on someone taking "a substantial part" of someone else's design and claiming it as their own. If your "original creation" bears even the slightest resemblance to the product you've copied—and you are caught selling it in the commercial marketplace—there could be legal problems.

Crafters often combine the parts of two or three patterns in an attempt to come up with their own original patterns, but often this only compounds the possible copyright problems. Let's imagine you're making a doll. You might take the head from one pattern, the arms and legs from another, and the unique facial features from another. You may think you have developed an original creation (and perhaps an original pattern

prove that his or her work is the original creation and that the two works are so similar that the alleged infringer must have copied it. This is not always an easy matter, for *original* is a difficult word to define. Even the Copyright Office has trouble here, which is why so many cases that go to court end up setting precedents.

In any copyright case, there will be discussions about "substantial similarity," instances where two people actually have created the same thing simultaneously, loss of profits, or damage to one's business or reputation. If you were found guilty of copyright infringement, at the very least you would probably be ordered to pay to the original creator all profits derived from the sale of the copyrighted work to date. You would also have to agree to refund any orders you might receive for the work in the future. In some copyright cases where the original creator has experienced considerable financial loss, penalties for copyright infringement have been as high as $100,000. As you can see, this is not a matter to take lightly.

you might sell), but you haven't. Because the original designer of any of the features you've copied might recognize her work in your "original creation" or published pattern, she could come after you for infringing on "a substantial part" of her design. In this case, all you've done is multiply your possibilities for a legal confrontation with three copyright holders.

"But I can't create my own original designs and patterns!" you moan. Many who have said this in the past were mistaken. With time and practice, most crafters are able to develop products that are original in design, and I believe you can do this, too. Meanwhile, check out Dover Publications' *Pictorial Archive* series of books (see A "Things to Do" Checklist with Related Resources). Here you will find thousands of copyright-free designs and motifs you can use on your craft work or in needlework projects. And don't forget the wealth of design material in museums and old books that have fallen into the public domain. (See sidebar, What's in the Public Domain? on page 270.)

This is a complex topic beyond the scope of this book, but any book on copyright law will provide additional information if you should ever need it. What's important here is that you fully understand the importance of being careful to respect the legal rights of others. As a crafts-business owner, you could possibly infringe on someone else's designs when you (1) quote someone in an article, periodical, or book you've written; (2) photocopy copyrighted materials; or (3) share information on the Internet. Following is a brief discussion of these topics.

1. **Be careful when quoting from a published source.** If you're writing an article or book and wish to quote someone's words from any published source (book, magazine, Internet, and so on), you should always obtain written permission first. Granted, minor quotations from published sources are okay when they fall under the Copyright Office's Fair Use Doctrine, but unless you completely understand this doctrine, you should protect yourself by

obtaining permission before you quote anyone in one of your own written works. It is not necessarily the quantity of the quote, but the value of the quoted material to the copyright owner.

In particular, never *ever* use a published poem in one of your written works without written permission. To the poet, this is a "whole work," much the same as a book is a whole work to an author. Although the use of one or two lines of a poem, or a paragraph from a book may be considered "fair use," many publishers now require written permission even for this short reproduction of a copyrighted work.

2. **Photocopying can be dangerous.** Teachers often photocopy large sections of a book (sometimes whole books) for distribution to their students, but this is a flagrant violation of the copyright law. Some publishers may grant photocopying of part of a work if it is to be used only once as a teaching aid, but written permission must always be obtained first.

   It is also a violation of the copyright law to photocopy patterns for sale or trade because such use denies the creator the profit from a copy that might have been sold.

3. **Don't share copyrighted information on the Internet.** People everywhere are lifting material from *Reader's Digest* and other copyrighted publications and "sharing" them on the Internet through e-mail messages, bulletin boards, and the like. *This is a very dangerous thing to do.* "But I didn't see a copyright notice," you might say, or "It indicated the author was anonymous." What you must remember is that *everything* gains copyright protection the moment it is created, whether a copyright notice is attached to it or not. Many "anonymous" items on the Internet are actually copyrighted poems and articles put there by someone who not only

violated the copyright law but compounded the matter by failing to give credit to the original creator.

If you were to pick up one of those "anonymous" pieces of information and put it in an article or book of your own, the original copyright owner, upon seeing his or her work in your publication, would have good grounds for a lawsuit. Remember, pleading ignorance of the law is never a good excuse.

Clearly there is no financial gain to be realized by violating the rights of a copyright holder when it means that any day you might be contacted by a lawyer and threatened with a lawsuit. As stated in my *Crafts Business Answer Book & Resource Guide:*

> The best way to avoid copyright infringement problems is to follow the "Golden Rule" proposed by a United States Supreme Court justice: "Take not from others to such an extent and in such a manner that you would be resentful if they so took from you."

Using Commercial Patterns and Designs

Beginning crafters who lack design skills commonly make products for sale using commercial patterns, designs in books, or how-to instructions for projects found in magazines. The problem here is that all of these things are published for the general consumer market and offered for *personal use* only. Because they are all protected by copyright, that means only the copyright holder has the right to profit from their use.

That said, let me ease your mind by saying that the sale of products made from copyrighted patterns, designs, and magazine how-to projects is probably not going to cause any problems *as long as sales are limited, and they yield a profit only to you, the crafter.* That means no sales through shops of any kind where a sales commission or profit is received by a third party, and absolutely no wholesaling of such products.

It's not that designers and publishers are concerned about your sale of a few craft or needlework items to friends and local buyers; what they are fighting to protect with the legality of copyrights is their right to sell their own designs or finished products in the commercial marketplace. You may find that some patterns, designs, or projects state "no mass-production." You are not mass-producing if you make a dozen handcrafted items for sale at a craft fair or holiday boutique, but you would definitely be considered a mass-producer if you made dozens, or hundreds, for sale in shops.

Consignment sales fall into a kind of gray area that requires some commonsense judgment on your part. This is neither wholesaling nor selling direct to consumers. One publisher might con-

What's in the Public Domain?

For all works created after January 1, 1978, the copyright lasts for the life of the author or creator plus 50 years after his or her death. For works created before 1978, there are different terms, which you can obtain from any book in your library on copyright law.

Once material falls into the public domain, it can never be copyrighted again. As a general rule, anything with a copyright date more than 75 years ago is probably in the public domain, but you can never be sure without doing a thorough search. Some characters in old books—such as Beatrix Potter's *Peter Rabbit*—are now protected under the trademark law as business logos. For more information on this, ask the Copyright Office to send you its circular, "How to Investigate the Copyright Status of a Work."

Early American craft and needlework patterns of all kind are in the public domain because they were created before the copyright law was a reality. Such old patterns may

sider such sales a violation of a copyright while another might not. Whenever specific guidelines for the use of a pattern, design, or how-to project are not given, the only way to know for sure if you are operating on safe legal ground is to write to the publisher and get written permission on where you can sell reproductions of the item in question.

Now let's take a closer look at the individual types of patterns, designs, and how-to projects you might consider using once you enter the crafts marketplace.

Craft, Toy, and Garment Patterns

Today, the consumer has access to thousands of sewing patterns plus toy, craft, needlework, and woodworking patterns of every kind and description found in books, magazines, and design or project leaflets. Whether you can use such patterns for commercial use

show up in books and magazines that are copyrighted, but the copyright in this case extends only to the book or magazine itself and the way in which a pattern has been presented to readers, along with the way in which the how-to-make instructions have been written. The actual patterns themselves cannot be copyrighted by anyone at this point.

Quilts offer an interesting example. If a contemporary quilt designer takes a traditional quilt pattern and does something unusual with it in terms of material or colors, this new creation would qualify for a copyright, with the protection being given to the quilt as a work of art, not to the traditional pattern itself, which is still in the public domain. Thus you could take that same traditional quilt pattern and do something else with it for publication, but you could not publish the contemporary designer's copyrighted version of that same pattern.

depends largely on who has published the pattern and owns the copyright, and what the copyright holder's policy happens to be for how buyers may use those patterns.

To avoid copyright problems when using patterns of any kind, the first thing you need to do is look for some kind of notice on the pattern packet or publication containing the pattern. In checking some patterns, I found that those sold by *Woman's Day* state specifically that reproductions of the designs may not be sold, bartered, or traded. *Good Housekeeping,* on the other hand, gives permission to use their patterns for "income-producing activities." When in doubt, ask!

Whereas the general rule for selling reproductions made from commercial patterns is "no wholesaling and no sales to shops," items made from the average garment pattern (such as an apron, vest, shirt, or simple dress) purchased in the local fabric store *may* be an exception. My research suggests that selling such items in your local consignment shop or craft mall isn't likely to be much of a problem because the sewing pattern companies aren't on the lookout for copyright violators the way individual craft designers and major corporations are. (And most people who sew end up changing those patterns and using different decorations to such a degree that pattern companies might not recognize those patterns even if they were looking for them.)

On the other hand, commercial garment patterns that have been designed by name designers should never be used without permission. In most cases, you would have to obtain a licensing agreement for the commercial use of such patterns.

Avoid this pitfall: In addition to problems in using copyrighted patterns, anyone who uses fabric to make a product for the marketplace has yet another concern: designer *fabrics.* Always look at the selvage of a patterned fabric. If you see a copyright notice with a designer's name and the phrase "for individual consumption only" (or similar wordage), *do not use this fabric to make any item for sale without first obtaining written permission from the fabric manu-*

facturer. In many instances, designer fabrics can be used commercially only when a license has been obtained for this purpose.

Be especially careful about selling reproductions of toys and dolls made from commercial patterns or design books. Many are likely to be for popular copyrighted characters being sold in the commercial marketplace. In such cases, the pattern company will have a special licensing arrangement with the toy or doll manufacturer to sell the pattern, and reproductions for sale by individual crafters will be strictly prohibited.

Take a Raggedy Ann doll, for example. The fact that you've purchased a pattern to make such a doll does not give you the right to sell a finished likeness of that doll any more than your purchase of a piece of artwork gives you the right to re-create it for sale in some other form, such as notepaper or calendars. Only the original creator has such rights. You have simply purchased the *physical property* for private use.

> **Avoid this pitfall:** Don't *ever* make and sell *any* replica in any material of a famous copyrighted character anywhere, such as the Walt Disney or Warner Brothers characters, Snoopy, or the Sesame Street gang. It's true that a lot of crafters are doing this, but they are inviting serious legal trouble if they ever get caught. Disney is particularly aggressive in defending its copyrights.

How-To Projects in Magazines and Books

Each magazine and book publisher has its own policy about the use of its art, craft, or needlework projects. How those projects may be used depends on who owns the copyright to the published projects. In some instances, craft and needlework designers sell their original designs outright to publishers of books, leaflets, or magazines. Other designers authorize only a one-time use of their projects, which gives them the right to republish or sell their designs to another market or license them to a manufacturer. If guidelines about selling finished

▼▼▼

Online Help

Today, one of the best ways to network and learn about business is to get on the Internet. The many online resources included in A "Things to Do" Checklist in the next section will give you a jump start and lead to many exciting discoveries.

For continuing help and advice from Barbara Brabec, be sure to visit her Web sites at www.crafter.com/brabec and www.IdeaForest.com. Here you will find a wealth of information to help you profit from your crafts, including newsletters, reprints of some of her crafts marketing and business columns, recommended books, and links to hundreds of other art and crafts sites on the Web.

You can also get Barbara's business advice in her monthly columns in *Crafts Magazine.*

▲▲

products do not appear somewhere in the magazine or on the copyright page of a book, you should always write and get permission to make such items for sale. In your letter, explain how many items you would like to make, and where you plan to sell them, as that could make a big difference in the reply you receive.

In case you missed the special note on the copyright page of this book, you *can* make and sell all of the projects featured in this and any other book in Prima's FOR FUN & PROFIT series.

As a columnist for *Crafts Magazine,* I can also tell you that its readers have the right to use its patterns and projects for money-making purposes, but only to the extent that sales are limited to places where the crafter is the only one who profits from their use. That means selling directly to individuals, with no sales in shops of any kind where a third party would also realize some profit from a sale. Actually, this is a good rule-of-thumb guideline to use if you plan to sell only a few items of any project or pattern published in any magazine, book, or leaflet.

In summary, products that aren't original in design will sell, but their market is limited, and they will never be able to command the kind of prices that original-design items enjoy. Generally speaking, the more original the product line, the greater one's chances for building a profitable crafts business.

As your business grows, questions about copyrights will arise, and you will have to do a little research to get the answers you need. Your library should have several books on this topic and there is a wealth of information on the Internet. (Just use your search button and type "copyright information.") If you have a technical copyright question, remember that you can always call the Copyright Office and speak to someone who can answer it and send you additional information. Note, however, that regulations prohibit the Copyright Office from giving legal advice or opinions concerning the rights of persons in connection with cases of alleged copyright infringement.

10. To Keep Growing, Keep Learning

Everything we do, every action we take, affects our life in one way or another. Reading a book is a simple act, indeed, but trust me when I say that your reading of this particular book *could ultimately change your life*. I know this to be true because thousands of men and women have written to me over the years to tell me how their lives changed after they read one or another of my books and decided to start a crafts business. My life has changed, too, as a result of reading books by other authors.

Many years ago, the purchase of a book titled *You Can Whittle and Carve* unleashed a flood of creativity in me that has yet to cease. That simple book helped me to discover unknown craft talents, which in turn led me to start my first crafts business at home. That experience prepared me for the message I would find a decade later in the book *On Writing Well* by William Zinsser. This author changed my life by giving me the courage to try my hand at writing professionally. Dozens of books later, I had learned a lot about the art and craft of writing well and making a living in the process.

Now you know why I believe reading should be given top priority in your life. Generally speaking, the more serious you become about anything you're interested in, the more reading you will need to do. This will take time, but the benefits will be enormous. If a crafts business is your current passion, this book contains all you need to know to get started. To keep growing, read some of the wonderful books recommended in the Resources. (If you don't find the books you need in your local library, ask your librarian to obtain them for you through the inter-library loan program.) Join one or more of the organizations recommended. Subscribe to a few periodicals or magazines, and "grow your business" through networking with others who share your interests.

Motivational Tips

As you start your new business or expand a money-making hobby already begun, consider the following suggestions:

- *Start an "Achievement Log."* Day by day, our small achievements may seem insignificant, but viewed in total after several weeks or months, they give us important perspective. Reread your achievement log periodically in the future, especially on days when you feel down in the dumps. Make entries at least once a week, noting such things as new customers or accounts acquired, publicity you've gotten, a new product you've designed, the brochure or catalog you've just completed, positive feedback received from others, new friendships, and financial gains.

- *Live your dream.* The mind is a curious thing—it can be trained to think success is possible or to think that success is only for other people. Most of our fears never come true, so allowing our minds to dwell on what may or may not happen cripples us, preventing us from moving ahead, from having confidence, and from living out our dreams. Instead of "facing fear," focus on the result you want. This may automatically eliminate the fear.

■ *Think positively.* As Murphy has proven time and again, what can go wrong will, and usually at the worst possible moment. It matters little whether the thing that has gone wrong was caused by circumstances beyond our control or by a mistake in judgment. What does matter is how we deal with the problem at hand. A positive attitude and the ability to remain flexible at all times are two of the most important ingredients for success in any endeavor.

■ *Don't be afraid to fail.* We often learn more from failure than from success. When you make a mistake, chalk it up to experience and consider it a good lesson well learned. The more you learn, the more self-confident you will become.

■ *Temper your "dreams of riches" with thoughts of reality.* Remember that "success" can also mean being in control of your own life, making new friends, or discovering a new world of possibilities.

Until now you may have lacked the courage to get your craft ideas off the ground, but now that you've seen how other people have accomplished their goals, I hope you feel more confident and adventurous and are ready to capitalize on your creativity. By following the good advice in this book, you can stop dreaming about all the things you want to do and start making plans to do them!

I'm not trying to make home-business owners out of everyone who reads this book, but my goal is definitely to give you a shove in that direction if you're teetering on the edge, wanting something more than just a profitable hobby. It's wonderful to have a satisfying hobby, and even better to have one that pays for itself; but the nicest thing of all is a real home business that lets you fully utilize your creative talents and abilities while also adding to the family income.

"The things I want to know are in books," Abraham Lincoln once said. "My best friend is the person who'll get me a book I ain't read." You now hold in your hands a book that has taught you many things you wanted to know. To make it a *life-changing book,* all you have to do is act on the information you've been given.

I wish you a joyful journey and a potful of profits!

A "Things to Do" Checklist with Related Resources

INSTRUCTIONS: Read through this entire section, noting the different things you need to do to get your crafts business "up and running." Use the checklist as a plan, checking off each task as it is completed and obtaining any recommended resources. Where indicated, note the date action was taken so you have a reminder about any follow-up action that should be taken.

Business Start-Up Checklist

☐ Call city hall or county clerk

☐ to register fictitious business name
☐ to see if you need a business license or permit
☐ to check on local zoning laws
(info also available in your library)

*Follow up:*_____

☐ Call state capitol

☐ secretary of state: to register your business name; ask about a license
☐ Department of Revenue: to apply for sales tax number

*Follow up:*_____

☐ Call your local telephone company about

☐ cost of a separate phone line for business
☐ cost of an additional personal line for Internet access

□ any special options for home-based businesses

*Follow up:*_____

□ Call your insurance agent(s) to discuss

□ business rider on house insurance
(or need for separate in-home insurance policy)
□ benefits of an umbrella policy for extra liability insurance
□ using your car for business
(how this may affect your insurance)

*Follow up:*_____

□ Call several banks or S&Ls in your area to

□ compare cost of a business checking account
□ get price of a safety deposit box for valuable business records

*Follow up:*_____

□ Visit office and computer supply stores to check on

□ manual bookkeeping systems, such as the
Dome Simplified Monthly
□ accounting software
□ standard invoices and other helpful business forms

*Follow up:*_____

□ Call National Association of Enrolled Agents at (800) 424-4339

□ to get a referral to a tax professional in your area
□ to get answers to any tax questions you may have (no charge)

*Follow up:*_____

□ Contact government agencies for information relative to your
business.

(See Government Agencies checklist.)

□ Request free brochures from organizations

(See Craft and Home-Business Organizations.)

☐ Obtain sample issues or subscribe to selected publications

(See Recommended Crafts-Business Periodicals.)

☐ Obtain other information of possible help to your business

(See Other Services and Suppliers.)

☐ Get acquainted with the business information available to you in your library.

(See list of Recommended Business Books and Helpful Library Directories.)

Government Agencies

☐ Consumer Product Safety Commission (CPSC), Washington, DC 20207. (800) 638-2772. Information Services: (301) 504-0000. Web site: www.cpsc.gov. (Includes a "Talk to Us" e-mail address where you can get answers to specific questions.) If you make toys or other products for children, garments (especially children's wear), or use any kind of paint, varnish, lacquer, or shellac on your products, obtain the following free booklets:

☐ *The Consumer Product Safety Act of 1972*
☐ *The Flammable Fabrics Act*

Date Contacted:_____Information Received:_____

*Follow up:*_____

☐ Copyright Office, Register of Copyrights, Library of Congress, Washington, DC 20559. To hear recorded messages on the Copyright Office's automated message system (general information, registration procedures, copyright search info, and so on), call (202) 707-3000. You can also get the same information online at www.loc.gov/copyright.

To get free copyright forms, a complete list of all publications available, or to speak personally to someone who will answer your special questions, call (202) 797-9100. In particular, ask for:

☐ Circular R1, *The Nuts and Bolts of Copyright*
☐ Circular R2 (a list of publications available)

Date Contacted:_____Information Received:_____

*Follow up:*_____

☐ Department of Labor. If you should ever hire an employee
or independent contractor, contact your local Labor Department, Wage & Hour Division, for guidance on what you must
do to be completely legal. (Check your phone book under
"U.S. Government.")

Date Contacted:_____Information Received:_____

*Follow up:*_____

☐ Federal Trade Commission (FTC), 6th Street and Pennsylvania
Avenue, NW, Washington, DC 20580. Web site: www.ftc.gov. Request
any of the following booklets relative to your craft or business:

☐ *Textile Fiber Products Identification Act*
☐ *Wool Products Labeling Act of 1939*
☐ *Care Labeling of Textile Wearing Apparel*
☐ *The Hand Knitting Yarn Industry* (booklet)
☐ *Truth-in-Advertising Rules*
☐ *Thirty-Day Mail-Order Rule*

Date Contacted:_____Information Received:_____

Follow up: _____

☐ Internal Revenue Service (IRS). Check the Internet at
www.irs.gov to read the following information online or
call your local IRS office or (800) 829-1040 to get the following booklets and other free tax information:

☐ *Tax Guide for Small Business—#334*
☐ *Business Use of Your Home—#587*
☐ *Tax Information for Direct Sellers*

Date Contacted:_____Information Received:_____

*Follow up:*_____

☐ Patent and Trademark Office (PTO), Washington, DC 20231. Web site: www.uspto.gov.

For patent and trademark information 24 hours a day, call (800) 786-9199 (in northern Virginia, call (703) 308-9000) to hear various messages about patents and trademarks or to order the following booklets:

☐ *Basic Facts about Patents*
☐ *Basic Facts about Trademarks*

To search the PTO's online database of all registered trademarks, go to www.uspto.gov/tmdb/index.html.

Date Contacted:_____Information Received:_____

*Follow up:*_____

☐ Social Security Hotline. (800) 772-1213. By calling this number, you can hear automated messages, order information booklets, or speak directly to someone who can answer specific questions.

Date Contacted:_____Information Received:_____

*Follow up:*_____

☐ U.S. Small Business Administration (SBA). (800) U-ASK-SBA. Call this number to hear a variety of prerecorded messages on starting and financing a business. Weekdays, you can speak personally to an SBA adviser to get answers to specific questions and request such free business publications as:

☐ *Starting Your Business* —#CO-0028
☐ *Resource Directory for Small Business Management*—#CO-0042 (a list of low-cost publications available from the SBA)

The SBA's mission is to help people get into business and stay there. One-on-one counseling, training, and workshops are available through 950 small-business development centers across the country. Help is also available from local district offices of the SBA in the form of free business counseling and training from SCORE volunteers. The SBA office in Washington has a special Women's Business Enterprise section that provides free information on loans, tax deductions, and other financial matters. District offices offer special training programs in management, marketing, and accounting.

A wealth of business information is also available online at www.sba.gov and www.business.gov (the U.S. Business Adviser site). To learn whether there is an SBA office near you, look under U.S. Government in your telephone directory, or call the SBA's toll-free number.

Date Contacted:_____Information Received:_____

*Follow up:*_____

☐ SCORE (Service Corps of Retired Executives). (800) 634-0245. There are more than 12,400 SCORE members who volunteer their time and expertise to small-business owners. Many crafts businesses have received valuable in-depth counseling and training simply by calling the organization and asking how to connect with a SCORE volunteer in their area.

In addition, the organization offers e-mail counseling via the Internet at www.score.org. You simply enter the specific expertise required and retrieve a list of e-mail counselors who represent the best match by industry and topic. Questions can then be sent by e-mail to the counselor of your choice for response.

Date Contacted:_____Information Received:_____

*Follow up:*_____

Craft and Home-Business Organizations

In addition to the regular benefits of membership in an organization related to your art or craft (fellowship, networking, educational conferences or workshops, marketing opportunities, and so on), membership may also bring special business services, such as insurance programs, merchant card services, and discounts on supplies and materials. Each of the following organizations will send you membership information on request.

☐ The American Association of Home-Based Businesses, PO Box 10023, Rockville, MD 20849. (800) 447-9710. Web site: www.aahbb.org. This organization has chapters throughout the country. Members have access to merchant card services, discounted business products and services, prepaid legal services, and more.

Date Contacted:_____Information Received:_____

*Follow up:*_____

☐ American Crafts Council, 72 Spring Street, New York, NY 10012. (800)-724-0859. Web site: www.craftcouncil.org. Membership in this organization will give you access to a property and casualty insurance policy that will cost between $250 and $500 a year, depending on your city, state, and the value of items being insured in your art or crafts studio. The policy includes insurance for a craftsperson's work in the studio, in transit, or at a show; $1 million coverage for bodily injury and property damage in studio or away; and $1 million worth of product liability insurance. This policy is from American Phoenix Corporation; staff members will answer your specific questions when you call (800) 274-6364, ext. 337.

Date Contacted:_____Information Received:_____

*Follow up:*_____

☐ Arts & Crafts Business Solutions, 2804 Bishop Gate Drive, Raleigh, NC 27613. (800) 873-1192. This company, known in the industry as the Arts Group, offers a bankcard service specifically for and tailored to the needs of the art and crafts marketplace. Several differently priced packages are available, and complete information is available on request.

Date Contacted:_____Information Received:_____

*Follow up:*_____

☐ Home Business Institute, Inc., PO Box 301, White Plains, NY 10605-0301. (888) DIAL-HBI; Fax: (914) 946-6694. Web site: www.hbiweb.com. Membership benefits include insurance programs (medical insurance and in-home business policy that includes some liability insurance); savings on telephone services, office supplies, and merchant account enrollment; and free advertising services.

Date Contacted:_____Information Received:_____

*Follow up:*_____

☐ National Craft Association (NCA), 1945 E. Ridge Road, Suite 5178, Rochester, NY 14622-2647. (800) 715-9594. Web site: www.craftassoc.com. Members of NCA have access to a comprehensive package of services, including merchant account services; discounts on business services and products; a prepaid legal program; a check-guarantee merchant program; checks by fax, phone, or e-mail; and insurance programs. Of special interest to this book's readers is the "Crafters Business Insurance" policy (through RLI Insurance Co.) that includes coverage for business property; art/craft merchandise or inventory at home, in transit, or at a show; theft away from premises; up to $1 million in both personal and product liability insurance; loss of business income; and more. Members have the option to select the exact benefits they need. Premiums range from $150 to $300, depending on location, value of average inventory, and the risks associated with one's art or craft.

Date Contacted:_____Information Received:_____

*Follow up:*_____

Recommended Crafts-Business Periodicals

Membership in an organization generally includes a subscription to a newsletter or magazine that will be helpful to your business. Here are additional craft periodicals you should sample or subscribe to:

☐ *The Crafts Report—The Business Journal for the Crafts Industry,* Box 1992, Wilmington, DE 19899. (800) 777-7098. On the Internet at www.craftsreport.com. A monthly magazine covering all areas of crafts-business management and marketing, including special-interest columns and show listings.

☐ *Craft Supply Magazine—The Industry Journal for the Professional Crafter,* Krause Publications, Inc., 700 E. State Street, Iowa, WI 54990-0001. (800) 258-0929. Web site: www.krause.com. A monthly magazine that includes crafts-business and marketing articles and wholesale supply sources.

☐ *Home Business Report,* 2949 Ash Street, Abbotsford, BC, V2S 4G5 Canada. (604) 857-1788; Fax: (604) 854-3087. Canada's premier home-business magazine, relative to both general and craft-related businesses.

☐ *SAC Newsmonthly,* 414 Avenue B, PO Box 159, Bogalusa, LA 70429-0159. (800) TAKE-SAC; Fax: (504) 732-3744. A monthly national show guide that also includes business articles for professional crafters.

☐ *Sunshine Artist Magazine,* 2600 Temple Drive, Winter Park, FL 32789. (800) 597-2573; Fax: (407) 539-1499. Web site: www. sunshineartist.com. America's premier show and festival guide. Each monthly issue contains business and marketing articles of interest to both artists and craftspeople.

Other Services and Suppliers

Contact any of the following companies that offer information or services of interest to you.

☐ American Express. For merchant account information, call the Merchant Establishment Services Department at (800) 445-AMEX.

Date Contacted:_____Information Received:_____

*Follow up:*_____

☐ Dover Publications, 31 E 2nd Street, Mineola, NY 11501. Your source for thousands of copyright-free designs and motifs you can use in your craftwork or needlecraft projects. Request a free catalog of books in the *Pictorial Archive* series.

Date Contacted:_____Information Received:_____

*Follow up:*_____

☐ Novus Services, Inc. For merchant account information, call (800) 347-6673.

Date Contacted:_____Information Received:_____

*Follow up:*_____

☐ Volunteer Lawyers for the Arts (VLA), 1 E. 53rd Street, New York, NY 10022. Legal hotline: (212) 319-2910. If you ever need an attorney, and cannot afford one, contact this nonprofit organization, which has chapters all over the country. In addition to providing legal aid for performing and visual artists and craftspeople (individually or in groups), the VLA also provides a range of educational services, including issuing publications concerning taxes, accounting, and insurance.

Date Contacted:_____Information Received:_____

*Follow up:*_____

☐ Widby Enterprises USA, 4321 Crestfield Road, Knoxville, TN 37921-3104. (888) 522-2458. Web site: www.widbylabel.com. Standard and custom-designed labels that meet federal labeling requirements.

Date Contacted:_____Information Received:_____

*Follow up:*_____

Recommended Business Books

When you have specific business questions not answered in this beginner's guide, check your library for the following books. Any not on library shelves can be obtained through the library's inter-library loan program.

☐ *Business and Legal Forms for Crafts* by Tad Crawford (Allworth Press)

☐ *Business Forms and Contracts (in Plain English) for Crafts People* by Leonard D. DuBoff (Interweave Press)

☐ *Crafting as a Business* by Wendy Rosen (Chilton)

☐ *The Crafts Business Answer Book & Resource Guide: Answers to Hundreds of Troublesome Questions about Starting, Marketing & Managing a Homebased Business Efficiently, Legally & Profitably* by Barbara Brabec (M. Evans & Co.)

☐ *Creative Cash: How to Profit from Your Special Artistry, Creativity, Hand Skills, and Related Know-How* by Barbara Brabec (Prima Publishing)

☐ *422 Tax Deductions for Businesses & Self-Employed Individuals* by Bernard Kamoroff (Bell Springs Publishing)

☐ *Homemade Money: How to Select, Start, Manage, Market, and Multiply the Profits of a Business at Home* by Barbara Brabec (Betterway Books)

☐ *How to Register Your Own Trademark with Forms*, 2nd ed., by Mark Warda (Sourcebooks)

☐ *INC Yourself: How to Profit by Setting Up Your Own Corporation*, by Judith H. McQuown (HarperBusiness)

☐ *Make It Profitable! How to make Your Art, Craft, Design, Writing or Publishing Business More Efficient, More Satisfying, and More Profitable* by Barbara Brabec (M. Evans & Co.)

☐ *Patent, Copyright & Trademark: A Desk Reference to Intellectual Property Law* by Stephen Elias (Nolo Press)

☐ *The Perils of Partners* by Irwin Gray (Smith-Johnson Publisher)

☐ *Small Time Operator: How to Start Your Own Business, Keep Your Books, Pay Your Taxes & Stay Out of Trouble* by Bernard Kamoroff (Bell Springs Publishing)

☐ *Trademark: How to Name a Business & Product* by Kate McGrath and Stephen Elias (Nolo Press)

Helpful Library Directories

☐ *Books in Print* and *Guide to Forthcoming Books* (how to find out which books are still in print, and which books will soon be published)

☐ *Encyclopedia of Associations* (useful in locating an organization dedicated to your art or craft)

- ☐ *National Trade and Professional Associations of the U.S.* (more than 7,000 associations listed alphabetically and geographically)

- ☐ *The Standard Periodical Directory* (annual guide to U.S. and Canadian periodicals)

- ☐ *Thomas Register of American Manufacturers* (helpful when you're looking for raw material suppliers or the owners of brand names and trademarks)

- ☐ *Trademark Register of the U.S.* (contains every trademark currently registered with the U.S. Patent & Trademark Office)

Glossary

Basting: Temporarily attaching two pieces of fabric together by hand or machine until they are sewn permanently. It is used when pinning will not adequately hold the pieces together or to give a realistic idea of how the seam will look when it is sewn.

Bent trimmers: Scissors that are usually at least 7 inches long with angled or "bent" handles that allow fabric to lie flat during cutting.

Bobbin: The spool around which the bobbin or lower thread is wound on a sewing machine.

Bobbin case: The plastic or metal case that holds the bobbin in a sewing machine. It can be removable or built-in.

Bonding: A way of producing fabric in which textile fibers are fused together with an adhesive or bonding agent.

Dressmaker's shears: See Bent trimmers.

Feed dogs: Metal bars with zigzag edges located on the surface of sewing machines under the needle and presser foot that draw the fabric through while sewing. They are matched by the presser foot.

Felt: Fabric, originally made from wool but now also manufactured from synthetics, that is made by agitating fibers with moisture, heat, and pressure rather than by weaving or knitting strands of fibers together.

Flax: The plant from which linen fabric is made.

Grain: The direction in which the threads composing the fabric run. Every woven fabric contains crosswise threads that are worked over and under sturdier lengthwise threads.

Hand: The feel of the fabric, including the weight (e.g., heavy, light, or drapey) and texture (e.g., smooth, soft, coarse, nubby).

Interfacing: Fabric that is used to reinforce and support outer fabric in crafts and clothing for the purpose of maintaining shape and firmness.

Invoice: An itemized list of goods shipped usually specifying the price and the terms of sale (see Net 30).

Ironing: Using the iron in a back-and-forth motion without a lot of pressure to remove wrinkles. It can be done with a dry iron or with steam.

Market saturation: The condition of having sold all of an item you are likely to sell at a certain price or in a certain location, or both.

Mission statement: A statement of intent, verbal or written, that defines and helps one perform an activity. In simple words, it explains what you want to do and can include how and when you want to do it.

Net 30: A term of sale used on invoices that means a customer must pay within 30 days of being billed.

Odd pricing: Giving the illusion of a lower price, such as by charging $19.95 instead of $20.

Off-grain: A term used to describe fabric when the lengthwise and crosswise threads are not at perfect 90-degree angles.

Overcast stitch: A hand stitch used for finishing raw edges of fabric by encasing them with thread.

Pinking shears: Shears that cut zigzag, ravel-resistant edges on fabric. They can also be used for decorative finishes.

Presser foot: A foot-shaped metal piece that puts pressure on the fabric from above so the feed dogs can draw it through.

Pressing: Using the iron to permanently shape and mold areas into place by applying pressure (and steam, if desired) in an up-and-down motion.

Retail selling: Selling directly to consumers at full price.

Rotary cutter: A new type of cutter that resembles a pizza cutter and can be used instead of shears for cutting fabric. Some people feel they are faster and more accurate.

Running stitch: The most basic hand stitch, done by evenly weaving the needle in and out of the fabric. It is used for basting or sewing flat seams together.

Seam gauge: A small metal ruler, usually $5/8 \times 6$ inches, with a sliding gauge used for calibrating the width of seams or other measurements in sewing.

Selvage: The woven border resulting at the lengthwise sides of the fabric when the crosswise threads reverse direction.

Serger: A specialty sewing machine that performs unique functions including sewing, trimming, and overcasting seams all in one motion. Some sergers also do decorative stitches and hems.

Setting the press: Allowing items to become cool and dry before moving them after ironing or pressing to "set" them or prolong the finished look.

Sewing scissors: Usually less than 7 inches in length with straight handles and one pointed and one rounded tip. They are used for clipping and trimming seams.

Slip stitch: A nearly invisible hand stitch that is used to join two folded edges or one folded edge to a flat surface, as in hemming.

Test marketing: Selling or giving away a sample amount of a product to see how consumers will accept it.

Topstitching: Stitching done on the surface by hand or machine that is always visible.

Vanity pricing: Pricing an item higher than necessary to make it appear more valuable.

Wholesale selling: Selling goods to someone at a discount who will then resell them to consumers at retail prices.

Word-of-mouth: A term used in advertising to describe the process of satisfied customers telling potential customers about products they like, thus prompting them to buy.

Resources

▼▼▼

Recommended Books

Following is a listing of books to help you in your craft sewing venture. Books without contact information in the listing are readily available in bookstores; self-published titles with contact information included are available only by mail from the author or publisher indicated.

Learning to Sew

Traditionally, sewing books do not sell well in bookstores like Barnes & Noble, so they are more available in fabric and craft stores. In addition, the Web site Amazon.com features, or can order, many sewing books. Don't forget your local library! All of the following books are easy to read and understand but also are very thorough.

101 Great Little Gifts by Sandra Foose (Oxmoor House, 1994). This has cute ideas and directions for simple projects. This is a good book for beginners because it contains doable projects that are also useful and attractive.

All about Wool, All about Silk, and *All about Cotton* by Julie Parker (Rain City Publishing, 1991). These are all excellent fabric references. They will help you understand the differences between fabrics, their characteristics, and their end uses.

The Complete Book of Sewing Shortcuts by Claire Shaeffer (Sterling, 1981). This book shows great shortcuts and techniques for just about every sewing situation. More than 800 step-by-step drawings aid beginners.

Sewing Essentials by Singer Sewing Reference Library (Cowles Creative Publishing, 1996). A colorful and well-illustrated book for beginners as well as experienced sewers.

Speed Sewing by Janice Saunders (Van Nostrand Reinhold, 1982). This helps anyone willing to try learning to sew at home to build self-confidence. It gives detailed descriptions of how sewing machines operate as well as instructions for many basic sewing techniques.

Setting Up Your Sewing Space

Setting up a workable and pleasant sewing space is very important whether you are sewing for fun or profit. I recommend taking time and care in arranging yours, and your efforts will pay off in the long run.

Dream Sewing Spaces by Lynette Ranney Black. (Palmer/Pletsch, 1996). Get it, read it, dream it, do it—this is the best and most comprehensive source available. Do not plan a sewing space without it!

Home Offices and Workspaces by Sunset Books (Lane Publishing, 1995). A good technical guide to arranging work stations and areas logically and conveniently.

More Splash Than Cash by Donna Babylon. (Windsor Oak, 1999). A must have if you need decorating ideas and advice.

Dreams, Goals, and Career Changes

Starting a new business or changing careers can be scary and intimidating, so here are some additional books that offer wonderful inspiration, assurance, ideas, and concrete advice.

Do What You Love, the Money Will Follow: Discovering Your Right Livelihood by Marsha Sinetar (Dell, 1989).

Get It All Done and Still Be Human by Robbie and Tony Fanning (Open Chain, 1990).

How to Raise a Family and a Career under One Roof: A Parent's Guide to Home Business by Lisa Roberts (Eden Jack Garden Calendar, 1997).

Making a Living without a Job: Winning Ways for Creating Work That You Love by Barbara Winter (Bantam Doubleday Dell, 1993).

Starting Over: How to Change Careers or Start Your Own Business by Stephen Pollan (Warner, 1997).

The Stay-at-Home Mom's Guide to Making Money: How to Create the Business That's Right for You Using the Skills and Interests You Already Have by Liz Folger (Prima Publishing, 1997).

What Are Your Goals? Powerful Questions to Discover What You Want Out of Life by Gary Blair (Wharton, 1997).

What to Say When You Talk to Yourself by Shad Helmstetter (Grindle, 1994).

Pricing

The Crafter's Guide to Pricing Your Work by Dan Ramsey (Betterway, 1991).

Sewing As a Home Business by Mary Roehr (Mary Roehr Books & Video, 500 Saddlerock Circle, Sedona, AZ 86336; (520) 282-4976, www.sewnet.com/maryroehr, 1996).

Marketing, Advertising, and Publicity

Dealing Effectively with the Media by John Wade (Crisp, 1992).

Home-Based Mail Order: A Success Guide for Entrepreneurs by William Bond (McGraw-Hill, 1990).

Making Money on the Internet by Alfred Glossbrenner (TAB Books, 1995).

Marketing on a Shoestring: Low-Cost Tips for Marketing Your Products or Services, 2nd edition by Jeffrey Davidson (Wiley, 1994).

Crafting

Visit bookstores, fabric stores, craft stores, libraries, and used-book shops for books on crafts. Here are a few of my favorites.

Crafting Lamps & Shades by Jodi Davis (Krause, 1998). Instructions for creating inexpensive and unique lamps and shades.

Great American Crafts for the Home by Julie Stephani (Krause, 2000). Instructions for the latest tips and techniques on home decor.

How to Dress a Naked Window by Donna Babylon (Krause, 1997) Step-by-step guide to creating numerous window treatments.

Sew & Go Baby by Jasmine Hubble (Krause, 1998). A collection of practical baby-gear projects.

Special Craft Sourcebooks

The following books contain annotated listings of sources for sewing and craft supplies. All are valuable resources for crafters whether you're craft sewing for fun or profit.

Crafts Supply Sourcebook by Margaret Boyd (Betterway Books, 1997).

Creative Machine Annual Guide to Resources. Open Chain Publishing, published annually.

Designer Source Listing by Maryanne Burgess (Carikean Publishing, 1996).

New York Theatrical Sourcebook by David Rodger (Broadway Press, 1998).

Sew Far, Sew Good by Heather Claus (Oracle Publications, 1998).

Sew Find It, Sew Craft It! by Joselyn Smith-Greene (J. Greene Enterprises, 1996).

Supplier Sourcebook for Creative Businesses by Sandy Redburn (Crafty Secrets Publications, 1996). Contains Canadian sources only.

Whole Costumer's Catalogue by Karen Dick (CBTB Press, 1996).

Craft Business

Business Forms and Contracts (in Plain English) for Crafts People by Leonard DuBoff (Interweave, 1993).

Crafter's Guide to Pricing Your Work by Dan Ramsey (Betterway, 1997). How to calculate the value of your time, materials, and handiwork to make money with your crafts.

Crafting As a Business: The Do-It-Yourself Guide to a Successful Crafts Business by Wendy Rosen (Chilton, 1994).

Crafting for Dollars: How to Establish and Profit from a Career in Crafts by Sylvia Landman (Prima Publishing, 1999).

The Crafts Business Answer Book and Resource Guide by Barbara Brabec (Evans, 1998). Answers hundreds of questions about starting, marketing, and managing a home-based business efficiently, legally, and profitably.

Crafts Market Place: Where and How to Sell Your Crafts ed. by Argie Manolis (Betterway, 1997). Includes listings of shows, craft malls, direct mail, retail stores, galleries, and much more.

Crafty Marketing by Sandy Redburn (Crafty Secrets Publications, 7231 120th Street, Delta, British Columbia, Canada V4C 6P5; (604) 597-8817). Creating maximum profits and potential from your craft business.

Creative Cash: How to Profit from Your Special Artistry, Creativity, Hand Skills, and Related Know-How, 6th ed., by Barbara Brabec (Prima Publishing, 1999). Contains dozens of moneymaking ideas and success secrets of more than 100 crafters and industry experts.

Handmade for Profit! Hundreds of Secrets to Success in Selling Arts and Crafts by Barbara Brabec (Evans, 1996). Tells how to sell your crafts to 16 different retail markets.

How to Be a Weekend Entrepreneur Making Money at Craft Fairs and Trade Shows by Susan Ratliff (Marketing Methods, 1994).

How to Put On a Great Craft Show, First Time and Every Time by Dianne and Lee Spiegel (FairCraft Publishing, PO Box 5508, Mill Valley, CA 94942).

How to Show and Sell Your Crafts by Kathryn Caputo (Betterway, 1997). This is billed as "the crafter's complete guide on how to display work at shows and make profitable sales." A must-read if you're going to do craft shows.

How to Start Making Money with Your Crafts, revised edition by Kathryn Caputo (Betterway, 1999). Completely updated with information on how to develop a product line, successfully sell at craft shows, and find markets for your work.

Made in America by Sue Gary and Connie Ulasewicz. (GarmentoSpeak, 1380 Tilton Road, Sebastopol, CA 95472; (707) 823-4001). Geared toward people who want to produce lines of clothing, but the information can also be used for manufacturing any sewn items. Written by two women who have been there, it's very down-to-earth and comprehensive.

Make It Profitable! How to Make Your Art, Craft Design, Writing, or Publishing Business More Efficient, More Satisfying, and More Profitable by Barbara Brabec (Evans, 2000).

Selling in Craft Malls by Patricia Krauss. (Showplace Marketing, 7046 Broadway, #360, Lemon Grove, CA 91945.)

Sewing As a Home Business by Mary Roehr (Mary Roehr Books & Video, 500 Saddle-rock Circle, Sedona, AZ 86336; (520) 282-4971; www.sewnet.com/maryroehr, 1996).

Business Books

Complete Work-at-Home Companion by Herman Holtz (Prima Publishing, 1994).

The Home-Based Entrepreneur: The Complete Guide to Working at Home, 2nd edition by Linda Pinson and Jerry Jinnett (Upstart, 1993).

Homemade Money, 5th edition by Barbara Brabec (Betterway, 1997). How to select, start, manage, market, and multiply the profits of a business at home. This valuable business reference has been dubbed the "home-business bible."

How to Run Your Own Home Business, 3rd edition by Coralee Smith Kern (VGM Career Books, 1994).

How to Start a Business without Quitting Your Job: The Moonlight Entrepreneur's Guide by Phillip Holland (Ten Speed Press, 1992).

Recommended Magazines and Newsletters

Learning to Sew

Check out newsstands, fabric stores, and libraries to preview copies of these publications, or call or write them to obtain a single issue. Then you'll be able to determine whether you want to subscribe. Ask other sewers what publications they like to read.

Bead & Button magazine
PO Box 1612
Waukesha, WI 53187-1612
Phone: (414) 796-8776
Fax: (414) 796-1383

Creative Sewing Magazine,
3500 Thayer Court
Aurora, IL 60504
Phone: (847) 697-4400

Cutter's Research Journal
6443 Ridings Road
Syracuse, NY 13206
Phone: (800) 93USITT

Designer's Network Newsletter
PO Box 820
Los Lunas, NM 87031

Dress
PO Box 73
Earleville, MD 21919
Phone: (410) 275-1619

Sewing Today Newsletter
PO Box 928
Altoona, PA 16603

Sew News
741 Corporate Circle, #A
Golden, CO 80401
Phone: (800) 289-6397
E-mail: sewnews@sewnews.com
Website: www.sewnews.com

This is probably the most popular all-around sewing magazine. If I could only subscribe to one, this would be it.

Threads
63 S. Main Street
Newtown, CT 06470
Phone: (203) 426-8171

Zig Zag
Viking sewing machines
31000 Viking Parkway
Westlake, OH 44145
Phone: (800) 446-2333

Crafts and Sewing

American Craft
American Craft Council
72 Spring Street
New York, NY 10012
Phone: (800) 724-0859

Arts & Crafts
Krause Publications
700 E. State Street
Iola, WI 54990
Phone: (800) 258-0929

Contemporary Doll Collector
Scott Publications
30595 Eight Mile
Livonia, MI 48152
Phone: (800) 458-8237

The Crafts Report: The Business Journal for the Crafts Industry
300 Water Street
Wilmington, DE 19801
Phone: (302) 656-2209

Creative Leisure News
2766 Ashley Court
Tremont, IL 61568
Phone: (309) 925-5593

Creative Machine Newsletter
PO Box 2634
Menlo Park, CA 94026
Phone: (650) 366-4440

Doll Crafter
Scott Publications
30595 Eight Mile
Livonia, MI 48152
Phone: (800) 458-8237

Embellishment
7660 Woodway Drive, Suite 550
Houston, TX 77063
Phone: (713) 781-6864

Embroidery Business News
3300 N. Central Avenue
Phoenix, AZ 85012
Phone: (602) 990-1101

Embroidery/Monogram Business
PO Box 1266
Skokie, IL 60076

Fiberarts
50 College Street
Asheville, NC 28801
Phone: (828) 253-0467

Great American Crafts
Krause Publications
700 E. State Street
Iola, WI 54990
Phone: (800) 258-0929

Handcrafts Illustrated
PO Box 509
Brookline, MA 02147
Phone: (617) 232-1000

Hand Woven
201 E. 4th Street
Loveland, CO 80537
Phone: (800) 272-2193

Home Embroidery
600 Harrison Street
San Francisco, CA 94107

Quilter's Newsletter Magazine
and *Quiltmaker*
741 Corporate Circle, Suite A
Golden, CO 80401
Phone: (800) 881-6634

Quilters Request Newsletter
PO Box 117
East Greenbush, NY 12061

Quilt World
PO Box 9001
Big Sandy, TX 75755
Phone: (800) 829-5865

Round Bobbin
2724 2nd Avenue
Des Moines, IA 50313
Phone: (800) 367-5651

Rubber Stampin' Retailer
136 W. Vallette, #6
Elmhurst, IL 60126
Phone: (630) 832-5200

Sew Beautiful
518 Madison Street
Huntsville, AL 35801
Phone: (256) 534-5200.

Sewing Professional
2724 2nd Avenue
Des Moines, IA 50313
Phone: (800) 367-5651

Stitches: The Magazine for the Commercial Embroidery Industry
9800 Metcalf Avenue
Shawnee Mission, KS 66212
Phone: (913) 341-1300

Total Embellishment Newsletter
142 Braewick Road
Salt Lake City, UT 84103
Phone: (801) 533-0481

Art and Crafts Shows

There are literally thousands of art and crafts shows nationwide, so the best way to research them is through the various publications listed here. Try to subscribe or obtain current issues so the information will be up-to-date. In addition, find show listings in craft magazines, local newspapers, from chambers of commerce, and on the Web sites listed in this chapter.

Craftmaster News
PO Box 39429
Downey, CA 90239
Phone: (562) 869-5882
Web site: www.craftmasternews.com.

Published monthly except January. Lists shows in California, Arizona, Nevada, Oregon, and Washington.

Machine Knitters Source magazine
3415 Custer, Suite 140
Plano, TX 75023
Phone: (800) 628-8047

Rubber Stamper
PO Box 420
Manalapan, NJ 07726
Phone: (800) 969-7176

SAC
PO Box 159
Bogalusa, LA 70429
Phone: (800) 825-3722

Published monthly. Contains national news and listings of art and crafts shows.

Where It's At
7204 Bucknell Drive
Austin, TX 78723
Phone: (512) 926-7954

Published monthly except December and January. Lists shows in Alabama, Arizona, Arkansas, Colorado, Georgia, Kansas, Louisiana, Mississippi, Missouri, New Mexico, Oklahoma, Tennessee, and Texas.

Where the Shows Are
PO Box 453
Edgewater, FL 32132
Phone: (904) 428-0173
Web site: www.artsandcrafts.com

Two different magazines are published quarterly. The first has listings for Florida, and the second includes New York, Pennsylvania, Maryland, Virginia, North Carolina, New Jersey, and a few listings for surrounding states.

Trade Magazines

Craft & Needlework Age and Craft Supply Magazine
700 E. State Street
Iola, WI 54990
Phone: (715) 445-2214

Craftrends
Primedia
741 Corporate Circle, Suite A
Golden, CO 80401
Phone: (800) 881-6634

Gifts & Decorative Accessories
345 Hudson Street
New York, NY 10014
Phone: (212) 689-4411

Giftware News
PO Box 5398
Deptford, NJ 08096
Phone: (856) 227-0798

Organizations

Craft Sewing

Included are organizations that most pertain to craft sewing. Check *The Encyclopedia of Associations* in your local library for others. I highly recommend joining and becoming involved with the organization or association of your choice. Camaraderie, networking, support, education, group insurance, resource libraries, newsletters, retreats, trade shows, discounts on supplies, and humanitarian projects are just some of the benefits.

American Craft Council
72 Spring Street
New York, NY 10012
Phone: (800) 724-0859
Membership

American Professional Crafters Guild
707 Kautz Road
St. Charles, IL 60174

American Sewing Guild
9140 Ward Parkway, Suite 200
Kansas City, MO 64114
Phone: (877) 422-6739
Web site: www.asg.org

American Quilter's Society
PO Box 3290
Paducah, KY 42002
Phone: (270) 898-7903

Costume Society of America
PO Box 70
Earleville, MD 21919
Phone: (410) 275-2329

Doll Makers Association
6408 Glendale Street
Metairie, LA 70003

Embroidery Trade Association
1199 S. Belt Line Road
Coppell, TX 75019
Phone: (800) 727-3014
Web site: www.homeembroidery.mfi.com

Handweavers Guild of America
3327 Duluth Highway, Suite 201
Duluth, GA 30096
Phone: (770) 495-7702
Web site: www.weavespindye.org

Home Embroidery Clubs
2751 Electronic Lane
Dallas, TX 75220
Phone: (800) 998-3334

Home Sewing Association
1350 Broadway, #1601
New York, NY 10018

Knitting Guild of America
PO Box 1606
Knoxville, TN 37901

Lace Guild
552 S. Murphy Avenue
Sunnyvale, CA 94086

Machine Knit America
PO Box 58668
Cincinnati, OH 45258

National Cloth Doll Makers Association
1601 Provincetown Drive
San Jose, CA 95129

National Craft Association
1945 E. Ridge Road, Suite 5178
Rochester, NY 14622
Web site: www.craftassoc.com

National Quilting Association
PO Box 393
Ellicott City, MD 21041

Ohio Arts & Crafts Guild
PO Box 3080
Lexington, OH 44904

Professional Needle Guild
PO Box 40236
Cleveland, OH 44140

Rhode Island Home Sewing Network
70 New Garners Neck Road
Swansea, MA 02777

Video Sewing Guild
PO Box 22597
Kansas City, MO 64113

Window Coverings Association of America
825 S. Waukegan Road, #A8-111
Lake Forest, IL 60045

Trade

Hobby Industry Association (HIA)
319 E. 54th Street
Elmwood Park, NJ 07407
Phone: (201) 794-1133
Web site: www.hobby.org.
A not-for-profit organization dedicated to building a stronger market for craft/hobby products. Industry leaders and the association's professional staff work together to implement a variety of industry growth initiatives, including sponsorship of an internationally acclaimed trade show, classes and workshops, and certification programs such as Certified Professional

Demonstrator (CPD) and Certified Professional Teacher (CPT). Members receive a newsletter, audiocassettes, and access to other resource materials. In addition, HIA performs continuous research on crafting and retains and oversees a public relations agency dedicated to promoting all aspects of crafting.

Offinger Management Company
PO Box 3388
Zanesville, OH 43702
Phone: (800) 889-8662
Web site: www.offinger.com.
A large umbrella management company for numerous craft organizations, shows, and publications on the wholesale and retail

levels. I highly recommend visiting its Web site or calling for more information on your specific area, whether you want to join an organization, exhibit your crafts at the wholesale or retail level, or attend craft-supply shows or retail shows for finished crafts.

Other craft-related organizations managed by the Offinger Management Company include The Association of Crafts and Creative Industries (ACCI), the National Needlework Association (TNNA), Society of Craft Designers (SCD), Miniatures Industry Association of America (MIAA), Ceramic Manufacturers Association (CerMA), and International Model-Hobby Manufacturer's Association (IMMA).

Craft Manufacturers

Clapper Communications Companies
2400 Devon Avenue, Suite 375
Des Plaines, IL 60018
Phone: (800) 444-0441
Web site: www.clapper.com
Publishes many craft magazines, including *Crafts 'n Things, Bridal Crafts, Painting, Pack-o-Fun*, and *The Cross Stitcher*. Their newsletter, *Clapper COMMUNique*, and their Web site (below), keep crafters up-to-date on craft news nationally.

Booth Design and Display Equipment Companies

Unless you live in a very large city, don't expect to find an abundance of booth design and display equipment in your

area. All of these companies produce catalogs and sell their products by mail order. Most will work with you to design a custom fixture if you need it.

ABELexpress
PO Box 668
Carnegie, PA 15106
Phone: (800) 542-9001
Corrugated cardboard display equipment; most items fold down for storage or travel.

Advantage Fixtures
4540 S. Pinemont Drive, Suite 110
Houston, TX 77041
Phone: (800) 543-7395
Brackets, shelving, fixtures, display cases, body forms, risers, hardware, wire display racks, as well as sign holders, streamers, tags—a one stop mail-order catalog for all your display needs.

Fred's Studio Tents & Canopies, Inc.
7 Tent Lane
Stillwater, NY 12170
Phone: (800) 998-3687
Web site: www.fstcinc.com.
Huge selection of tents, canopies,
awnings, and accessories for craft
show exhibits.

Nomadic Instand
7400 Fullerton Road, Suite 134
Springfield, VA 22153
Phone: (800) 732-9395
Lightweight, portable, and completely
collapsible display systems.

Novelcrafts
PO Box 1168
Rogue River, OR 97537
Phone: (541) 582-3208
Wire display products.

Renfro-Franklin Co.
525 W. Brooks Street
Ontario, CA 91762
Phone: (800) 334-0937
All types of freestanding and attachable
wire display racks.

Skyline Portable Displays
3355 Discovery Road
Eagan, MN 55121
Phone: (800) 328-2725

Traverse Bay Display Co.
4366 Deerwood Drive
Traverse City, MI 49686
Phone: (800) 240-9802
Countertop, freestanding, and custom-
designed corrugated cardboard displays.

Wyrefab, Inc.
PO Box 3767
Gardena, CA 90247
Phone: (310) 523-2147
Wire display racks

Sewing Machine Manufacturers

All the major sewing machine manufacturers produce quality machines in all
price ranges. First make a list of your individual needs, and then call for the dealer
nearest your area.

Baby Lock; (800) 422-2952,
www.babylock.com

Bernina; (800) 405-2739,
www.berninausa.com

Brother; (800) 42 BROTHER,
www.brother.com

Elna; (800) 848-3562, www.elnausa.com

Husqvarna Viking; (800) 358-0001,
www.husqvarnaviking.com

Janome-New Home; (800) 631-0183,
www.janome.com

Pfaff; (800) 997-3233,
www.pfaff-us-cda.com

Singer; (800) 968-1502,
www.singersewing.com

Iron Manufacturers

Black & Decker
6 Armstrong Road
Shelton, CT 06484
Phone: (800) 231-9786

Euro-Pro
178 West Service Road
Champlain, NY 12919
Phone: (800) 798-7395

Hamilton Beach (Proctor-Silex irons)
Spring Road, Highway 17 North
Washington, NC 27889

LauraStar
PO Box 112246
Tacoma, WA 98411
Phone: (253) 761-0924

Rowenta
196 Boston Avenue
Medford, MA 02155
Phone: (781) 396-0600
Web site: www.rowentausa.com.

Lighting Manufacturers

Duro-Test Corporation
9 Law Drive, Suite 11
Fairfield, NJ 07004
Phone: (800) 289-3876

Environmental Lighting Concepts
(Ott-Lites)
1214 W. Cass Street
Tampa, FL 33606
Phone: (800) 842-8848
Web site: www.ott-lite.com

Ventilation Manufacturers

Harmony Products
360 Interlocken Boulevard, Suite 300
Broomfield, CO 80021
Phone: (800) 869-3446
Freestanding air conditioners

Cabinet and Furniture Manufacturers

Koala Cabinets
9631 N.E. Colfax
Portland, OR 97220
Phone: (800) 547-8025

Horn of America (cabinets)
PO Box 608
Sutton, WV 26601
Phone: (800) 882-8845

Sew/Fit Co.
5310 W. 66th Street, Unit A
Bedford Park, IL 60638
Phone: (800) 547-4739
This company sells sturdy but lightweight and collapsible cutting tables.

Handler Textile
103 Eisenhower Parkway
Roseland, NJ 07068
Phone: (888) 618-2555
Web site: www.htc-handler.com
This firm distributes the Big Board cutting and pressing board that folds for travel or storage.

Craft Suppliers

Listed are some popular craft suppliers and their specialties, if appropriate. Unless specifically noted, most are open to both retail and wholesale buying depending on quantities purchased. In addition, display and classified ads in craft magazines are one of the richest sources for suppliers.

Setting Up Your Sewing Space

Aleene's Craft Supplies
PO Box 9500
Buellton, CA 93427
Phone: (800) 825-3363

Amazon Dry Goods
2218 E. 11th Street
Davenport, IA 52803
Phone: (800) 798-7979

Atlanta Thread and Supply
695 Red Oak Road
Stockbridge, GA 30281
Phone: (800) 847-1001

B & G Lieberman
2420 Distribution Street
Charlotte, NC 28203
Phone: (800) 438-0346

Back Street, Inc.
3905 Steve Reynolds Boulevard
Norcross, GA 30093
Phone: (678) 206-7373

Bee Lee Co.
PO Box 36018
Dallas, TX 75235
Phone: (800) 527-5271
Snaps and other decorative findings.

Calico Moon Handcrafts
Nancy Ingerson
1919 State Street
Salem, OR 97301
Phone: (800) 678-7607

Carol's Zoo
992 Coral Ridge Circle
Rodeo, CA 94572
Phone: (510) 245-2020
Stuffed animal patterns, fake furs,
stuffing, plastic eyes.

Coats & Clark
4135 South Stream Boulevard
Charlotte, NC 28217
Phone: (704) 329-5800
Thread and trims.

Fabric Depot
700 S.E. 122nd Avenue
Portland, OR 97233
Phone: (800) 392-3376
All types of crafting and sewing supplies.

Five T's Embroidery Supply
PO Box 484
Mecedon, NY 14502
Phone: (315) 986-8434

Garden of Beadin'
PO Box 1535
Redway, CA 95560
Phone: (800) 232-3588
Beads and other findings.

Golden Hands Industries
PO Box 720279
Atlanta, GA 30358
Phone: (800) 998-1392
Ironing board pads, covers, and other
pressing supplies.

Hard to Find Sewing Supplies
142 Medford Avenue
Patchogue, NY 11772
Phone: (516) 475-8282

Johnson Ruffler Machines, Inc.
2323 Lake Wheeler Road
Raleigh, NC 27603
Phone: (800) 662-6471

June Tailor
PO Box 208
Richfield, WI 53076
Phone: (800) 844-5400
Pressing, quilting, and craft supplies.

Kreinik Metallic Threads
3106 Timanus Lane, Suite 101
Baltimore, MD 21244
Phone: (800) 537-2166
Web site: www.kreinik.com
Decorative threads.

Make It Easy Sewing & Crafts
2012 Queen Avenue South
Minneapolis, MN 55405
Phone: (612) 377-7560
Web site: www.make-it-easy.com
Patterns and books.

Make It Southwest Style
191 Big Horn Ridge Circle Northeast
Albuquerque, NM 87122
Phone: (505) 856-9585

Martha Pullen Co.
518 Madison Street
Huntsville, AL 35801
Phone: (800) 547-4176
French hand sewing and heirloom fabric
and supplies.

Michaels Arts & Crafts Stores
Web site: www.michaels.com.

Norden Crafts
502 Morse Avenue, Unit K
Schaumburg, IL 60193
Phone: (847) 891-0770

Nustyle Quilting Frame Co.
PO Box 61
Stover, MO 65078
Phone: (800) 821-7490

Olfa Products Group
PO Box 747
Plattsburgh, NY 12901
Phone: (800) 962-6532

Rotary cutters, replacement blades,
fabric weights, and cutting mats.

One & Only Creations
PO Box 2730
Napa, CA 94558
Phone: (800) 262-6768
Presewn muslin doll bodies ready for
stuffing and dressing.

Peruvian Bead Co.
1601 Callens Road
Ventura, CA 93003
Phone: (805) 642-0952

Quilting from the Heartland
111 E. 5th Street
Starbuck, MN 56381
Phone: (800) 637-2541
Quilting patterns and supplies.

South Star Supply
PO Box 90147
Nashville, TN 37209
Phone: (800) 288-6739

Office Supplies, Packaging, Bags, Labels, Printed Forms, and Other Paper Supplies

Luckily most of these items are available through mail order if you cannot find them in your area. Be advised that paper and paper products are heavy, so if you're buying in quantity, it might be worth making a road trip to pick items up instead of paying for shipping. Be sure to get catalogs, shop, and compare prices. One company may have low prices on some items and comparatively high prices on others. Make sure you're comparing apples with apples, though!

Associated Bag Company
400 W. Boden Street
Milwaukee, WI 53207
Phone: (414) 769-1000
All types and sizes of bags, boxes, and
packaging materials.

Charm Woven Labels
2400 W. Magnolia Boulevard
Burbank, CA 91506
Phone: (800) 843-1111
Cloth labels for crafts or garments.

Consolidated Plastics Company
8181 Darrow Road
Twinsburg, OH 44087
Phone: (800) 362-1000
Plastic products including bags,
containers, bottles, and shipping
materials.

Discount Package Supply
2415 South Roosevelt, Suite 101
Taupe, AZ 85282
Phone: (800) 373-7713
Packing and shipping materials.

The Drawing Board
Phone: (800) 210-4431

General Label Mfg.
PO Box 640371
Miami, FL 33164
Phone: (800) 944-4696
Woven and printed cloth labels.

Glenside Tape & Label
641 Lancaster Pike, Suite 1002
Frazer, PA 19355
Phone: (610) 647-7288

Gift Box Corporation of America
225 Fifth Avenue, #1226
New York, NY 10010
Phone: (800) GIFT-BOX
Boxes, bags, and ribbon.

Heirloom Woven Labels
PO Box 428
Moorestown, NJ 08057
Phone: (856) 722-1618

National Bag Company, Inc.
2233 Old Mill Road
Hudson, OH 44236
Phone: (800) 247-6000

NEBS Small Business Catalog
500 Main Street
Groton, MA 01471
Phone: (800) 225-6380.

Northwest Tag & Label
2435 S.E. 11th Avenue
Portland, OR 97214
Phone: (503) 234-1054

Office Max (locations vary)
Phone: (800) 788-8080

Office Depot (locations vary)
Phone: (800) 685-8800

On Paper (locations vary)
Phone: (800) 820-2299

Paper Direct (locations vary)
Phone: (800) A-PAPERS

Paper Showcase
PO Box 8465
Mankato, NM 56002
Phone: (800) 287-8163
Preprinted business forms.

Penny Wise Office Products
(locations vary)
Phone: (800) 942-3311

Premier Papers (locations vary)
Phone: (800) 350-7290

Quill Office Supplies (locations vary)
Phone: (800) 789-1331

Reuben Schneider Co.
1926 W. North Lane
Phoenix, AZ 85021
Phone: (800) 755-0097
Colorful and decorated bows, bags, and boxes.

Russell & Miller, Inc.
PO Box 2152
Santa Fe Springs, CA 90670

Phone: (800) 231-9600
All types of merchandising products including signs, labels, bags, banners, display materials, and more.

Staples Office Supplies (locations vary)
Phone: (800) 333-3330

Sterling Name Tape Co.
9 Willow Street
Winsted, CT 06098
Phone: (860) 379-5142

UARCO Computer and Office Supplies
(locations vary)
Phone: (800) 435-0713

Viking Office Supplies (locations vary)
Phone: (800) 421-1222

Recommended Web Sites

Many of the resources in this chapter list Web sites, but these are my top picks for general sewing and craft sites that will lead you to numerous links, chat rooms, and other Web sites on sewing and crafting. If you're a novice on searching the Web or don't have much time, Barbara Brabec's site, www.crafter.com/brabec, is the best place to start. Barbara offers an online newsletter called *CraftsBiz Chat,* a variety of crafts-business articles, infor-

mation about her books, and links to hundreds of other crafts-business sites.

www.CraftShop.com

www.crafter.com/brabec

www.lilyabello.com/sewdir.htm

www.quiltropolis.com

www.sewnet.com

www.sewnews.com

Recommended Videos

Some people learn by seeing rather than reading, so here are some videos that teach sewing. If you like to watch techniques rather than read about them, consult your TV and cable listings for sewing shows. The Home and Garden Channel on cable television, PBS, and many other stations host sewing programs.

Learn to Sew the White Way
Viking Sewing Machines
31000 Viking Parkway
Westlake, OH 44145
Phone: (800) 446-2333
This is a very basic sewing video aimed at beginners.

Pressing to Perfection
Mary Roehr
Mary Roehr Books & Video
500 Saddlerock Circle
Sedona, AZ 86336
Phone: (520) 282-4971
www.sewnet.com/maryroehr
Teaches the principles of pressing using tailoring as a point of reference, but the skills pertain to any aspect of sewing or crafting whenever you use your iron.

You Can Make It
Pam Tripaldi
PO Box 247
Walnutport, PA 18088
Phone: (888) 576-2739
Web site: www.youcanmakeit.com
Available are five different videos ranging in difficulty from beginning to advanced sewing.

Recommended Mail-Order Sources

Fabric

There aren't as many fabric stores as there used to be, and although purchasing fabric by mail isn't as much fun as feeling the textures and seeing the beautiful colors on a grand scale, shopping by mail order is the next best thing if you can't find what you need in your area. Some of these sources have stores as well as catalogs, and I have visited most of them or ordered from many of their catalogs, so I know they sell quality fabrics at affordable prices.

Apple Annie Fabrics
566 Wilbur Avenue
Swansea, MA 02777
Phone: (508) 678-5187

B & J Fabrics
263 W. 40th Street
New York, NY 10018
Phone: (212) 354-8150

Baer Fabrics
515 E. Market Street
Louisville, KY 40202
Phone: (800) 769-7776

Britex
153 Maiden Lane
San Francisco, CA 94108
Phone: (415) 392-2910

Calico Corners
203 Gale Lane
Kennett Square, PA 19348
Phone: (800) 213-6366
Web site: www.calicocorners.com.

Cy Rudnick's Fabrics
2450 Grand Avenue
Kansas City, MO 64108
Phone: (816) 842-7808

Fabric Mart
511 Penn Avenue
Sinking Spring, PA 19608
Phone: (800) 242-3695

Fashion Fabrics Club
10490 Baur Boulevard
St. Louis, MO 63132
Phone: (800) 468-0602

Fishman's Fabrics
1101-43 S. Desplaines Street
Chicago, IL 60607
Phone: (312) 922-7250

G Street Fabrics
12240 Wilkins Avenue
Rockville, MD 20852
Phone: (800) 333-9191

Josephine's Dry Goods
921 S.W. Morrison
Portland, OR 97205
Phone: (503) 224-4202

Kunin Felt
300 Lafayette Road
Hampton, NH 03843

Phone: (800) 292-7900
Web site: www.kuninfelt.com

Pendleton Wool Outlet
1307 S.E. Court Place
Pendleton, OR 97801
Phone: (800) 568-3156

Rosebar Textile Co. Inc.
93 Entin Road
Clifton, NJ 07014
Phone: (800) 631-8573

Sawyer Brook Distinctive Fabrics
PO Box 1800
Clinton, MA 01510
Phone: (800) 290-2739

Vogue Fabrics by Mail
618 Hartrey Avenue
Evanston, IL 60202
Phone: (800) 433-4313

Waverly
Phone: (800) 423-5881
Web site: www.decoratewaverly.com

Craft Supply Catalogs

The following companies sell via mail order and publish lengthy catalogs that are good sources for many craft items. If you are interested in quantity buying, ask for wholesale pricing and policies.

Clotilde
PO Box 3000
Louisiana, MO 63353
Phone: (800) 772-2891

Craft Wholesalers Catalog
77 Cypress Street SW
Reynoldsburg, OH 43068
Phone: (800) 666-5858

Dover Needlecraft Catalog
31 E. 2nd Street
Mineola, NY 11501
Phone: (516) 294-7000

Nancy's Notions
333 Beichl Avenue
Beaver Dam, WI 53916
Phone: (800) 833-0690

Zim's Catalog of Craft Supplies
4370 S. 3rd West
Salt Lake City, UT 84107
Phone: (801) 359-5821

Sewing Kits

These companies sell kits for all types of pillows, stuffed animals, tote bags, hats, simple accessories, and more. They are geared for beginners or people who want easy, all-inclusive projects. If you live in a remote area where supplies are difficult to find, or if you want a prepackaged project that several people can complete at the same time (e.g., getting together with some friends who also want to learn to sew), these resources might be for you.

Haan Crafts
506 E. Second Street
Otterbein, IN 47970
Phone: (800) 422-6548
Web site: www.haan.com

Lama
17530 Frederick Street
Mount Airy, MD 21771
Phone: (800) 876-8870

Pineapple Appeal, Inc.
2879 W. Highway 14
Owatonna, MN 55060
Phone: (800) 321-3041
Web site: www.pineappleappeal.com

Sew Kits by Lida
PO Box 500
Harleton, TX 75651
Phone: (800) 882-5487

Stanwood Products, Inc.
PO Box 465
Batavia, NY 14021
Phone: (800) 782-6966
Web site: www.stanwoodkits.com

To Sew
PO Box 1835
Fort Collins, CO 80522
Phone: (800) 824-5278

Sewing Shows, Getaways, and Retreats

Sewing shows, getaways, and retreats are fun and stimulating ways to learn to sew. Most offer products as well as classes, so you can combine learning, shopping, and vacationing all in one trip. Don't worry if the addresses aren't in your immediate area; many offer seminars across the country in several locations. These are the most popular venues for people who want to learn to sew or to sharpen their skills.

America Sews
11760 Berea Road
Cleveland, OH 44111
Phone: (216) 252-2037

American Stitches
1385 Clyde Road
Highland, MI 48357
Phone: (800) 594-9029

Craft and Sewing Festivals
2022 S. 2100 East, Suite 201
Salt Lake City, UT 84108
Phone: (800) 717-8789

Creative Arts & Textiles Shows
4539-A Clover Drive
Clemmons, NC 27012
Phone: (336) 778-1157

Creative Festival
PO Box 1772
Medford, OR 97501
Phone: (541) 245-1296
Web site: www.creativefestival.com

Creative Inspirations
PO Box 369
Monroeville, PA 15146
Phone: (800) 249-3154
Web site: www.sewingevents.com

Creative Machine Newsletter Cruise
PO Box 2634
Menlo Park, CA 94026
Phone: (650) 366-4440

European Fashion Study Tour
Colorado State University
311 Gifford Building
Fort Collins, CO 80523
Phone: (970) 491-5360

International Quilt Festival
7660 Woodway Drive, Suite 550
Houston, TX 77063
Phone: (713) 781-6864

Martha's Sewing Market and
Martha's School of Art Fashion
518 Madison Street
Huntsville, AL 35801
Phone: (800) 547-4176

Needlearts and Design Fall Fair
2701 Fairview Road
Costa Mesa, CA 92628
Phone: (888) 622-5376

NeedleArts Adventures
PO Box 331
Crownsville, MD 21032
Phone: (410) 923-3415
Web site: www.needlearts-adventures.com

Oregon Sewing Retreats
c/o Sacramento City College
3835 Freeport Boulevard
Sacramento, CA 95822
Phone: (916) 558-2292

Original Sewing & Craft Expo
26612 Center Ridge Road
Westlake, OH 44145
Phone: (800) 699-6309
Web site: www.sewncraftexpo.com

Original Sewing Fair
PO Box 25191
Portland, OR 97298
Phone: (503) 292-0420

Pacific International Quilt Festival
PO Box 667
New Hope, PA 18938
Phone: (215) 862-5828

Sewing and Stitchery Expo
7612 Pioneer Way East
Puyallup, WA 98371
Phone: (253) 445-4575

Sewing in the Sun
PO Box 331
Crownsville, MD 21032
Phone: (410) 923-3415

Sew 'n' Go Tours
741 Corporate Circle, Suite A
Golden, CO 80401
Phone: (800) 881-6634

Sewing and Quilting Craft Exposition
2487 Spring Street, Suite 5
Redwood City, CA 94063
Phone: (800) 472-6476

Sew Unbelievable Seminars
Phone: (800) 301-1110
Web site: www.husqvarnaviking.com

STITCHES
Great Fiber Getaways
PO Box 777
Wayzata, MN 55401
Phone: (847) 277-0490
Web site: www.stitchesgetaways.com
E-mail: stitchsinc@aol.com

The Sewing Workshop
2010 Balboa Street
San Francisco, CA 94121
Phone: (415) 221-7397

Using Your Library—The Best Resource of All!

If I had to choose one favorite resource, it would be my public library. Aside from supplying books for people's reading pleasure, libraries contain reference sections that are constantly updated and virtually unlimited in their potential for finding information. Call or visit the reference librarian, a professional who is trained to know how to use all the information systems. This person's help can be invaluable, whether you are looking for a company's phone number or trying to find out what craft shows are held in your state each year. The more you use the library, the more you'll learn, and, in general, almost all their services are free.

If you need to see a book or publication that your local library doesn't own, many libraries offer a service called interlibrary loan that lets you order the item from another library. I have ordered and read hundreds of books using this system— books that I only want to read once and don't want to add to my home library. It has saved me hundreds if not thousands of dollars. In addition, most libraries now have computers that are hooked up to the Internet so you can rent time and surf the Web if you're not hooked up at home yet.

Index

Accent pillows
    layout, 102–103
    materials, 100–102
    popularity, 99–100
    profit potential, 102
    sewing, 104–106
Achievement log, 276
Advertising. *see also* Marketing; Publicity
    direct mail, 197–198
    free, 198
    magazines, 197
    newspapers, 197
    word-of-mouth, 196
American Association of Home-Based Businesses, 284
American Crafts Council, 284
American Express, 241, 287
American Sewing Guild, 3–4
Aprons
    layout, 110–111
    materials, 107, 110
    pattern drawing, 107–109
    personalizing, 114
    profit potential, 110
    sewing, 112–114
Arena, Barbara, 241–242
Arts & Crafts Business Solutions, 285
Attorneys, 235–238
Auto insurance, 252

Backstitching, 64
Basting, 73
Bazaars, 157–158
Bedding and upholstered furniture law, 256–257
Beeswax, 26, 71–72
Bent trimmers, 22
Booths
    closing down, 176–177
    designing, 163–168
    location, 161–162
    no-no's, 168–171
    protecting, 168
    setting up, 168–171
    size, 161–162
    space application, 163
Boslough, Susan, 156–157
Brabec, Barbara, 157, 202, 274

Brochures, 195
Bulletins, 196
Business. *see also* Sales
    books, recommended, 288–289
    cards, 194–195
    checking accounts, 238–239
    hobby *vs.*, 216–217
    knowledge, 275–276
    legal forms
        corporations, 225–226
        LLC, 226
        partnerships, 224–225
        sole proprietorships, 224
    motivation, 276–278
    name
        registration
            failure to, 229
            federal, 230
            local, 227–229
            state, 229–230
        selecting, 228–229
    organizations, 284–286
    plans
        assistance, 137
        components, 234–235
        importance, 134–135
        sample, 135–136
    policies, 148
    procedures, 189
    services, 287–288
    start-up checklist, 278–280
    success, ensuring, 148–151
    supplies, 188

Cabinets, 45, 47
Care Labeling Laws, 255
Carpets, 51
Cash boxes, 175
Chairs, 46–47
Chalk, tailor's, 25
Checking accounts, 238–239
Checks
    accepting, 173
    bad, 246–248
Cloths, press, 36
Clutter control, 55

Color, 167
Competitive pricing, 146–147
Computers, 189–190
Consignment
    financial risks, 245
    published patterns, 270
    sales tax, 220
    state laws, 242
Consignment shops, 179, 181
Consumer Product Safety Act, 252–253
Consumer Product Safety Commission, 253, 280
Consumer safety laws, 252–254
Contract negotiation, 236–237
Coomer, Rufus, 245
Copyrights
    definition, 258
    deposits, 265
    how-to-projects, 273–275
    infringement, 236
    Internet, 268–269
    notice, 256
    office, 280–281
    patterns, 268–273
    protection, 262–264
    public domain, 268–269
    registration, 264–265
    respecting, 265–269
Corkboards, 48
Corporations, 225–226
Cost of living, 150
Cotton
    characteristics, 28
    covers, 36
The Crafter's Guide to Pricing Your Work, 151
Craft fairs
    booths
        closing down, 176–177
        designing, 163–168
        location, 161–162
        no-no's, 168–171
        protecting, 168
        setting up, 168–171
        size, 161–162
        space application, 163
    checklist, 161
    customer education, 170–171
    evaluating, 160–161, 177
    finances, 172–176
    records, 177–178
    sales
        advice, 172
        pitch, 172
    security, 174
    tax collection, 221

Crafting process, streamlining, 180
Craft malls
    description, 178–180
    financial risks, 245–246
    tips, 159
Crafts organizations
    lists, 284–286
    merchant status, 240–241
The Crafts Report-The Business Journal for the Crafts Industry, 286
Craft Supply Magazine, 286
Creativity, 16–17, 164–165
Credit cards
    advantages, 239
    merchant status, 240–241
        banks, 240
        card companies, 241
        crafts organizations, 240–241
        ISO, 241–242
    at shows, 173–175
    transaction fees, 243
Curiosity, 118
Customer education, 170–171
Cutting
    space, 44–45
    tips, 70
    tools, 21–24

Dealing Effectively with the Media, 208
Debit cards, 173
Deliveries, 169
Department of Labor, 281
Designs. *see* Patterns
Dining room, linens
    layout, 98
    materials, 95–97
    sewing, 98–99
Direct mail, 197–198
Directories, 289–290
Discounts, 147
Disney characters, 273
Dover Publications, 287
The Drawing Board, 192
Dreams
    importance, 117–118
    living, 276–277
    naysayers, 119–120
    tempering, 277
Dressmaker's shears, 22

Efficiency, 186, 189
Electricity, 54

Ellis, Bonnie, 16
Embroidery scissors, 22
Equipment. *see* Tools
Eyeglass case
   customizing, 89
   ease, 81–82
   layout, 84–86
   materials, 82–86
   profit potential, 83
   sewing, 86–87

Fabrics
   construction, 31
   designer, 272–273
   facts, 30
   flammability, 254
   glues, 27
   grain, 32, 67–68
   interfacing, 33
   layout, 69–70
   natural fibers, 27–29
   preshrinking, 67
   raveling, 88
   special surfaces, 32–33
   synthetic fibers, 29–31
   washing, 67
Failure, fear of, 277
Fair Use Doctrine, 267–268
Fear, 214, 277
Federal Trade Commission
   contacting, 281
   labels, 255
   mail-order sales, 257–258
Finances
   craft fairs, 172–176
   importance, 121
   risks
      accepting, 244
      consignment, 245
      at craft malls, 245–246
Flammable Fabrics Act, 254
Flea markets, 157–158
Fluorescent lights, 52
Flyers, 195
Fray Check, 27, 66
Furniture, 46–47

Galleries, 181–184
Garage sales, 154
Gateway, 190
General partnership, 224
Give-a-ways, 192

Giving, 129–132
Glossary, 251–253
Glues, fabric, 27
Goals
   defining, 118–119
   importance, 117–118
   setting, 120
Good Housekeeping, 272
Government agencies, 280–284
Grain
   description, 32
   straightening, 67–68
Grant, Patrick, 50
Gray, John, 12
Great American Crafts, 180

Handmade for Profit, 157
Hand sewing
   basting, 73
   beeswax, 71–72
   knot tying, 72–73, 75
   needle threading, 71
   overcast stitch, 74
   ripping, 76–77
   slipstitch, 74
   tread removal, 77
   tying off, 75
Hand Woven, 9
Hess, Mary, 16
Hobbies, definition, 216
Holiday boutiques. *see* Home shows
Home Business Institute, Inc., 285
Home-business organizations, 284–286
Home Business Report, 286
Homeowner's insurance, 249–250
Home shows
   description, 155
   tax collection, 221–223
   tips, 155
   zoning laws, 233
How-to-projects, 273–275

Idea notebook, 140
Income. *see* Pricing
Independent contractors, 237
Ingerson, Nancy, 187
Insurance
   auto, 252
   crafts, 249, 251–252
   homeowner's, 249–250
   importance, 248–249

Insurance, *continued*
   liability, 250–251
   renter's, 249–250
Intellectual property
   copyright
      deposits, 265
      how-to-projects, 273–275
      infringement, 236
      Internet, 268–269
      notice, 256
      patterns, 268–273
      protection, 262–264
      public domain, 268–269
      registration, 264–265
      respecting, 265–269
   definitions, 258
   patents, 258–259
   trademarks, 259–261
Interfacing, 33
Internal Revenue Service
   contacting, 281–282
   hobby definition, 216
   self-employment, 217
Internet
   advantages, 158–159
   copyright laws, 268–269
   sales tax, 223
   trademark searches, 260
Ironing board covers, 36
Irons
   dropping, 78
   maintenance, 80
   selecting, 34–35
IRS. *see* Internal Revenue Service

Kamoroff, Bernard, 225
Kitchen, linens
   description, 90–91
   fraying, 94
   layout, 92
   materials, 91
   sewing, 93–94
Knits, 31
Knot tying, 72–73, 75

Labels, requirements, 254–256
Liability insurance, 250–251
Lighting, 52–54
Limited liability company, 226
Limited partnership, 224
Linen, 29

LLC. *see* Limited liability company
Logos, 192–193

Machine sewing
   backstitching, 64
   seams
      finishes, 65–66
      technique, 61–63
   threading, 59–60
   topstitching, 66–67
Magazines
   advertising, 197
   how-to-projects, 273–275
   publicity, 202–203, 205
   recommended, 286–287
   selling to, 260
Mail order, 257–258
Marketing. *see also* Advertising; Publicity
   benefits, 196
   brochures, 195
   bulletins, 196
   business cards, 194–195
   flyers, 195
   logos, 192–193
   newsletters, 196
   portfolios, 195
   sales *vs.*, 191–192
Markets
   changing, 150–151
   testing, 148–149
Marking tools, 24–25
Measuring tools, 20–21
Media. *see specific types*
Men Are from Mars, Women Are from Venus, 12
Merchant status
   banks, 240
   card companies, 241
   crafts organizations, 240–241
   SOS, 241–242
Metcalfe, Margaret, 122–123
Moseley Bankcard Services, 173
Motivation, 129, 276–278

Napkins
   dining room
      layout, 98
      materials, 95–97
      sewing, 98–99
   kitchen
      description, 90–91
      fraying, 94
      layout, 92

materials, 91–92
sewing, 93–94
Napoleon, 227
National Association of Enrolled Agents, 218
National Craft Association, 240–241, 285–286
Natural fibers, 27–29
Naylor, Michele Cokl, 182–183
Naysayers, 119–120
Networking, 198, 200
Newsletters, 196
Newspapers
advertising, 197
publicity, 202–203, 205
Notebook, idea, 140
Novus, 241, 287

Odd pricing, 146
Ott-Lites, 53–54
Overcast stitch, 74
Overhead, 144

Pacific Card Services, 173
Paints, safety, 253
Partnerships, 224–225, 236
Patchwork, 8–9
Patent and Trademark Office, 282
Patents
definition, 258
granting, 258–259
Patterns. *see also specific projects*
access, 271
copy righted, using, 269–272
famous characters, 273–275
modifying, 266
Pegboards, 48
Periodicals. *see* Magazines
Personal liability, 250–251
Peter Rabbit, 270
Photocopying, 268
Pillows. *see* Accent pillows
Pincushions, 26
Pine come promotion, 207
Pinking shears, 22
Pins
safety, 50
types, 25–26
use, tips, 61, 112
Placemats
dining room
layout, 98
materials, 95–97
sewing, 98–99

kitchen
description, 90–91
fraying, 94
layout, 92
materials, 91–92
sewing, 93–94
Plans. *see under* Business
Portfolios, 195
Positive thinking, 277
Potter, Beatrix, 270
Press cloths, 36
Pressing
equipment (*see* Irons)
importance, 77
procedures, 78–79
space, 44
surfaces, 34–36
temperature, 78
Press releases, 202–204
Pricing
common practices, 146–147
crafter's wages, 142–143, 150
indicators, 149–151
material cost, 143–144
overhead, 144
psychology, 145–147
sales tax, 222–223
self-worth and, 141–142
time tracking, 144
Product liability, 250–251
Products
criteria, 137
finding, 138–140
Psychology, pricing, 145–147
Public domain, 270–271
Publicity. *see also* Advertising; Marketing
description, 198
networking, 198, 200
press releases, 202–204
public speaking, 200–202
radio, 206–207
teaching, 208–209
television, 205–206, 208
Public speaking, 200–202
Pullen, Martha, 133

Quilts, 271

Radio, 206–207
Rags, sewing with, 6–7
Ramsey, Dan, 151
Rayon, 30–31

Record keeping, 145, 216, 218
Regulations
    federal
        bedding, 256–257
        consumer safety laws, 252–254
        furniture, 256–257
        labels, 254–256
    local
        breaking, 227
        licenses, 230
        registration, 227–229
    state
        breaking, 227
        consignment, 242
        registration, 229–230
    telephones, 230–231
    zoning, 232–233
Renter's insurance, 249–250
Retreats, 4
Reynolds, Phyllis, 15
Ripping, 24, 76–77
Rotary cutters
    description, 21–24
    safety, 50
    seam ripping, 76–77
Rotary mat, 24
Rotary Point Cutters, 76–77
Rounding up, 146
Ruler, 20–21

S*AC Newsmonthly*, 286
Safety
    consumer laws, 252–254
    sewing, 49–51
Safety deposit boxes, 235
Sales
    bazaars, 157
    consignment
        published patterns, 270
        state laws, 242
        store, evaluating, 179
    craft fairs
        booths
            closing down, 176–177
            designing, 163–168
            location, 161–162
            no-no's, 168–171
            protecting, 168
            setting up, 168–171
            size, 161–162
            space application, 163
        checklist, 161
        customer education, 170–171
        evaluating, 160–161, 177

        records, 177–178
        tax collection, 221
    crafting *vs.*, 185–188
    craft malls, 178–180
    crafts fairs
        advice, 172
        finances, 172–176
        pitch, 171–172
        security, 174
    financial risks
        accepting, 244
        consignment, 245
        at craft malls, 245–246
    flea markets, 157–158
    galleries, 181–184
    garage, 154
    home, 155–157
    Internet
        advantages, 158–159
        credit cards, 243
        sales tax, 223
    mail order, 257–258
    marketing *vs.*, 191–192
    pricing
        common practices, 146–147
        factors
            crafter's wages, 142–143, 150
            material cost, 143–144
            overhead, 144
            psychology, 145–147
            self-worth and, 141–142
            time tacking, 144
        indicators, 149–151
        tax inclusion, 222–223
    products, 137–140
    tax
        consignment, 220
        craft shows, 221
        home shows, 221–223
        Internet, 223
        licenses, 219–220
        wholesale, 220–221
    transitioning to, 129–132
    wholesale, 184–185
Savings and Loans, 238
Schedules, 186–187
Scissors
    care, 23
    cutting with, 70
    quality, 23
    types, 22
SCORE, 283
Seams
    finishes, 65–66
    gauges, 20

rippers
   alternate, 76–77
   description, 24
   safety, 50
   traditional, 76
   sewing, 61–63
Security, 174
Self-employment
   benefits, 132–133
   disadvantages, 133–134
   skills, 131
Self-employment taxes, 217–219
Self-expression, 10–11
Serger, 38
Service Corps of Retired Executives, 283
Sew Hilarious, 14
Sewing
   accomplishment, sense of, 11–12
   breaks, 187–188
   community benefits, 15–16
   ease of, 9–10
   hand (*see* Hand sewing)
   impact, 5–6
   machine (*see* Machine sewing)
   other activities, 7–8
   other needle crafts, 8–9
   problem solving, 14
   projects
      aprons, 106–114
      dining room linens, 95–99
      eyeglass case, 81–88
      pillows, 99–106
   from rags, 6–7
   scissors, 22
   self-expression through, 10–11
   therapeutic aspects, 12–13
   work schedules, 186–187
Sewing machines
   buying, 37–39
   cabinet, 45, 47
   features, 40
   maintenance, 37–39
   manuals, 58–59
   operating (*see* Machine sewing)
   parts, 58
   sales, 39
   used, 40
Sew News Magazine, 8
Sew of the Cure, 16
Shears. *see* Scissors
Signs, tips, 165
Silk, 28
Skills. *see* Talents
Slipstitch, 74
Small Business Administration, 282–283

Small Time Operator, 218, 225
Social Security
   hotline, 282
   taxes, 215
Sole proprietorships, 224
Sparling, Glenda, 4–5
Specials, 147
Stephani, Julie, 180
Stitches
   back, 64
   length, 60–61
   overcast, 74
   reverse, 64
   slip, 74
   top, 66–67
Storage, 45, 48–49
Stress, 149–150
Success, tips, 187
Sunshine Artist, 287
Supplies, 188
Synthetic fibers, 29–31

Table linens
   description, 88–89
   uses, 98
Tailor's chalk, 25
Talents, assessing, 124–125
Tape measure, 20
Taxes
   record keeping, 216, 218
   sales
      consignment, 219–220
      craft shows, 221
      home shows, 221–223
      Internet, 223
      licenses, 219–220
      wholesale, 220–221
   self-employment, 217–219
   social security, 215
Teaching, 208–209
Telephones, 230–231
Television, 205–206, 208
Temperature
   pressing, 78
   room, 54
Test marketing, 148–149
Textile Fiber Products Identification Act, 255
Thimbles, 26
Threads
   bobbin filling, 115
   changing colors, 115
   empty spools, 115
   knot tying, 72–73, 75
   needle, 71

Threads, *continued*
  removing, 77
  selecting, 33
  snips, 22
Time management, 122–123, 186–187
Tools. *see also* Sewing machines
  for booths, 169–170
  costs, 143–144
  cutting, 21–24
  hand, 25–27
  list, 21
  marking, 24–25
  measuring, 20–21
  pressing (*see* Irons)
  tips, 19–20
Topstitching, 66–67
Toy patterns, 271
Toy safety, 253
Trademarks
  definition, 258
  infringement, 236
  protection, 259–261
  searches, 260
Threading, 59–60
Tying off, 75

Vacations, 187–188
Vanity pricing, 147
Varnishes, safety, 253
Vita-Lite, 52
Volunteering, 161
Volunteer Lawyers for the Arts, 287–288

Wade, John, 208
Wall treatments, 52

Warner Brothers' characters, 273
Washing, 67
Wastebaskets, 55
Weaving, 9
Wholesale
  offers, evaluating, 184–185
  sales tax, 220–221
Widby Enterprises USA, 288
Woman's Day, 272
Wool, 28–29
Workspace
  available, 42–43
  changing, 130
  checklist, 44
  clutter control, 55
  comforts, 50
  efficient, 46–48
  electricity, 54
  flooring, 51
  importance, 41
  lighting, 52–54
  needs analysis, 42
  organizing, 45
  project designation, 44–45
  storage, 45–46, 48–49
  temperature control, 54
  wall treatments, 52

Yardsticks, 21
*You Can Make Money from Your
  Hobby,* 133

Zieman, Nancy, 15
Zoning, 232–233

About the Author

MARY ROEHR is an internationally known author, consultant, and teacher who has shown thousands of students how to tailor, press, alter clothing, and create sewing businesses of their own. She earned her B.S. degree in Clothing and Textiles in 1972 and has been sewing and selling crafts for more than 25 years. Ms. Roehr writes articles for many popular sewing publications, appears regularly on PBS, and has authored five books and a video on these subjects.

About the Series Editor

BARBARA BRABEC, one of the world's leading experts on how to turn an art or craft hobby into a profitable home-based business, is the author of six books, including the national bestseller *Creative Cash,* 6th ed. (Prima). She regularly communicates with thousands of creative people through her Web site and monthly column in *Crafts Magazine.*

To Order Books

Please send me the following items:

Quantity	Title	U.S. Price	Total
_____	Decorative Painting For Fun & Profit	$ __19.99__	$ _____
_____	Holiday Decorations For Fun & Profit	$ __19.99__	$ _____
_____	Woodworking For Fun & Profit	$ __19.99__	$ _____
_____	Knitting For Fun & Profit	$ __19.99__	$ _____
_____	Quilting For Fun & Profit	$ __19.99__	$ _____
_____	Soapmaking For Fun & Profit	$ __19.99__	$ _____
_____	Craft Sewing For Fun & Profit	$ __19.99__	$ _____
_____	_____	$ _____	$ _____

Subtotal	$ _____
7.25% Sales Tax (CA only)	$ _____
7% Sales Tax (PA only)	$ _____
5% Sales Tax (IN only)	$ _____
7% G.S.T. Tax (Canada only)	$ _____
Priority Shipping	$ _____
Total Order	$ _____

FREE
Ground Freight
in U.S. and Canada

Foreign and all Priority Request orders:
Call Customer Service
for price quote at 916-787-7000

By Telephone: With American Express, MC, or Visa,
call 800-632-8676, Monday–Friday, 8:30–4:30
www.primapublishing.com

By E-mail: sales@primapub.com

By Mail: Just fill out the information below and send with your remittance to:
Prima Publishing ▪ P.O. Box 1260BK ▪ Rocklin, CA 95677

Name _____

Address _____

City _____ State _____ ZIP _____

MC/Visa/American Express# _____ Exp. _____

Check/money order enclosed for $ _____ Payable to Prima Publishing

Daytime telephone _____

Signature _____